Library Partnerships
with Writers and Poets

Library Partnerships with Writers and Poets

Case Studies

Edited by Carol Smallwood *and* Vera Gubnitskaia

Foreword by Patti Gibbons

McFarland & Company, Inc., Publishers

Jefferson, North Carolina

RECENT MCFARLAND WORKS ALSO OF INTEREST: *Teaching Technology in Libraries: Creative Ideas...*, edited by Carol Smallwood and Lura Sanborn (2017); *Library Partnerships with Writers and Poets*, edited by Carol Smallwood and Vera Gubnitskaia (2017); *Library Volunteers Welcome!*, edited by Carol Smallwood and Lura Sanborn (2016); *Continuing Education for Librarians: Essays*, edited by Carol Smallwood, Kerol Harrod and Vera Gubnitskaia (2013); *Job Stress and the Librarian*, edited by Carol Smallwood and Linda Burkey Wade (2013); *Marketing Your Library*, edited by Carol Smallwood, Vera Gubnitskaia and Kerol Harrod (2012); *Mentoring in Librarianship: Essays*, edited by Carol Smallwood and Rebecca Tolley-Stokes (2012); *Women on Poetry*, edited by Carol Smallwood, Colleen S. Harris and Cynthia Brackett-Vincent (2012)

ISBN (print) 978-1-4766-6539-9
ISBN (ebook) 978-1-4766-2922-3

LIBRARY OF CONGRESS CATALOGUING DATA ARE AVAILABLE

British Library cataloguing data are available

Printed in the United States of America

McFarland & Company, Inc., Publishers
Box 611, Jefferson, North Carolina 28640
www.mcfarlandpub.com

Table of Contents

Part VII: Classes and Workshops

Part VIII: Outreach

Foreword

Patti Gibbons

By design, libraries attract literary-minded book lovers and people seeking information for work, school, and leisure. Librarians have long recognized that the intersecting needs that bring people to the library present them with an opportunity to tap into ready-made audiences when promoting library activities and events. Well before the advent of "If you like X, you might also enjoy Y" virtual concierge tactics, libraries pioneered similar matchmaking campaigns to offer library users wider services that strengthen literary appreciation and help writers hone their skills. Libraries provide an open venue where literary groups can attract members, explore common interests, and develop a sense of community. Through and through, libraries and writers are obvious partners, and together they foster personal enrichment and add to the collective body of creative literary work.

Over the span of the eight parts of this book, editors Carol Smallwood and Vera Gubnitskaia skillfully curate insightful contributions and seasoned advice from nearly fifty authors who uncover and survey the many ways writers and libraries can collaborate and reinforce each other's missions. Rich with case studies and practical how-to advice, this book ponders the elements that make the relationship a success and examines the needs of both the creators and the custodians of books.

For librarians, the book delivers both a reflective look and pragmatic instruction on how to develop outreach strategies that inspire. The book delivers examples of highly effective programs that can be adopted and repeated elsewhere. Enriching the project is a standout apportioned to poets that looks at ways libraries inspire and promote their work, and how poets attract people responsive to verse to the library. Further providing unique insight and taking the book beyond the instructive realm of a handbook, *Library Partnerships with Writers and Poets* devotes chapters to collection development that help librarians understand their role in capturing the history that provides insights into the writer's creative process.

Library Partnerships with Writers and Poets covers ways library activities can vitalize the creative and professional development of writers and poets. In addition to encouraging the artistic process, authors explore opportunities libraries have to celebrate finished works through author talks, festivals, and other literary-themed events that delight library users and honor the writer's accomplishments.

Throughout the book, contributors continually illustrate the symbiotic and supportive relationship between writers and libraries. Recognizing the natural collaborative fit, *Library Partnerships with Writers and Poets* illustrates how librarians play a key role in sponsoring and directing the partnership that helps libraries flourish and promotes the work and appreciation of contemporary writers and poets. This important collection of voices invigorates the long marriage between libraries and authors.

Patti Gibbons, head of collection management at the University of Chicago Library's Special Collections Research Center, is a member of the American Library Association and the American Alliance of Museums. She contributed to the *Handbook of Research on Disaster Management and Contingency Planning in Modern Libraries* and has reviewed books for *RBM: A Journal of Rare Books, Manuscripts, and Cultural Heritage and Collection Management.*

Preface

Libraries, writers, and poets have long had a close working relationship. Rapid changes in technology have not changed the importance of this cooperation: book talks and readings are as popular as ever, and the ways librarians support local writers with workshops, festivals, and widely varied community events is evident in these essays. The forty-four contributors and one forewordist are from all across the United States.

It is fitting that Patti Gibbons from the University of Chicago Library has written the foreword since the University of Chicago Press is famous for *The Chicago Manual of Style*—the origin of the many editions of this classic for writers can be traced to 1891 when the press opened. Besides being a librarian, Patti is a writer and reviewer of note.

The twenty-nine essays are divided into eight parts: Partnerships, Writers Groups, Author Talks, Festivals, Collections, Poetry, Classes and Workshops, and Outreach.

Academic Libraries Reach Out to Writers and Poets

Aline Soules

In November 2015, the library at California State University, East Bay supported the annual "write 50,000 words in a month" sponsored by NaNoWriMo (National Novel Writing Month) by offering a weekly place for participants to write each Sunday afternoon through November. The library "registered" its location on the NaNoWriMo website as a place for writers and turned the gathering into an "event" with a kick-off on November 1 and a celebration of success on November 29. Each week, the library hosted from a dozen to two dozen writers, not always the same people. Regardless of who came, the library provided a place of "writing safety" where that week's group of writers "wrote alone together" and made progress on their works.

The cost of this event was minimal: the time of a librarian who was already on staff, use of a meeting space on Sunday afternoon when demand is generally low, and, for the celebration, cookies, which were homemade by the librarian, but could have been purchased from a budget, if needed. The benefits to the library were significant: writers, who were not part of the university, learned about a library that was barely on their radar screens, the library received goodwill from attendees, the word will likely spread more extensively in the community as attendees talk about their positive library experience, and the goodwill should grow as the library turns this into an annual event.

Libraries have long partnered with the arts to enhance and enrich their communities; however, those efforts have often centered on public libraries. Today, academic libraries are engaging more proactively in supporting the arts in their university and wider communities.

Key factors for an academic library seeking to partner on community efforts for writers and poets include:

- information resources and services for writers
- suitable space for people to gather
- a strong and interested creative writing program on campus
- a community of writers (on campus and off) that value library offerings and programs

Library contributions include:

- access to information resources

- access to reference and other services within the building and (sometimes) via instant messaging, e-mail, or social media
- the use of available space
- financial support
- librarians interested in partnering with their campuses and wider communities
- creative ideas from all partners in the programs and projects

Information Resources and Services

Most public university libraries extend privileges to unaffiliated community members, including Internet access, borrowing privileges, in-house use of electronic resources and noncirculating items, and reference and other staff services within the building. Depending on the library's level of engagement in social media, that outreach can also be available to the community at large. Dole and Hill (2012) of the Ottenheimer Library at the University of Arkansas at Little Rock conducted a web-based survey of community users to gather information on demographics and the perception of the value of those privileges. They also analyzed the costs and benefits of extending such services. They discovered that community users often have some connection to the university and are generally satisfied and value the privileges. While recognizing the challenge of measuring goodwill and social capital, they concluded that there might be an increase in goodwill and, potentially, a willingness to donate to development efforts (276). Regardless of whether broader community members wish to "pay back" through donations, academic libraries generally offer types of resources not available in local public libraries to all comers. Access to such materials is critical for writers who need to conduct research for their projects. The obvious example is the author of historical novels, but all writers, even poets, need to complete research to ensure that they convey accurate information and can provide a citation to back it up, if needed.

Librarians now provide a wealth of "guides" to direct specific types of writers, e.g., poets, to valuable resources. These guides are possible not just because of the World Wide Web, but also because of a service called LibGuides. Many academic libraries use the LibGuides platform to provide users with a compilation of useful material on a particular topic, e.g., poetry. These materials include links to key websites; suggested databases for searching; links to library catalogs; suggestions of print and e-books of poetry or on the craft or writing and poetics; links to YouTube videos and podcasts; suggestions of who to follow on Twitter, Facebook, and other social media venues; and, potentially, current news feeds, such as Credo's Topic Page on Literature. Examples of LibGuides include:

- *Poetry Research,* created by Leslie Madden at Georgia State University's library
- *Poems and Poets: Finding Poems,* created by Amanda Watson at New York University's library
- *Poetry,* created at Tulsa Community College (author not given)
- *Poetry Center,* Sierra Nevada College (author not given)

At Sierra Nevada College (this last example), the Poetry Center is located in the Prim Library and funded by grants from the Nevada State Library and Archives and the Institute of Museum and Library Services. The grants enabled the acquisition of more than 500 volumes of poetry. The Center also received a donation of about 3,000 volumes. The Poetry Center's collections and programs are open to the general public and the Center offers free access to all Nevada residents. The Poetry Center's resources are listed on their LibGuide, which also contains a media example.

Academic libraries leverage their collections on behalf of writers. Special collections are often strong attractions, offering unique materials that are either local in nature or not found in the local public library. At Hamilton College Burke Library, New York, for example, where Academic Centers, such as the Writing Center, are on the opposite side of the campus, libraries have developed innovative approaches to serving writers and other creators. Their *Apple & Quill* program highlights the creative work of students and faculty. Students participate in writing workshops, but go one step further, using the library's makerspace to create physical books, as well as sharing writing through organized reading events that involve students and faculty. Open mic sessions are also offered. The program has further expanded to new endeavors, such as exploring oral history through song, and semester-long themed programming. These draw community members to the library and increase the use of special collection materials. Forrest (2015) explains that "when librarians create programs that incorporate library resources, renewed life is given to underused collections and to the library itself" (389). Add to that future plans to expand to other arts, e.g., photography, sculpture, painting, and writers discover opportunities to immerse themselves in a broad range of arts to enrich their own writing.

Creative writing programs in English Departments make extensive use of collections, particularly special collections. Pavelich (2010) provides information about areas where special collections are critical: historical fiction, which requires extensive research, some of which will ideally come from primary sources; editorial interventions, where creative writers can explore not only the finished work, but editorial files that show the development of a work from manuscript to published book; drafts, which educate students about the revision process; different versions, which foster discussions about the choices writers and poets make; and self-publishing and alternative book forms, which explore the book as medium, along with chapbooks, pamphlets, and other formats.

Space

Academic libraries have long occupied extensive spaces, but, as architectural redesigns focus more on people spaces and less on book stacks, opportunities for innovation increase. Traditionally, libraries have partnered on providing reading series by local, national, and international authors. Partners include the English Department on campus, local public libraries, non-profit writing organizations involved in writing, interested "Friends" groups, or any group or organization with an interest in writing and in listening to live readings. Setting up such readings is relatively simple. All that's needed is the space, some water for the readers, and marketing. Refreshments, while they can enhance the post-reading experience by fostering conversation, are not essential, and can be scaled to budget. Marketing is more important in order to ensure a good-sized audience. Often, the featured reader can help with that, putting out the word on his/her blogspace to draw in fans to supplement marketing by the libraries and by the various funding partners of the reading series.

Such gatherings are also a great opportunity to create an interplay between noted authors and student writers. At the University of Tennessee, Knoxville, the *Writers in the Library* is a long-running reading series that showcases the work of novelists, poets, and other literary figures. The partnership includes the University Libraries, the university's Creative Writing Program, and the John C. Hodges Better English Fund. Each semester, several readings are sponsored. They are free, the public is invited, and the program has evolved from being a venue for local writers (including students) to a showcase for award-winning national and international authors. Their readers have included Pulitzer Prize winners, a U.S. Poet Laureate, and authors of *New York Times* bestsellers. The final event each year features winners of the John C. Hodges Graduate Writing Prizes in fiction and poetry.

Summer is another opportunity to make use of library space when it's less in demand for university students and functions. A number of universities offer programs for high school students, some of which partner with the library as part of the experience. Whether a summer camp, a summer bridge program to help students transition to university, or an integrated pre-college program that offers college credit, high school students benefit from being on a university campus, having privileges in the library, and sometimes meeting in the library for their creative writing and other classes.

Libraries also bring partners into library spaces to create synergies through various types of Writing Centers. The Poetry Center at Sierra Nevada College is just one example. The John Fowles Center for Creative Writing works with the library, offering its prestigious reading series in the Henley Reading Room in the campus' Leatherby Libraries. Even though Chapman University is a private institution, all events are free and open to the public. With guest writers such as Salman Rushdie, Lawrence Ferlinghetti, Elizabeth George, and Luisa Valenzuela, interest and attendance are high.

Team members of the *Library as Incubator Project* completed their library degrees at the University of Wisconsin–Madison and went on to found this broad initiative. On their "Team" page, they describe their project as "a collaborative effort that involves the time, skill, and dedication of many individuals and organizations," and go on to explain: "We rely on a long list of partners, guest writers, and volunteers to do what we do, as well as an army of creative makers and librarians who share their work and ideas with us." The "Libraries" page lists a mix of libraries (public, university, even an airport library), all engaged in exciting, innovative efforts in areas such as digital humanities.

Creative Writing Programs and Libraries

Creative writing programs have grown by leaps and bounds. According to *Education News'* Career Index on Creative Writing Schools, there are 328 accredited creative writing schools in the U.S. alone. A list of key schools is offered in the *Poets & Writers* MFA Programs Database. For the library, forging partnerships with these programs is essential and achievable. Often, our great writers, poets and others, are affiliated with universities because making a living solely as a creative writer is possible only for the very few. The MFA Programs Database lists key faculty in each program: Mark Doty at New York University in Paris, Tony Hoagland at the University of Houston—the list goes on. Great writers are great readers and they encourage and require their students to read in the genres the students aspire to create. The library is an important element in these programs and library liaisons can forge rich relationships. The partnerships can involve workshops, help with independent studies, support for literature courses, use of special and other collections (see above), reading series, contests, and, above all, community. An example is at Mills College in Oakland, California, which emphasizes not only students' growth as writers and readers of poetry, and their awareness of the contemporary poetic field, but also provides opportunities to publish, teach, and engage in community work. Located in the San Francisco Bay Area, there are ample opportunities to participate in local events, many of which center in libraries around the area.

Many creative writing programs offer contests for students, contests that are often funded by individual donors or larger foundations. Sometimes, librarians who liaise with these programs are participating judges. For example, for some years, I have been privileged to be one of the judges of the De Clercq poetry competition for undergraduates at California State University, East Bay. As a writer of poetry and other genres, as well as a librarian and liaison to the English Department, I have credentials as a writer, as a librarian, and as a literature major, all of which provide a suitable background to engage in this unique opportunity to read the work of our students and learn what moves them.

Poet/Librarians

There are, in fact, many librarians who are also creative writers. An article written by Erin Dorney (2014) entitled "Librarian as Poet/Poet as Librarian" in the online journal *In the Library with the Lead Pipe*, explores these two facets. Erin, herself, was Assistant Professor and Outreach Librarian in the library at Millersville University in Pennsylvania from 2008 to 2014, where she coordinated library marketing communications. She left the library to become a free-lance writer, assistant to a textile designer, continue marketing communications for a local organic market, and found *The Triangle*, a volunteer-run literary organization. Like many of us, she has masters in both librarianship and creative writing. In speaking about her time as a librarian and poet, she explained that, at first, she tried to keep the roles separate, fearing that her creative writing would undermine her professionalism. In time, she realized that her two roles intersected and influenced each other.

Poet/librarians, both in public and academic libraries world-wide, include the famous as well as the unknown, and have included over the years Audre Lorde (Caribbean-American), Jorge Luis Borges (Argentine), Philip Larkin (English), and many others. The website, *Leaves of Bark*, documents "the nexus between poetry (the spoken and written word) and librarianship (the keepers of libers, of books, of bark)." There are dozens of us. In Dorney's article, she focuses particularly on Patrick Williams, Associate Librarian, Subject Specialist for English and other subjects at Syracuse University Libraries.

Williams leverages technology and social media extensively in his dual work. He began writing poetry before he worked as a librarian, but thinks that "the same set of impulses" drew him to both worlds. His doctoral project at the University of Texas at Austin explored the online social lives of poets and fiction writers. In January 2014, he launched *Really System*, an online journal of poetry and extensible poetics (see his "RS_Lab" page for an explanation of extensible poetics). Key here is his view of the balance and interaction of the two roles of librarian and poet. Poetry is relevant to his daily work as a librarian. His reference and instruction activities support the university's strong English and Writing programs, he is welcomed by the writing community, and he states that "many of my most productive talks and connections with people happen at readings and other literary events," which often take place in the library.

Another area of intersection occurs in Williams' choice of projects. In his interview with Dorney, he described his involvement in making videos of the university's Raymond Carver Reading Series available through the university's online repository (academic libraries have become major players in the management and organization of such repositories). He also spoke of his support of small presses and independent poetry publishers in his collection development work; and his promotion of poetry as a visible part of the library community by making poetry books and journals (and poetry-related special collections) a part of any class, event, or interaction in which he is involved. He knows that his poetry strengths improve his ability to think creatively and out of the box, something he believes will help libraries remain vibrant and sustainable. Williams basically pulls together all the elements discussed in this article into a cohesive whole to create a synergistic partnership that reaches out to provide writers and poets with an enriched set of resources and services.

It is also possible to take outreach even further. Williams is only one example of a librarian who promotes poetry materials in classes, events, and other interactions, but, as librarians' instruction role becomes more visible to a wider public, writer/poet/librarians leverage opportunities to teach in environments other than the library. In some cases, they teach creative writing classes in their universities as a result of their library work with those programs and their dual role, which generally includes an MFA in Creative Writing. Other opportunities exist beyond the university. For example, I currently teach a class called *Writing in Many Forms* for the Osher Lifelong Learning Institute. In 2000, the Osher Foundation began to focus on "more mature" students with a joy of learning and a desire to stay in touch with a wider world. They affiliate with and house classes in universities across the nation, but their programs are uniquely their own. Students in my classes range from their sixties through their nineties. Many of them write memoir and do they have tales to tell! They enrich my world and, when I bring back my experiences with these students into my daily library work, I have new perspectives, particularly when teaching my information literacy courses where students are eighteen. My current goal is to put some of these disparately aged students together.

Making It Happen

What do you need in order to forge partnerships and synergies for writers and poets? The predominant requirements are

- desire
- energy
- the ability to network
- a project or an overall plan
- persistence

This is not about a large budget. It is true that if you want to bring in Pulitzer Prize winning poets, like the University of Tennessee, Knoxville, you need money for honoraria and travel expenses, but a modest program that begins with local writers and creates community often requires no more than a welcome handshake and a round of applause after a reading. Many local writers are delighted to share their work with students and with the public at large. The best timing is often when authors have just published a new book. If you partner with the author and your local bookstore, you can reap benefits from premiering the author's new work, while providing the author and the bookstore with the potential for post-reading sales.

Network in the library to build enthusiasm for your ideas. Network on campus to build support and audience. Network with your university's fundraising arm, if you're truly ambitious and want to create a donation fund. Network with your local public library, local bookstores, local historical societies, local branches of your state writing organization (most states have one), local authors, anyone who can help you achieve your goals. Most organizations are happy to work with librarians, valuing their creativity, their willingness to work to make projects come to life, and their ability to promote both their projects and their partners.

Conclusion

It is ironic that in these times when schools and colleges are focused on science, technology, engineering, and mathematics, and the humanities, in general, receive less emphasis, creative endeavors, such as writing and poetry, are more talked about than ever, push technological innovation through digital projects, and engage a wider audience than ever before. Whether it's the easy communication of the World Wide Web, the increased speed between submission and e-publication (for poetry in particular), or the rise of self-publishing, more people are writing and sharing than ever. Academic libraries are in a unique position to partner with creative writing programs and authors (many of whom must work in academia to make a living). Partnerships for writing fit well into the increasing emphasis on outreach by academic libraries to build goodwill and social capital, and the number of poet/librarians (and other author/librarians) who straddle both worlds provide academic libraries with the expertise to make it happen.

Works Cited

Dole, Wanda V., and J. B. Hill. 2012. "Assessing the Good Will of Community Users in an Academic Library." *New Library World,* 113 (5–6): 270–280.

Forrest, Lisa A. 2015. "Going Analog and Getting Artsy: Programming in the Academic Library." *College & Research Libraries News,* 76 (7): 387–391.

Pavelich, David. 2010. "Lighting Fires in Creative Minds: Teaching Creative Writing in Special Collections." *College & Research Libraries News,* 71 (6): 295–313.

From Fieldwork to Framework

Preparing for Library Outreach to Writers and Poets

John Glover

Connecting with writers and poets is a different enterprise from serving many other kinds of patrons. The reader wants to find a good book, the teacher needs to identify appropriate material for her students, the government official wants to study the history of a municipal issue, and the job-seeker needs to be pointed to career databases. A creative writer, whether she is just starting her first short story or finishing assembling her third book of poems, has needs that encompass all these and more. As with any reference transaction, however, the questions that creative writers present to you may be only tangentially connected to their actual needs.

Supporting writers and poets, whether answering basic questions or planning an outreach framework, is neither more nor less complicated than working with other patrons. It does have some special characteristics you can plan for, improving the impact of your efforts. A fundamental part of this planning is learning about your audience—who they are and how they have been served in the past.

Studying the Terrain

Begin by learning something about the creative writers in your area. Presumably you have already studied your community, or conducted some community analyses of your own, but unless you work in an arts-heavy community, or have a position explicitly tied to serving writers and poets (such as liaison to or bibliographer for a creative writing program), likely this study has not focused primarily on this population. Where are the writers and poets likely to be found in your community? If you are at an academic institution, places to start gathering information include:

- English departments
- Creative writing programs, within English, independent, or otherwise
- Rhetoric/composition programs, if separate from English
- Student newspapers, literary journals, or other media programs
- Clubs, trade organizations, or honor societies for creative writers
- Campus writing centers

- After-school activity centers
- Community arts or writing centers

If you are a public librarian, while your creative writers may be everywhere, chances are good that they already number among your library's regular patrons, or can be found nearby. Study course listings at local writing or art centers, community colleges, or municipal offerings. Look for membership lists, if public, associated with local writing organizations, whether on their websites or via activity on social media, in printed newsletters, etc.

This kind of research can be immediately helpful, in that it can provide names for mailing lists or mass e-mails, etc. Perhaps more importantly, however, it can help you identify gatekeepers, like writing program coordinators, club presidents, or influencers, whether poets on advisory boards or writers with large numbers of followers on social media.

What has your library offered for writers and poets in past? If you are taking over duties from a colleague or predecessor, try to get any information she is willing to provide, whether in conversation or by sharing past notes, files, etc. If you are in a new position, or this kind of outreach is new to your library, try checking the library's website or archives for evidence of past activities:

- Writer's groups
- Readings by local or visiting writers or poets
- Courses taught at the library
- Collection development connected with local literature
- Reading lists or other reader's advisory tools associated with writing

As you have time, it is a good idea to learn something about the literary history of the area you serve. How much time to spend on this depends on how important that history is to your patrons, and how easy this history is to locate. Large cities may have had many overlapping literary communities over the years, and it could take a lifetime to study the history of writers and poets in places like Chicago, Los Angeles, New York, etc. (Hughes 2011, 276). By the same token, towns or smaller cities may have only modest extant literary histories, and the effort to ferret it out can be greater than what is gained by doing so. Search for this kind of information in:

- Literary histories or biographies of creative writers in your community, state, or region
- Magazines, newsletters, broadcasts, or other periodicals created in your community that are specifically targeted at writers or poets
- Websites or blogs run by local historians or local literary community members
- Histories of your community, whether published, oral, online, or in archives
- Print or digital indexes of local news sources

Observing the Wildlife

In terms of understanding how to fulfill your creative writing patrons' needs, it is necessary to see what they are actually doing, if that is feasible. One approach is to read what they are writing, whether they are published by high-status literary journals or making their work available on blogs, forums, or websites like Wattpad. While you will not have time to read everything that your patrons are writing, skimming some of it and seeing where it is published or posted can help you evaluate your collections and consider what sorts of services your poets and writers may need that your library is not yet offering. It is particularly important in an academic setting to read books or articles by your faculty about creative writing pedagogy, if any are available, to acquaint yourself with your faculty's ideas about what student writers need in the way of information literacy.

Along the same lines, another way to familiarize yourself with activities of local writers and poets is to attend some of their public events. This may mean sitting in quietly as an observer at a workshop, participating in a NaNoWriMo writing marathon at a coffee shop, attending readings given by your writers or poets, or attending a local open mic, where both experienced and new writers read their work to an audience. These events provide a ready-made opportunity to interact with patrons individually or in small groups and learn something about them, and perhaps their specific needs, that may not emerge clearly from websites or newsletters.

If you are able to win a grant, secure funding from your library, or pay on your own behalf, attending a writing conference provides the opportunity to get a much broader view of the population of creative writers generally. Such events can be found around the country in cities large and small, as well as in some towns and rural areas. While these events are intended for writers and poets, they often have programming tracks or other events that are useful for librarians or readers, whether meeting authors who do not come to events like the American Library Association annual conference, learning about small presses that may fit your patrons' needs but don't tend to get reviewed in publications like *Library Journal* or *Publisher's Weekly*, or listening to panels about the education of writers that can help you to evaluate the quality of your own library's holdings and services. You can find more information about writing conferences in various places:

- Association of Writers & Writing Programs (AWP) website
- Poets & Writers website
- *The Writer*
- *The Writer's Chronicle*
- *Writer's Digest*

Aside from these opportunities for interacting with writers, what other options do you have for information-gathering? Perhaps the most obvious are those associated with duties that bring you into contact with patrons. Whether answering a reference question or responding to a collection development request, opportunities will occasionally present themselves, and it pays to be ready with follow-up questions or offers of information about creative writer-related services your institution might be piloting. This is especially helpful when you are working with very new writers and poets, who may not belong to any group, association, academic program, etc., some of whom you might thus not encounter otherwise.

Deep Background

Part of preparing for library outreach to writers and poets is understanding their history. Many librarians believe that familiarity with literature—recent or past, genre or literary, print or online—prepares them to engage with poets and writers, but this is a fundamental mistake. Received ideas about would-be novelists struggling with typewriters in Parisian garrets, or an ethereal poet wandering fields lonely as a cloud, have little to do with the experience of most writers you will encounter as a librarian. While a few of your patrons may write in near-total isolation, you are more likely to encounter patrons who write at least occasionally in some kind of group context.

For librarians working at universities and colleges, the most important context to understand is that of the academic creative writing program. You may already have reached out to your students or faculty, but do you understand how their environment is structured, and why it exists? Here are some starting places.

- Eric Bennett's *Workshops of Empire* (2015) is one of several recent works that has considered the impact of the Cold War on the literary arts and how government funding and influence shaped the MFA environment.
- *MFA vs. NYC: The Two Cultures of American Fiction* (2014) is a collection of essays edited by Chad Harbach that describes and differentiates between university MFA programs and professional/New York publishing.
- Junot Díaz's "MFA vs. POC" (2014) is an essay centered on issues of race and difference in writing education and is a useful window into the world of young/new writers and poets of color.
- Mark McGurl's *The Program Era* (2009) is an already-seminal study of the growth of U.S. creative writing programs, and how that growth shaped writing and writing culture in the U.S. from the end of World War II onward.
- The AWP occasionally surveys its membership, and the most recent survey results are available on their website, providing statistical insights into creative writing programs across the country.

It doesn't hurt to do some writing of your own, as well, if you have the time and inclination. Whether you do this solo or as part of a course or degree is another question, but it pays to have some practical experience with your patrons' milieu. In this case you have some advantage over librarians working with patrons involved in complex or expensive activities that would take serious investments of time or money to dabble in, whether restoring vintage cars, casting bronze statues, or learning how to build houses. All it takes is a little time and some writing materials.

Baiting the Trap

Having spent time studying your community's writers, learning the needs of writers generally, and understanding the context of writers and writing in the early 21st century, what now? Below are three types of outreach you can engage in, all of which require some work on your part, but none of which will strain your library's budget, and which can provide value for your patrons, both the creative writers and everyone else. Whether they will constitute the entirety of your outreach, or only a part of it, or serve as a stepping stone to innovative partnerships, is up to you and your library to decide.

First Bait: Resource Guide

The particular mixture of library resources that writers and poets need in order to flourish is a complex one, whether your creative writers are doing background research, seeking markets for publication, or learning how to edit their own work. Without guidance, many writers can take a long time to become familiar with all of the types of resources they may need, or want to have available (Glassman). Even writers who have participated in major writing workshops, programs, or residencies have blanks in their knowledge, because inevitably formal training has to skew toward something, whether developing writing craft, learning how to self-publish, or becoming a professional writer.

Public and academic libraries regularly construct pathfinders for a range of needs, whether locally called research guides, resource guides, or LibGuides (to name one currently popular platform), and creating such a tool for creative writers is a substantive form of outreach that is easy to work into your schedule. What should you include? The needs you see among writers in your community should dictate this, but possibilities might include:

- Resources from your collection pertaining to writing
  - Technique advice
  - Market resources
  - Background research
- Suggestions for high-interest areas of your collection for writers and poets
- Lists of online publication resources, lists, or tools
- Lists of local associations, centers, or reading series

How often you update this guide depends on what type of guide it is, and how much time you have to devote to it. A static guide that gives fundamentals of using the library with writers and poets in mind may require little upkeep, except perhaps for changing out title suggestions as new material becomes available. A dynamic guide with many references to resources outside of the library, or that is focused primarily around providing current information, may require regular updating, monthly or otherwise, in order for it to remain current and useful.

Second Bait: Venues

Reading series are helpful in providing your patrons, creative writers and otherwise, direct contact with poets and writers. Depending on where your library is located, there may already be one or more local reading series for poets and writers. You can typically find listings of these in newspapers, newsletters, writing program websites, event websites like Meetup, and so on. Some questions that bear researching are:

- What sort of series is it? Literary craft talks, or readings from stories, poems, etc.?
- Do the speakers address needs you've identified for your community?
- Is attendance limited to a certain audience?
- Can low-income members of your community attend? Consider cover/ticket prices, but also the cost of parking or transit, and whether public transit reaches the venue.

Can your library afford to host a literary reading, or a series of them, bringing in outside speakers and offering refreshments? If so, there are many resources on event planning that can guide you through the steps for this, from websites like ProgrammingLibrarian.org to books with checklists for everything from effective PR to sample budgets (Dowson and Bassett 2015, 189). If funds are tighter, two low- or no-cost options may meet your needs.

A reading, or reading series, centered on local poets and writers can be run in rooms with a range of sizes and configurations. As you will have identified local writers at this point, take a look at their websites, or simply get in contact with them, to learn their availability for speaking. Some writers or poets will only present at events where they are paid, but others will present at no cost, or will make exceptions for library/community events. Be sure to be clear in advance with your reader(s), and with library administration, about how or if you can accommodate writers and poets who wish to sell books at the event.

Another time-honored tradition is that of the open mic event, where the library provides (or partners with another community organization to provide) a space for aspiring or established creative writers to read their work to an audience.

Whichever kind of reading your library decides to sponsor, if this is your first time running such event, don't bite off more than you can chew. Consider starting with a "pilot" reading, well-advertised in advance, with a low or modest expense. Running a reading series is not necessarily difficult once you have it under way, but it can be helpful to run one event, and in a follow-up meeting with colleagues, identify challenges and work out practices or policies to handle them, if they are not in place already. Some questions to consider include:

- What is your room capacity?
- Will you actually use amplification, or are the acoustics satisfactory?
- What level of material will you allow/encourage, and is it appropriate for all ages?
- Can the library provide refreshments? If not, how will you handle, or does policy permit, potluck-style snacks?
- Will staffing this event be part of your and your colleagues' regular duties, or is it "extra," overtime, or volunteer time?
- Can you put together a temporary display of related author materials from your collection for the event, or around the same time as the event?

Third Bait: Education

What do your writers and poets need to learn about? While your collection undoubtedly contains a range of material that can support their education, there are unique benefits for learning and dialogue with in-person instruction, or supporting a group viewing of distance/remote instruction (Brophy and MacFarlane 2015, 139). Depending on your patrons' interests, and their level of accomplishment and commitment, there are many possibilities for topics:

- Research skills
- Sources of inspiration
- Fundamentals of literary technique
- Background/historical research skills
- Advanced literary technique
- Traditional publishing
- Self-publishing

You may or may not yourself be offering these courses, and likely there are also authors in your area who can provide training. Formally they might consist of one-off talks, series of talks, or workshops. Note that the self-help-for-writers industry, along with the charging-writers-for-advice industry, has been going strong for well over a century at this point, so consider carefully whom you invite to speak or teach at your library, particularly if they charge for editing, advice, classes, etc., and be clear on what your library's policy is about presenters "advertising for themselves" in such settings. What constitutes a service and what constitutes a scam can at times be difficult to parse, and one person's resource may be another's con artist.

A Framework for Outreach

Piloting some of the outreach types outlined above will provide an idea of what your community of poets and writers need from your library. Whether you choose to pursue some or all of these, or pursue your own innovative initiatives, you have a range of options that can come together to make a year's worth of outreach. The trick will be learning how to take the feedback you get from that first year, while pursuing that outreach, and using it to shape the next year—before it arrives.

Works Cited

Association of Writers & Writing Programs. "2009–2010 AWP MFA Survey." Accessed January 28, 2016, https://www.awpwriter.org/application/public/pdf/survey/AWPMFASurvey10.pdf.

Bennett, Eric. 2015. *Workshops of Empire*. Iowa City: University of Iowa Press.

Brophy, Kevin, and Elizabeth MacFarlane. 2015. "Redesigning the Lecture in a Cyber World: A Creative Writing Case Study." In *Creative Writing and Education*, 138–149. Bristol, UK: Multilingual Matters.

Díaz, Junot. "MFA vs. POC." Page-Turner. *The New Yorker*, April 30, 2014. Accessed January 29, 2016. http://www.newyorker.com/books/page-turner/mfa-vs-poc.

Dowson, Ruth, and David Bassett. 2015. *Event Planning and Management: A Practical Handbook for PR and Events Professionals*. London, UK: Kogan Page.

Glassman, Julia. "Research Support for Creative Writers: Bolstering Undergraduate Fiction and Poetry Through Library Instruction." *College & Research Libraries News* 75, no. 11 (2014). Accessed January 28, 2016. http://crln.acrl.org/content/75/11/602.full.

Harbach, Chad, ed. 2014. *MFA vs NYC: The Two Cultures of American Fiction*. New York: Faber and Faber.

Hughes, Evan. 2011. *Literary Brooklyn: The Writers of Brooklyn and the Story of American City Life*. New York: Henry Holt.

McGurl, Mark. 2009. *The Program Era*. Cambridge: Harvard University Press.

The Library as a Community of Writers and Readers

STANLEY L. KLEMETSON

In the context of a library, a community could be defined as a group of people with shared interests. Initially, libraries were exclusive communities with a narrow focus. The first part of this chapter provides a brief history of the change from a narrow focus to a broad public focus. The second part contains an example of a modern community of writers and readers in the context of Holiday Book Signing events that often take place in libraries across the country. The final, third, part draws comments from a variety of authors and publications.

History of the Change

The earliest libraries contained records of commercial transactions, or inventories kept on clay cuneiform tablets or papyrus, with some records dating back to 2600 BC. The Library of Alexandria in Egypt functioned as a major center of scholarship from the third century BC until the Roman conquest in 30 BC.

In the 17th and 18th centuries, there were many new libraries across Europe open only to scholars, but books could not be lent. As secular literature became available, there was a greater need for lending libraries. Private and commercial subscription libraries were created. The materials tended to focus on specific non-fiction subject areas.

The American Library Association was founded on October 6, 1876, to provide leadership for the development, promotion, and improvement of library and information services and the profession of librarianship. (American Library Association, 2015). In 1886, the estate of New York Governor Samuel J. Tilden was utilized to establish the New York Public Library as the first official U.S. Public Library. It is currently one of the largest library systems in the world (New York Public Library, 2015).

Andrew Carnegie inspired and funded the growth of free public libraries. The first of his libraries was built in 1889 in Braddock, Pennsylvania. By 1929, he had supported the building of 1689 libraries in the United States and a thousand more in other countries. Equally important were the efforts of the Women's Clubs that lead the community efforts to make the construction and support of the libraries possible (Eduscapes, 2015).

It was believed by Carnegie, and other library benefactors, that just providing a library would elevate the educational level of common people and propel them to higher literary achievements. When statistics did not support these beliefs, libraries developed new services to address the needs of the "common man." Some of these included reference services, children's programs, reader's advisory services, the creation of traveling libraries to rural areas and the sharing of materials between libraries (Eduscapes, 2015).

Case Study of Writers and Readers

Libraries are dedicated to providing free and accessible information to all and have a key role in creating an environment that promotes literacy for all ages and backgrounds. In short, libraries have become community learning centers with the goal of bringing together people with shared interests.

The following case study is provided as an example of library outreach to writers and the benefits to readers. The data was collected from a holiday book signing at Orem Public Library in Orem, Utah. It was organized by Nathan Robison, programming librarian, with the support of the following authors: Ally Condie, Michael Jenson, David Powers King, Dan Wells, Nathan Hale, Christine Hayes, Heather B. Moore, Josi S. Kilpack, and Julie Olson (Klemetson, 2015).

The first two surveys included in the study present the comments from the writers. The next two contain the comments from the readers who came to visit with the authors and to get their books signed. Finally, there is a summary of an interview with Ally Condie about her experiences working with the library outreach events.

Writers' Survey 1: Why Should Writers/Authors Meet with Readers at the Library?

Answers:

- It's great for the exchange of ideas, outreach, sense of community and promoting literacy.
- To encourage library patronage and learn more about what readers want.
- Libraries are such rich environments for sharing ideas and love of reading.
- One-on-one personal interactions and great environment.
- It extends the purpose of the library in regards to fostering a reading community.
- To make personal connections with others and to share reading/writing experiences.
- It is where the books are.
- It is fun.

Writers' Survey 2: How Do You Benefit from Meeting Your Readers?

Answers:

- It's nice to connect with readers—to learn from them, and to know what spoke to them in the stories we write.
- I get an opportunity to meet my fan base and get more exposure.

- Connecting with your readers is a huge highlight for both parties and provides valuable speaking time.
- It helps remind me who my readers are, what they like, and why they read.
- Readers' interaction is both fun and necessary. I love being a reader and a writer at library programs.
- That is one of the main reasons I write—to connect with readers and encourage reluctant readers, especially tween boys, to find books that speak to them.
- Great to get feedback on my books and to talk about writing and publishing. I frequently go to the library to write and to meet with other writers for a write-in.
- As an author, I get to meet readers, hear feedback, and answer questions.
- It buoys me up to know people who enjoy my work.

The authors appreciated the community relationship that was created between them and the readers. They wanted to promote the love of reading in those who talked to them, and they received the benefit of talking to other authors as well as sharing their experiences. Authors indicated that they liked to learn from their readers what resonated with them in the stories that they wrote. It was also their opportunity to give guidance to those readers who wanted to become writers themselves. It became a mutually beneficial activity.

Readers' Survey 1: Why Should Writers/Authors Meet with Readers at the Library?

Answers:

- It encourages us to follow our dreams and shows us that if they can do it so can we.
- They get inspiration and story ideas. We can let authors, know that we appreciate them.
- I can meet writers in the genre I like. I also can network and talk about books.
- My friends are signing books. It helps to spread the word about their books.
- It is a great experience to meet the ones that created the books you love.
- I can learn more about their books and what's coming out in the future.
- What is better than a signed book?
- I think it is cool to meet real authors.
- It is always more enjoyable reading if there is a personal connection.
- It is a comfortable setting and not as much pressure to buy their books, though the option is available.

Readers' Survey 2: How Do You Benefit from Meeting Writers?

Answers:

- I get encouraged that one day I too can become a published author.
- I am shy; they are scary. I did not talk to them much.
- I learn about new books and local writing opportunities and communities.
- It is interesting to hear them talk about various things.
- I think they are all great.
- You can thank them. It is fun to hear what they have to say.
- Through their personalities and our discussion, I decide what to read.

- My friends and family benefit by having signed books.
- Authors have an amazing nourishing energy that keeps me going.
- I love knowing how down-to-earth, normal, and kind they are. I just love meeting the people who make the magic.
- I get excited about reading.

Readers develop a closer bond to the books they are reading when they can talk to the author and get to know why they wrote their books. Avid readers are also the ones who have questions about becoming writers themselves and talking to a published author can be very beneficial and uplifting. The interaction between writers and readers creates the community that allows for the exchange of ideas and shared interests.

Interview with Ally Condie

Ally Condie writes novels for middle school and young adult readers. As a former high school English teacher, she brings excellent practical experiences to her novels. The following interview focuses on the questions asked of all authors involved in the Holiday Book Signing event.

What are the benefits for you to come to these events?

Answer: Writing is so solitary that I love any chance to be out in the community. Librarians are pivotal to our success because they are the ones that determine what books to buy and to put on the shelves, what to book talk or to emphasize. It is great to meet the librarians and the people to whom they recommended my books. It is a chance to interact on a personal or professional level. From the readers' perspective, it is a chance to interact with someone who likes what I have made. If they liked my book, it is fun for them to ask me their questions. Since I write for young adults, it is an extra fun group because they always ask questions. I used to teach high school so this is a group that I like, and I want to give them a chance to ask their questions.

How do the people that come to see you benefit?

A: It is a humbling experience for an author. Some readers like my book and just wanted to meet the author. Some want to interact on a deeper level. This may be the first book that they have read all of the way through. As a former teacher, I always tried to find the right match for my students. I hope that my books help people enjoy reading. Some want to be writers, and this gives them the opportunity to ask about writing. They have come to ask an author about the writing process. A common question is how old were you when you started to write.

How does the library benefit from these events?

A: It generates excitement around the library. A library is unique. It is such a gathering center for the community. It is not a bookstore so people can come to look at books without feeling awkward about reading parts of books and not buying any. It is a crossroad, a place for public discourse.

What can an author do to help the library?

A: When I have a new book coming out, I talk to my friends at the library and determine if they want to host an event. If they do, I am the first to sign up and then solicit other authors to participate in the event.

The following two experiences between readers and writers highlight the importance of these types of events for the community. Mary, 14, and Sarah, 11 were going skiing on the day of the book signing, but when they found out that their favorite author, Ally Condie, was signing the books they wanted to buy, they postponed the trip to the mountain until after they bought her books, had them signed and got their picture taken with her. Jacob, 4, wanted a graphic novel published by Nathan Hale. As he signed his book, Nathan drew a picture of a little devil. Jacob was thrilled. These experiences between writers and readers strengthen their love of books and reading.

Comments and Experiences

Orson Scott Card was first introduced to science fiction and fantasy when he was a young child exploring the local library in Santa Clara, California (Porschet, 2015).

Cheryl Kaye Tardif said, "Reading inspired me. I wanted to create stories just like my favorite authors. I wanted people to be lost in them, affected by them, scared by them. I still want that. I take great pleasure from a fan who says one of my novels made them cry. That is the hugest compliment" (Tardif, 2015).

"Good writers have a passion for words. They read because they enjoy a well-constructed sentence, a powerful paragraph, and a compelling story. Reading works by talented authors encourages a good writer to become better. When a writer tells us he or she dislikes reading, we know that this is an individual courting disaster—and rejection. Books, magazine, and other media should excite you. Libraries and bookstores should be your sacred temples" (Tameri Guide for Writers, 2015).

"In their fifth annual survey of 32,000 children and young people aged between eight and 18, the National Literacy Trust found enjoyment of reading and frequencies of reading are both at their highest levels in nine years. This follows a series of major campaigns and initiatives including Bookstart, the Summer Reading Challenge, the Young Reader Programme and National Literacy Trust Hubs, which have combined with the advocacy for a succession of powerful Children's Laureates to create momentum and to encourage children to read more from a young age. Children and young people who read daily outside of class are five times more likely to read above expected levels for their age compared with young people who never read outside class (National Literacy Trust, 2015).

Author Joel Savage said "Let these great modern library buildings increase your appetite to read." "Many get happiness in doing different things. Gardening, cleaning, cooking, listening to music, participating or watching sports and reading, add happiness to man's life and takes away boredom. However, I take reading as a priority among all activities, since reading enlightens, educates, provides information and aware our consciousness of whatever is going on around us. Just imagine, without reading how can we follow our choice of career professions?" (Savage, 2015)

Author Jim Cherry stated, "If you're a writer you've been writing most of your life. I made that conscious decision when I was 12 or 13. I've been writing and keeping diaries and since then … over 40 years."

"I was always the shy kid reading poetry. I was reading Thoreau and Walt Whitman when I was a freshman in high school. My school records did not reflect anything good. I was always cutting classes, but my mom said she could always find me at the library" (Aurora Public Library, 2015).

"Don't just dream of your book on the library shelf—make sure it circulated. Most writers begin as readers in the library, and today, libraries are doing much of what publishers used to do for their authors—and more" (Association of Writers & Writing Programs, 2015).

From early times libraries have served many functions beyond acquiring and lending books. "The early Carnegie buildings of the 1880s were community centers with swimming pools and public baths, bowling alleys, billiard rooms, even rifle ranges, as well as book stacks.... In short, the library has always been a place where informational and social infrastructures intersect within a physical infrastructure that (ideally) supports the program" (Mattern, 2015).

The Orem Public Library published author interviews conducted by library staff. The following questions and responses that relate to writing and library outreach were extracted from those interviews (Orem Public Library, 2015).

Brandon Mull:

- What do I need to do to become a writer? "Read a lot and write a lot until you figure out what kind of stories you want to tell and what you sound like as a story teller."
- Why do you write? "My head is full of stories. Some seem more interesting and fun to me than many of the books I read and movies I see. Writing is my way to share them."

Katharine Coles

- How does one become a poet? "The short answer is that you become a poet first by reading, then by writing.
- How did you become a poet? "I knew I wanted to be a writer as soon as I realized by the age of seven that the books and poems I loved were written by actual people. The writing comes in response—both from the idea that 'I want to do that.' But also usually from the urge to have a conversation with a particular other poem or set of poems."

Sarah Eden

- What are the characteristics of a good story, character, etc.? "That is not a question that can be answered in a single paragraph. However, one thing I think is crucial to good writing is authenticity. Too many writers employ a tight-fisted control over their plot, characters, setting, etc., forcing the story to take the shape they, the author, want it to take rather than letting the characters act the way they ought to act and allowing the plot to play out in a way that is natural, even if it isn't convenient. Sometimes that means letting characters make stupid mistakes or behave in ways the author would not. Often that means the plot does not take the shape the author had anticipated, and it means more work. But, in the end, a story that isn't authentic doesn't work."

Julie Olson

- What inspired you to make a career in illustration? "I have always loved to draw. I was not the best artist in class, but I worked hard and practiced. I also loved stories. My dad would read us kids Mark Twain's words and use all of the right accents and expressions. I finally realized that expressing a story through pictures was truly my calling."

Carol Lynch Williams

- What makes a good story? "As a writer, I have to be interested in my character. Since I spend a lot of time in the book, I want to love whom I am working with. Therefore, the character is important to me. I also have to care emotionally about what my character is going through."

Lisa Mangum

- What advice do you have for aspiring writers seeking to improve the quality of their writing? "First, read. Read everything you can get your hands on. Read books in your genre; read books out of your genre. Read well-written books and poorly written books. The more you read, the more you develop an instinct for what works and what does not. It also helps when you know what kind of stories are being published and which trends are waxing and waning.... The second bit of advice is to write. The more you write, the more practice you have writing. Perhaps that sounds too basic, but sometimes the only way to become better at a skill is to just practice every day.... Don't tell yourself that everything you write has to be perfect the first time.... Writing is a process, not perfection.... Attend writing conferences and network with other writers."

Josi Kilpack

- What is your advice to aspiring writers? "Learn the craft! Then, learn your craft. In addition, when you finish with that, learn your craft some more. The only thing more frustrating to me than reading a poorly written book by a new novelist (I do contest judging and free-lance editing) is reading a poorly written book by a seasoned writer. Just like a surgeon, a plumber, or a police officer, there are skill sets that are necessary for a writer to be good at what they do. Learn those skills. Take writing courses at a local college, attend writer's conferences, read books on writing, read great books and take note of why you love them. Never stop doing these things, never stop improving, and never believe you know it all, because you don't."

Chris Crowe

- When did you know that you wanted to be a writer? "The summer between 6th and 7th grade. I was doing a lot of reading—old science fiction and most of the Sherlock Homes stories by Conan Doyle—and it occurred to me that it would be interesting to be the person on the other side of the book, to be the writer, not the reader. Of course, I had no idea what that would entail, but I did pound out a few pages on my dad's old Underwood typewriter that summer."
- What advice to you have for aspiring professional writers? "Richard Peck likes to say something like 'You can't become a writer if you're not a reader.' I agree with him on that. It is essential for aspiring writers to read widely, not just in their favorite genre but also in all kinds of books. A successful writer must also have the self-discipline required to write. I have learned, again and again, that the real work of writing is in revision, and in order to revise well, I have to rely on a smart,

trusted reader who will tell me the truth about the manuscript. Good writers have to embrace revision and refuse to send off a manuscript before it is ready. When I think I am finished with a manuscript, I know that I'm really only just beginning the work."

Dan Wells

- How do you become a writer? "By writing. Becoming a published writer takes longer, but it is still the same basic process: write, and then write more, then write more, and then keep writing, and every story will get better, and every book will get stronger and eventually it will happen. Quality will out. Always be writing, always be submitting, and always be looking for the next opportunity to read."

Ally Condie

- Do you have any advice for aspiring writers? "Write every day, or close to it. Be disciplined about it and take it seriously. If you are not good yet, do not despair. Give yourself the time you need each day and over the years to get better. It's okay if it takes time, but make sure you're putting in the time."

Closing Comments

Libraries have always provided more than books. With close to 175,000 libraries across the United States there are diverse library services tailored to fit their community needs. A few of the services provided at the Orem Public Library related to writers and readers include the following: author interviews, Utah Valley Writers group, Society for Children's Book Writers and Illustrators, Story time, Reading Education Assistance Dogs (R.E.A.D.), Children's Summer Reading program, Shakespeare for Kids, Teens Summer Reading Program, Orem Reads, Book Club, Book Talk and Signing. These are but a sampling of what might be found to create the community between writers and readers.

Works Cited

American Library Association. 2015. "Mission & History." Retrieved 31 December 2015. http://www.ala.org/aboutala/missionhistory.

Association of Writers & Writing Programs. 2015. "R152. Libraries Influence Readers, Writers, and Communities." Retrieved 31 December 2015. https://www.awpwriter.org/awp_conference/event_detail/3824.

Aurora Public Library. 2015. "Writer 'Under the Influence of Rock and Roll' to Appear at Library Author Fair." Retrieved 31 December 2015. http://www.aurorapubliclibrary.org/about-the-library/news-press-releases/columns-by-amy-roth/writer-under-the-influence-of-rock-and-roll-to-appear-at-library-author-fair/.

Eduscape. 2015. "History of Libraries." Retrieved 31 December 2015. http://eduscapes.com/history/contemporary/1900.htm.

Klemetson, Stanley L. 2015. Holiday Book Signing Event at Orem Public Library, Orem, Utah on December 5, 2015. Personal interviews with writers and readers.

Mattern, Shannon. 2014. "Library as Infrastructure." Retrieved 31 December 2015. https://placesjournal.org/article/library-as-infrastructure/.

National Literacy Trust. 2015. "Reading Levels Hit Nine Year High as Record Number of Children Enjoy Reading Every Day." Published 20 May 2015. http://www.literacytrust.org.uk/media/6647_reading_levels_hit_nine_year_high_as_record_numbers_of_children_enjoy_reading_every_day.

New York Public Library. 2015. "History of the New York Public Library." Retrieved 31 December 2015. http://www.nypl.org/help/about-nypl/history.

Orem Library. 2015. "Author Interviews." Retrieved 31 December 2015. http://oremlibrary.org/index.php/calendarfind-upcoming-events/author-interviews.

Porschet, Martha Whitmer. 2015. "Orson Scott Card—What Influences This Science Fiction Writer." Retrieved 31 December 2015. http://www.hatrack.com/research/student-papers/porschet.shtml.

Savage, Joel. 2015. "The Influence of Technology on Public Libraries." Retrieved 31 December 2015. https://joelsavage1.wordpress.com/2015/04/26/the-influence-of-technology-on-public-libraries/.
Tameri Guide for Writers. 2015. "Influences, Good and Bad." Retrieved 31 December 2015. http://www.tameri.com/workshop/influences.html.
Tardif, Cheryl Kaye. 2015. "What Influenced Me to Become a Writer?" Retrieved 31 December 2016. http://www.cherylktardif.com/what-inspired-me-to-be-writer/.

Bridging the Gap

A Playwright, Sneak Peek and Production of a Performance

JEN PARK *and* JAMES W. PHILLIPS

Mount Saint Mary College is a small liberal-arts college located in Newburgh, New York, with a student body of approximately 2500 students. MSMC hosts more than 50 undergraduate programs that lead to a bachelor of arts or bachelor of science, as well as master's degree programs in education, business, and nursing. With a wide range of academic disciplines, the library understands there is a need for diverse programming on campus in order to appeal to each area of study. The Kaplan Family Library at Mount Saint Mary College continuously looks for opportunities to partner with divisions on campus in order to create or assist with programs that would result in bringing the college community physically into the library.

Recognizing the need for novel programs that would foster interest in library programs and services throughout the collegiate community, Barbara Petruzzelli, library director, approached director of theatre James Phillips in the fall of 2011 about a low-cost new initiative: the Sneak Peek. Petruzzelli described the Sneak Peek to be a short preview of the upcoming theatre production. Phillips, an assistant professor in the Division of Arts & Letters at the time, was amenable to this program as it would give the actors in the upcoming theatre production some practice in front of a live audience a few days before opening night. Since the inception of the Sneak Peek, this event has grown from a one-time program to being held each semester. Despite staffing changes within the library, the Sneak Peek has continued to be a successful event that has created the basis to a strong relationship between MSMC Theatre and the library.

Sneak Peeks

The purpose of the Sneak Peek, from the point of view of the library, is to bring the collegiate community into the library while giving a preview of the upcoming theatre performance. As information professionals, librarians understand the importance of patrons reaching a level of comfort with the library and staff in order for the space and resources to be adequately utilized. The theatre department saw the Sneak Peek as an opportunity for the theatre group to practice acts within the upcoming performance.

The ability to practice in front of a live audience was particularly enticing since many of the actors were first semester students at MSMC. With the multiple goals of the Sneak Peek events established the departments moved forward with forming the logistics needed to carry them out.

One of the most enticing aspects of the Sneak Peek was that the cost of the program was minimal. The only costs associated with the Sneak Peek were the promotional materials. Time spent creating and disseminating promotional materials were taken into account as well, but the overhead was small enough to not concern budgetary restrictions.

Library Staff Assigned to Event

The library staff originally dedicated to creating a successful Sneak Peek was the library director and the administrative assistant. Through title changes and the library employing new staff, the Kaplan Family Library currently has one librarian dedicated to outreach activities. These outreach activities include creating and strengthening partnerships with the campus community and promoting events the library sponsors or co-sponsors. The librarians also have liaison areas dedicated to the divisions and schools at MSMC. Coincidentally, the Division of Arts & Letters' liaison librarian is the outreach librarian. Therefore, just one librarian is dedicated to the entirety of the Sneak Peek which allows for even communication and a smaller possibility of mistakes being made. The Library Director is still involved, but as an administrator rather than an event organizer.

The administrative assistant has continued to work on the logistics behind the scenes. This includes contacting Information Technology department with any technology requests needed for the event, generating a work order with Facilities staff to have the layout of the event space organized properly, and ensuring that the room is arranged properly. She is also available to assist as needed on the day of the Sneak Peek.

Logistics

The duties between the two departments were discussed and split evenly. With the Sneak Peek taking place in the library, the library became responsible for creating and distributing the promotional materials and logistical setup. Phillips was responsible for coordinating a date and time that the actors were available to produce the Sneak Peek as well as relaying the information to the actors regarding where and when the Sneak Peek would take place. Any costumes, properties or furniture pieces needed were the responsibility of MSMC Theatre. Generally, the actors perform in full costume, but only the essential props and furniture are used.

In order to engage patrons informally with the Sneak Peek, it was decided that the event would be conducted in an open area. The Kaplan Family Library has an all-purpose area that can be set up in such a way that patrons are still able to walk through the area without being intrusive. This open setup allowed patrons who were studying or passing through the library a chance to be exposed to a theatrical event. The setting also created an open invitation to the Sneak Peek while keeping the Sneak Peek itself informal. Patrons were able to come and go as they pleased during the short Sneak Peek without disturbing the actors.

Technology was not needed for the Sneak Peek events. In the future, should the Sneak Peek need microphones, the library is able to accommodate this request. However, this would diminish the informality the event warrants. Additionally, not using a microphone keeps the volume of the event to a minimum, thus allowing for the noise level to be less intrusive to patrons who are studying. To date, the library has yet to receive a noise complaint from patrons when a Sneak Peek is being performed.

The Sneak Peek Schedule of Events

The benefit of bringing a group to a non-library event is being able to inform them of library services and programs they may not be aware of. The Sneak Peek opened with a welcome from the director of the library who used the time to inform the attendees of such services and programs. She then introduced the director of the theatrical production who thanked everyone for coming to the Sneak Peek and gave an introduction of the portions of the play the actors would be showcasing. The theatre director turned the "stage" over to the actors and introduced the first part of the Sneak Peek.

Phillips selected three to five scenes from the production that could be performed by the available actors. These scenes are typically from the first half of the play so as not to give away the ending. Each scene opens with a short introduction from the director. When the actors have completed the last scene, the director introduces the actors and they take a curtain call, much like at the end of a full performance. He then gives information relating to the show including where and when the show will take place as well as information about ticket purchasing and price.

Promotion and Marketing

The library created and disbursed the promotional materials based on the marketing plan used for special events. This plan includes a timeline for the creation of the materials as well as their specific placement around campus. In addition to the physical resources, digital materials were also designed.

The theatre department created the posters for the fall production and hung them around the campus. Rather than design a second poster showcasing information about the Sneak Peek, a small neon sign was made with the logistical Sneak Peek information: place, date, and time. Work-study students from the library placed the small sign on the fall production posters throughout the campus.

The digital promotion included e-mail, social media outlets, and campus-wide digital signage. Along with an image depicting the play, the e-mail contained information about the upcoming production along with information about the Sneak Peek event. This e-mail was sent to faculty and staff one week before the Sneak Peek. The second e-mail was sent to the same group with the addition of the student listserv three days before the Sneak Peek. Finally, on the day of the Sneak Peek, the last e-mail sent highlighted the event place and time.

Using the wording from the e-mail as well as the graphics, a promotional slide was created for the library's digital signage system as well as the campus-wide digital signage system. This slide was placed on the signage system the same day the first e-mail promoting the Sneak Peek was sent out. Information regarding the Sneak Peek was highlighted in the slide, although there was also basic information about the theatre production. This slide was also posted to the library's Facebook page.

The last piece of digital promotional material was placed on the portal to the college. Here, there are postings of upcoming events and information that is made available to the college community. The same information that was sent through the e-mail about the Sneak Peek was placed on the Portal. This was completed one week before the event.

Signage for the day of the Sneak Peek is important as well. The library placed the posters with the neon Sneak Peek signs in front of the entrance points of the building to let people know where and when the Sneak Peek would be held. With several entrance points in the building, staff at each service station in the library was made aware of the event time and place in order to assist as needed.

The End Result of the Sneak Peek

As stated earlier, Sneak Peeks take place each semester during the week of the production. This generally means that the Sneak Peek is taking place in the open space of the library between mid-terms and finals—a time when many of the spaces in the library are being heavily used for student work. The library is conscious of the implications that may arise from its space being used in a disruptive and loud manner to promote an event, but it had not received complaints from patrons yet. In fact, while the Sneak Peek has attracted a formal attendance of audience members seated in the seats set up in front of the "stage," many times patrons studying in the library will wander to the space out of curiosity and end up watching the Sneak Peek in its entirety.

The Sneak Peeks provide a chance for students to perform in front of a small audience with very low stakes. Theatre productions at Mount Saint Mary are typically scheduled for only three nights, so the opportunity to perform in front of an audience before opening night is extremely valuable. In comedies the actors begin the process of learning where the laughs will come and how to hold the action to allow the laughs time to crest. In more dramatic pieces they learn how the audience will respond to the story and their characters. According to MSMC student Rebecca Gordils, "The Sneak Peeks have always kind of been a little ice breaker for me into how the audience will perceive the show. I'm always excited to see their reactions, no matter how different they are from what I was expecting, and then I am able to assess my performance and how I'm portraying my character or scene."

MSMC Theatre also uses the Sneak Peek as a way to market the upcoming production. The neon-colored announcements attached to the posters add visual interest and increase the likelihood of people giving a second look to the poster. After the posters have been hanging for a month, the splash of color and text freshen the look and help the poster stand out among a crowd of other advertisements. At the performance the production is introduced to both those specifically attending the Sneak Peek and those passing by or studying close to the event. For some, the Sneak Peek is their first knowledge of an upcoming production.

Playwright Residency

With successful Sneak Peek events carried out each semester since 2011, with the exception of one semester when it was logistically not possible due to the relocation of the library from one building to another, the Division of Arts & Letters approached the library about a co-sponsorship opportunity for the fall of 2015. *The Women of Lockerbie* playwright, Deborah Brevoort pays close attention to rights requests received through Dramatists Play Service, and noticed that Mount Saint Mary had submitted a request for November performance dates. Brevoort contacted Phillips on September 5, 2015, offering to arrange an artistic residency during the rehearsal period. The offer was accepted, with the understanding that the visit was contingent upon securing funding. The visit was conceived to have three components: classroom discussion, a public event, and rehearsal visitation. The Division of Arts and Letters, MSMC Theatre's academic home, was asked to contribute to help support the classroom portion of the event, and the library was asked to host and contribute to support the public event. Both groups were eager to assist and agreed to the hosting and funding requests. After further discussions with all the parties involved, the visitation was finalized with just five weeks to plan the logistics of the event. The two departments began to move forward with the marketing and promotion of the playwright's visit as well as the Sneak Peek that would take place one month after her visit.

Because of the short time between securing funding and the agreed-upon date of the residency, much of the planning was done after the event had already been scheduled. Under normal circumstances an event like this would be planned months ahead, with venues and content determined before finalizing an agreement with the playwright, but the opportunity to have Brevoort come to the college was too valuable an experience to allow a condensed planning period to interfere. MSMC Theatre and the library staff have experience planning and executing events, and that experience was vital in creating a schedule on such short notice. Both organizations were flexible and willing to improvise as necessary, and Brevoort was extremely accommodating with her schedule and requests.

It was important that the college maximized the day of Brevoort's residency with minimal fatigue being caused on the part of the author. Therefore, the residency was to be composed of three parts: classroom discussion, a public event and a rehearsal visitation. The classroom discussion was planned with members of the Division of Arts and Letters and was the first event of the residency, taking place in the morning. The public event was co-sponsored with the library for an afternoon discussion and the rehearsal visitation was slated for the normally scheduled rehearsal time that evening.

The content of the public event was largely left to Brevoort, who had expressed a willingness to discuss the content of the play and the story of its conception. She has experience speaking for both educational and public audiences, so she was well equipped for such a presentation even with limited preparation time. Her one request for her talk was to have access to a DVD and projector, as her talk began with a clip from a DVD of a *Nightline* episode from December 1998 that featured the laundry project of the women of Lockerbie, Scotland. Both MSMC Theatre and the library staff moved quickly to finalize the details of the residency, and within a week most of the planning had been confirmed. Brevoort supplied a title to her talk, "The Writer's Impulse and the Writing of The Women of Lockerbie," and promotional efforts began.

Promotional Items for Brevoort's Visit

The previous long partnership between the library and MSMC Theatre allowed the day of the residency and public talk to be well promoted throughout the campus. The college marketing department, in consultation with MSMC Theatre, handled outside promotions and website content. The condensed timeline made it difficult to saturate all local media, but the event was able to be advertised in the local newspaper, the *Times Herald-Record*.

Since Brevoort's visit was tied to the upcoming Sneak Peek as well as MSMC Theatre's production of *The Women of Lockerbie*, it was important to keep promotional materials for her discussion consistent with the upcoming events. Although new promotional materials were created using the same templates as the Sneak Peek materials, the main difference was the content of the items. While it was important to convey that the playwright's visit was tied in to the Sneak Peek as well as the Fall Theatre production, it also had to be noted that this was going to be a talk given by the person whose work would be viewed. Brevoort's visit was promoted using the same timeline and resources as were used for the Sneak Peek.

Public Discussion

Brevoort's talk lasted approximately ninety minutes, including ample time for questions and discussion. After sharing the video clip of the laundry project that inspired her to write *The Women of Lockerbie*, which would be produced by MSMC Theatre later that semester, she explained how this topic that she had not heard before was able to foster a story idea. She further explained that she did the opposite of what most playwrights do—she did not research the topic. Rather, she wrote the play from what she knew of the facts from the video segment she had watched and then added in the characters and materials as she saw fit. This idea to not research the topic before writing is generally not found to be promoted by libraries but her feeling of being strongly compelled to write creatively on the topic resonated with the audience. She then shared her struggle in getting the play produced, finally accepting an offer that resulted in a poorly received premiere production. It was only years afterward that the play started to find an audience without the support of strong critical reviews.

Brevoort's candid discussion regarding her struggles as a playwright was refreshing. Rather than glossing over her work, she gave a thorough account of the struggles she faced as a playwright. The takeaway from her talk was that the playwright development and production business is incredibly difficult to break into and aspiring playwrights must be prepared for many obstacles that are necessary to overcome when trying to break into the business.

While the attendance for the talk was less than hoped for, those in attendance found Brevoort's struggles and her perseverance, as well as the true events behind *The Women of Lockerbie*, inspiring. For most, the play was the introduction to the Laundry Project and showing the video made a great impact. Brevoort's presentation and subsequent discussion with the audience members adequately tied the three events together. For the audience to be able to ask questions about the author's pursuit of production, to then be able to watch a short production of the play, and then be one of the fortunate attendees to see the sold-out theatre production was an incredible and immeasurable experience.

A Strong Partnership

There are clear benefits for MSMC Theatre. The willingness of the library to help fund Brevoort's residency and host a public talk made the event possible. MSMC Theatre simply does not have the funding to make these types of residencies possible. The library's willingness to host the public talk also provided far greater visibility to the residency and the performances of *The Women of Lockerbie*. The library is a central hub on campus, visited by a large proportion of the student body and faculty/staff. The publicity efforts of the library staff provided far greater exposure to the campus community than would have been true had the event been solely sponsored by MSMC Theatre.

The partnership between the Kaplan Library and MSMC Theatre started small, but as the relationship developed, new programming was developed and more resources were committed to expanded collaboration. When Petruzzelli approached MSMC Theatre about a Sneak Peek neither organization was committing to anything beyond that single event. The success of the Sneak Peek encouraged both organizations to commit to Sneak Peaks for each of MSMC Theatre's productions. The collaboration between the library staff and MSMC Theatre grew and evolved with each event. Promotional and logistical needs and responsibilities were clarified over time and made as consistent as possible given the particular requirements of each theatre production.

When the opportunity to host a playwright residency arose, the relationships developed through the Sneak Peeks made possible the commitment of funds, space and staff time. The initial inquiry by Petruzzelli asking to partner with MSMC Theatre laid the groundwork for a relationship that has grown with time. Even with staffing changes at the library trust between the two organizations is high, and a "can do" attitude has developed regarding almost every request. It is unlikely that the playwright residency would have been approved without the success of and experience gained through the Sneak Peeks.

Librarian as Volunteer
United Way ReadingPals Program

Sarah Cissé

Every professional writer had to learn to write. But before they could learn to write, they had to learn to read. Upon consideration one realizes that without reading, there is no writing. Indeed, studies point out a strong correlation between early reading skills and the development of good writing skills. The ability of a child to visually discriminate between letters and then words is a strong predictor of writing development and a measure of the foundation stage of writing skills itself. Children tend to learn letters as members of a set which suggests that visual processing is important in determining those who will become better writers (Bourke, Davies, Sumner and Green 2014).

It has been found that even as early as kindergarten the grammatical skills of children are a great predictor of the quality of their writing. Positive and significant correlations between grammatical understanding and writing were identified in a study of adolescent students with a history of language impairment (Silverman, Coker, Proctore, Harring, Piantedosi and Hartranft 2015). Simply reading good quality texts can bring the world of imagination and creativity to life which provides students with great opportunities for writing (Robertson 2015). The greater the lexical awareness, such as derivations and opaque expressions in students' reading, the greater the use of derivations in their own writing (Tonne and Pihl 2015). This correlation extends beyond elementary grades through the educational career and into college, where low reading ability can hinder technical writing skills (Collins, Onquegbuzie and Jiao 2014). Even reading poetry can contribute to the writing curriculum, in that poems written for children have a distinct pattern or structure on which they can model their own writing. By emulating poems that they enjoy reading, students may engage in a deeper analysis of the poems and begin to internalize the linguistic and poetic structures used by the poets. Writing can be nurtured through the regular and intentional reading of poetry in classrooms at all grade levels (Rasinski 2014).

United Way ReadingPals Program

In July 2015 I received an e-newsletter which included a brief mention of the ReadingPals program through the United Way of Broward County. ReadingPals pairs volunteers with elementary aged children to practice reading throughout the school year. The newsletter talked about how volunteer mentors can make a lasting impact, and how successful the previous year had been for the program. I had recently worked with elementary aged children at the university library where I work and truly enjoyed the experience. It dawned on me that as a librarian I might be the perfect candidate to volunteer for the ReadingPals program. Having never done volunteer work before, but always having wanted to, I knew that this program could be the perfect way to begin. Not surprisingly for a librarian, I had always loved to read. I remember many lovely afternoons spent sitting on the floor of my elementary school library browsing through Nancy Drew books. I wanted to help children to experience the same enjoyment, and so I wanted to know more about the program.

Mentoring is described as an intense, instructional relationship in which the mentor serves to enhance the development of the mentee through the provision of information, assistance, support and guidance. The mentoring relationship is usually structured around activities, such as observation, demonstration, conferencing, and affirmation (Ross 2014). It is widely acknowledged as a powerful technique and is often used at significant transitions in education, such as moving from primary to secondary education, secondary to the university level, or into the work-force. Mentoring may involve outside partners, for example, university students or successful working persons often mentor kids in school to support, encourage and raise their aspirations. Other variations, such as peer mentoring, may involve older students mentoring younger ones within or across the school sector. However, mentoring programs do have certain limitations, as well as, costs. Mentors not only have to be trained, but training must be of a high quality and also closely supervised at all stages. It is essential that any mentor recognize their limitations and are aware of when issues would be best referred. This also applies to the trainers, who should be keenly aware of program lines of referral and supervision (McFarlane and Wroe, 2014).

Mentoring and volunteerism are activities that many librarians take part in. The library environment, which often relies on the assistance of volunteers on a daily basis, serves to encourage some librarians to become involved in such activities themselves. If time, cash and travel are limited, one may consider volunteering locally. Volunteering in general can give you a new perspective, valuable skills and important contacts. Consider volunteer mentorship with a regional library association which can provide opportunities to give back to the profession (La Chappelle and Wark 2014).

Lorna Eguia, a librarian at the American Corner library at the University of San Carlos in the Philippines, was just launching her mobile library service, Books in Bags (BiB), when the country was hit by Typhoon Haiyan in early November 2013. As her family was being evacuated, she grabbed a kit from BiB along with emergency supplies. The stories and other materials in the BiB kit were a welcome treat for the children in the shelter where Eguia stayed for two days during the typhoon. She also rallied volunteers to ramp up her program so she could provide what she calls "bibliotherapy" to children displaced by the storm. Due to a great deal of experience with storytelling workshops and seminars, Eguia was ready with an arsenal of storytelling techniques designed to capture kids' attention that she terms H.I.T.: stories to HEAL emotion, soul, and spirit; to INSPIRE in spite of disasters; and to TRANSFORM the mind-set of children and their families (Library Journal, 2015). Another volunteer program, "Book Blast" which is hosted by The Kidgits Club, celebrates books and the joy of reading. Children are able to enjoy an afternoon of arts and craft activities, treats and book readings at the local mall. Local librarians in the community are among many who volunteer their time to read for the kids (Banda 2014). Librarians volunteer their time not only in local libraries, but also in libraries around the world. After visiting Malawi as a volunteer in 2009, Suffolk librarian Lesley Martin (2015) returned to establish a library for the Good News Orphanage in rural southern Malawi, near Mozambique. She researched the steps to setting up and running a library in an African country, mobilized volunteers, and solicited book donations. Future plans for the library include making it available to the wider community for local children and adults to use.

Improving communities is the central focus of many charitable organizations. United Way Worldwide, the parent organization for ReadingPals, improves lives by mobilizing the caring power of communities around the world to advance the common good. The organization advances the common good by creating opportunities for all. Their main focus is on education, income and health, which they promote as the building blocks for a good quality of life and a strong community. United Way's mission is to improve lives and strengthen communities, which is powered by the enthusiasm and dedication of 2.6 million volunteers. These volunteers are ordinary people who donate their time and skills to create lasting solutions that improve the lives of everyone. Improving communities requires, not only money, programs and policies, but the willingness of people from all walks of life to volunteer wherever they are needed the most (United Way).

On the local level, United Way of Broward County provides solutions for the challenges faced by people in various communities. Their goal is to help children and youth reach their full potential through quality education; give families the support they need through financial education; and also teach people to make sound decisions about their health. United Way, along with community volunteers who are experts in their fields, identifies specific needs, partners and funding to develop programs which deliver measurable results. Through collaboration, the best people, ideas, skills and resources are brought together to find solutions to complex challenges for long-term positive change in Broward County (United Way of Broward County).

ReadingPals, just one United Way of Broward County program, is an early literacy initiative targeted towards children in kindergarten through third grade. The program pairs volunteer mentors with young children struggling with reading skills, focuses on making sure that these children are exposed to literature and are reading at grade level by the end of the third grade. Almost a third of Florida's grade three students in public school cannot read at minimally proficient levels. Ultimately, these children are four times more likely to drop out of high school. Volunteers, focused on improving third grade reading scores, each commit 25 hours to working with children in pre-kindergarten and first grade. The United Way trains and deploys volunteer "reading pals" who dedicate one hour a week for 25 weeks to read to a child. ReadingPals also provides approximately 15 books for each child to take home for their personal library. Currently the program is in 14 public schools and six childcare sites, which reaches more than 300 children (United Way of Broward County).

Becoming a ReadingPals Volunteer Mentor

Once I applied for the ReadingPals program through the online form on their website I was scheduled to attend a training and information session about the program. The online form asks for basic information such as:

- Name
- Address
- Email address
- Phone number
- The ability to volunteer for one hour a week during school hours (8:30–2:30 p.m.)
- ReadingPals status (new or returning)
- Desire to be notified about other volunteer opportunities
- Fingerprinting for Level 2 security clearance
- Training date, time, duration (2 hours) and location

On the day of training, after finding my way to the training site at the School Board of Broward County in downtown Fort Lauderdale, I was issued a temporary visitor's photo ID at the security reception desk. I was then directed to another area of the building to have fingerprinting done before training began. Once fingerprinted, I went back to the reception area to wait for training to begin. Not surprisingly, security in this Board of Education building was extremely high, with many restricted areas. This meant that all trainees had to be escorted in groups to the training room on a higher floor.

I had arrived to the site early, so I sat in the lobby to wait, checking my phone and wondering what to expect from the training session. In the meantime the organizers of the training had arrived, and with a flurry of activity the lobby was suddenly a "pop-up" photo studio. The pictures they took of us with the lobby wall as backdrop were to become our ReadingPals ID badges, should we accept the challenge. After signing a release that allowed my image to be used in United Way publications, a small group of us were escorted up to the training room where we waited for the trainer and other trainees to arrive.

Once we were assembled, the trainer introduced herself and welcomed us to the training session. We were given training materials, which included the ReadingPals volunteer manual, a children's book and a short exercise pamphlet to go with it. The manual covered topics such as:

- Becoming a ReadingPal
- Books
- Children's safety
- Tips for the first and last day of being a volunteer
- How to be an effective listener
- Qualities of an effective mentor
- Diversity
- Tips for reading with children

The trainer asked us about past mentorship experiences, which allowed new participants to hear about the past experiences of returning mentors. We also viewed a short United Way video about the program. However, a good portion of the training session was a review and discussion of the guidelines, and expectations for working with students. We were given the opportunity to ask questions about how the program operated, the students who were involved, and how we would work with the student's school during the course of the ReadingPals year. Volunteers were made aware that the voluntary commitment was 1 hour a week for 25 weeks during the school year. Mentors were made aware that during and after the program there would be no contact with the student outside of their school. So, the importance of developing a relationship with the child through healthy interaction during the sessions was stressed.

For the remaining portion of the training session we were asked to break into small groups of 2 or 3 to practice reading and responding with each other, simulating an actual ReadingPals session. The trainer emphasized that this was essential to understanding what an actual session entailed and how we were expected to interact with a student. As a trainee I found that this exercise, as both reader and responder, was a very quick way to understand exactly what would be expected of me with an actual student. I realized that I would have to actively engage the student, and think of ways to keep the student interested in the book we were reading, for an entire hour. As I flipped through the ReadingPals manual later on, I gave serious thought about whether this was something I could not only do, but do well. I realized that it was important to be able to be fully present and committed to the student during the sessions for the entire school year. I determined that not only could I be all of those things, but more importantly, I wanted to be. I wanted to help a student improve their reading skills and I somehow knew that I would enjoy the process, maybe even more than the student!

I left the training feeling motivated and elated about my decision to be a ReadingPals volunteer mentor. After the training the coordinator of the program sent email updates regarding security clearance. Once cleared, I received a letter stating that I had been screened by Broward County, FBI and FDLE and approved for "Level 2 Clearance," which allowed me to serve as a mentor at a Broward County Public School campus during the school day. I was asked to take this letter with me to the school on the first day of volunteering. Soon after receiving clearance, I was asked to choose two schools where I wanted to volunteer, one of which I was eventually assigned to. I chose the two sites based on my work schedule, with which I had a bit of flexibility, and the proximity of the schools to my home and workplace. After the training, materials provided and frequent communication with the program coordinator, I felt adequately prepared for my first day of volunteering.

On the first day of volunteering I met the school's ReadingPals coordinator in the front office, where I signed in, and was given the ID badge created on the day of training, and session materials such as:

- ReadingPals curriculum for the year
- Exercises and vocabulary lists for each book to be read
- Mini white-board, marker and eraser
- Crayons

I was shown where the books were housed in the school's media center, and then escorted to my ReadingPal's classroom to meet the student for the first time. When I got to the classroom, I was introduced to the teacher, who let us know that the student I was originally assigned to work with was not at school that day. Since there were other students on a waiting list who were in need of a ReadingPals mentor, I was quickly assigned to another student.

We met in a specially designated room for the sessions. I began by asking the student some questions so that we could get to know each other a little bit before reading the assigned book. I asked about her age, birthday, parents, and siblings. The student was very excited to be out of her normal classroom setting, and curiously explored the space we were in. She wasn't immediately interested in reading the book, however, once she noticed the bright, colorful pictures in the book she became curious about the story. She followed along as I read, and answered questions I raised about the story, as well as, asked her own questions. After we finished reading the story, she suggested we play some games, so I used the white board I was supplied with so that she could draw pictures based on the story and play tic-tac-toe with me. We continued to talk about the story, and I reminded her that we would read the same book again next week.

When it was time for her to go back to class, she did not seem to want to leave. She explored the room some more for a few minutes, and lingered in the hallway when we got to her classroom door. As her teacher encouraged her to go back into the classroom, I said goodbye and reminded her that I would see her the following week at the same time. Before the next session, I re-familiarized myself with the lesson plan. We would be reading the same book again, but would be working through different exercises during the session. I also contacted the program and school coordinator for advice about how to handle behavioral issues during the sessions.

At the start of session two, the student seemed eager to leave her classroom to join me, but seemed disappointed that we would be reading the same book again. Hence, it was more difficult to gain her attention as I began reviewing the book with her. I tried asking her questions to see what she remembered about the story from the week before. Once again, she was drawn to the bright colors and images, and became willing to participate. At the end of the session I told her that I had a gift for her, and presented her with the book. She resisted taking the book, and seemed disappointed, as if she had expected another type of gift. Back at her classroom, I handed the book to the teacher, emphasizing that the book belonged to her, as the label inside the front cover stated.

To my great surprise at the beginning of the third session she announced that she had read a book since our last session. She explained that she had read the book that I gave her, with her mother. She seemed proud as well as aware of the importance of the activity. As I pulled out a new book she immediately asked if she could take it home as well, and was eager to label and write her own name in the front cover, which she did with great care. She showed even more interest in this second book, tried to read along and answer all of my questions about the story-line or those which related the story to her own life. I was thrilled that I could see what I hoped was the beginning of her love for reading and an interest in books after only 2 sessions. Most likely, her mother's interest and participation at home was a huge part of her change of attitude. Without this input her interest level and participation during the next sessions may not have changed. Participants in Lynch's 2009 study stated that parental involvement in the development of student literacy is very important, but not all parents are involved as others. Many of the teachers informed parents of ways they could help support children's development at home, such as reading them stories and asking them questions, however, some stated that they were unsure of exactly what to advise parents. Overall, parents were viewed as a means to support school literacy-based activities and teachers wanted more knowledge on how to better inform parents (Lynch, 2009).

Conclusion

The first few sessions of my ReadingPals mentoring were already proving to be highly rewarding for both of us. My hope was that each future session would lead to even greater interest, participation and the ability to read the books on her own. The plan was to work with her for the entire school year, for one hour a week. Based on our first interactions,

I knew that while this would be challenging on many levels, I could expect great rewards. For the student the reward might be not only learning to read, but loving to read. For me the reward would be the honor of playing a part in the process. Writing about this mentoring experience was a constant reminder that it was crucial that she not only learn how to read, but enjoy it so much that she would one day be compelled to write about her own experiences.

Works Cited

Banda, Danielle. 2014. "Book Blast Enchants Children." *Valley Morning Star*, Feb. 15.
Bourke, Lorna, Simon Davies, Emma Sumner, and Carolyn Green. 2014. "Individual Differences in the Development of Early Writing Skills: Testing the Unique Contribution of Visuo-Spatial Working Memory." *Reading & Writing* 27 (2):315–335. doi: 10.1007/s11145-013-9446-3.
Collins, Kathleen M. T., Anthony J. Onwuegbuzie, and Qun G. Jiao. 2014. "Reading Ability as a Predictor of African American Graduate Students' Technical Writing Proficiency in the Context of Statistics Courses." *Journal of Negro Education* 83 (2):135–146.
"Community Builders: Bibliotherapist." 2015. *Library Journal* no. 140 (5):61.
La Chapelle, Jennifer, and Laura Wark. 2014. "I've Got My MLIS, Now What? Further Educational Opportunities for LIS Professionals." *Partnership: The Canadian Journal of Library and Information Practice and Research* 9 (1):1–4.
Lynch, Jacqueline. 2009. "Preschool Teachers' Beliefs About Children's Print Literacy Development." *Early Years* 29 (2):191–203. doi: 10.1080/09575140802628743.
Martin, Lesley. 2015. "Good News Library: Establishing a Library in Malawi." *The School Librarian* 63 (1):13–15.
McFarlane, Penny, and Nina Wroe. 2014. *KidsKope Peer Mentoring Programme*. Jessica Kingsley Publishers, http://www.myilibrary.com.ezproxylocal.library.nova.edu?ID=639353 (4 December 2015).
Rasinski, Timothy. 2014. "Tapping the Power of Poetry." *Educational Leadership* 72 (3):30–34.
Robertson, Pauline. 2015. "Reading Is the Key to Unlock Learning." *English 4–11* (53):19–20.
Ross, William. 2014. *Mentoring African American Males: A Research Design Comparison Perspective, African American Male Series*. Charlotte, NC: Information Age.
Silverman, Rebecca D., David Coker, C. Patrick Proctor, Jeffrey Harring, Kelly W. Piantedosi, and Anna M. Hartranft. 2015. "The Relationship Between Language Skills and Writing Outcomes for Linguistically Diverse Students in Upper Elementary School." *The Elementary School Journal* 116 (1):103–125. doi: 10.1086/683135.
Tonne, Ingebjørg, and Joron Pihl. 2015. "Morphological Correspondences in the Reading-Writing Relation Among L2 Learners." *Reading Matrix: An International Online Journal* 15 (1):206–219.
United Way. http://www.unitedway.org/.
United Way of Broward County. http://www.unitedwaybroward.org/readingpals.

Hosting a Writing Club for Teen Writers at Your Library

HEATHER BOTELHO

Almost two years ago, I was approached by a teen looking for a writing group in the area. We live in a suburb of the Dallas–Fort Worth Metroplex, and I thought I would surely find something for her. Upon searching for a group that was both close by and for her age group, I found nothing. This was the first instance that made me start to consider hosting a writing club for teens at the library. Over the next six months, I began to plan and advertise our Teen Writing Group that started in the summer of 2014. Since starting the club, I have made adjustments to fit the needs of the teens in my group. This chapter will follow the process of starting the club from conception, including how to identify interest in your community, to planning the program, to extending the experience for the teens by creating a collaborative work and putting their writing in print.

Identifying Interest in Your Community

When that first teen expressed interest in joining a writing group for her age, it was the first I had heard any mention of it. I wasn't sure that I would be able to maintain enough attendance to justify starting a club as attendance at teen programs at the time was sporadic at best. I took her information and told her if I determined that there was enough interest and if I could find available time in our programming schedule, I would let her know.

Over the next six months, I had another teen approach with the same question of looking for a writing group for her age, which confirmed that I would be starting a writing club. I started paying close attention to the conversations teens were having in the library. I sometimes heard them talk about creative writing for class. I made sure to mention to these teens that the library would soon have a club for them to help them with their writing. I often heard the teens in my Teen Advisory Group (TAG) talk about National Novel Writing Month, commonly known as NaNoWriMo, held in November. An informal survey of the social media used by the teens who come into my library showed that several of them were on Wattpad, a website for sharing stories. I knew that writing fanfiction was popular with the teens in TAG, and I was able to confirm with a few of them that they would be interested in joining a writing group.

In planning the Teen Writing Group, I had a few considerations. First was if I would have enough people attending to make the program worth the time and effort. This will be something you have to decide for yourself. I determined that the ideal size for this group would be similar to a typical in-person book club. Since the writing club's inception, I have averaged about eight teens in attendance each month. This size has been perfect for our group. In the hour that the club runs, everyone has time to share their writing if they choose to do so, and the group is small enough that even shy teens feel more at ease. With a small group being the goal, it is easy to maintain the writing club and justify its continuation. You may determine that you need to have a larger group to justify starting a club at your library, or you may find that you have a lot of interest. I do want to caution against having a group that is too large. When I was planning my writing club, one of my goals was to create an environment where the teens felt comfortable, where they all felt enough trust to share their work, and where no one was left out due to time constraints. In the month with the largest attendance of almost 20 teens, this was difficult to achieve, so I recommend thinking of your writing club like a book club, where bigger isn't necessarily better.

Structuring Your Writing Club

There are different ways you can structure your writing club, depending on your goals for the program and the needs of your teens. Some writing clubs may be more instructional, focusing on the mechanics of writing good stories, such as developing good characters or using descriptive words to show what is happening in the story. You may try a workshop method where teens bring in a story they are already writing and as a group you work on improving it. Your program may be an amalgam of methods, which I think gives teens the best, most well-rounded experience. This is the basic structure of the program I host:

- Writing to a prompt for 2 to 5 minutes
- Sharing their writing
- Writing activity or game for the rest of the time
- Door prize drawing

The supplies needed to run a writing club are simple, which makes this a cost-effective program. Many attendees will bring their own laptop or tablet, but you should still provide computers if possible. WiFi will allow them to save anything they write during the program to a cloud storage service, such as Google Drive or Dropbox, or they can use their own flash drive. Some writers prefer to write their first drafts by hand, so you should have notepads and pens or pencils available. The only other thing you need is refreshments!

I always begin with a writing prompt. I filled a large vase with a hundred prompts that I selected from the website Writer's Digest. Although the writers often complain about the short time they are allowed for writing, my goal is to encourage them to stop editing themselves as they write and jump into the action. I have noticed that teens who have come to the group many times before are more likely to get to the crux of the prompt in the amount of time given, which indicates that the time limits are working.

After they finish writing, I encourage them to share what they just wrote. It is important to set guidelines before sharing begins. The guidelines that I have set are as follows:

- No one is forced to share their story. However, many teens will start to share their writing as their trust and comfort in the club increase.
- Writers can choose if they want feedback. Writers can also choose if they want positive feedback only, negative feedback only, or both. All of the listeners must adhere to the wishes of the writer.
- Even when giving negative feedback, the listeners must focus their comments on the story and be respectful of the writer.

One last note about sharing stories is that I always share what I wrote. I emphasize to my teens that I am just as much of an amateur as they are. I tell them I am not a published author, unless they count the poem in the magazine *Teen Ink* when I was their age, and I am not formally trained in creative writing. Do not feel that you have to be an expert writer in order to form a writing group. There is a multitude of resources available in print and online for improving your writing. Be sure to make these resources available to your writers as part of your club.

After they have shared their writing from the prompt, we either write a longer piece around an activity or we play an oral storytelling game, which I will cover in the following sections. The program ends with a door prize drawing for a book. I make a selection of donations or Advanced Reader's Copies available. Many authors have stated that reading a lot is crucial to being a good writer, and I like to not only reward my writers for their hard work but also make sure they all have a book at home that they don't have to worry about returning on time.

The entire program lasts one hour, not including the time it takes for setup and take-down. This is usually enough time to allow everyone to complete the activities while still having time to chat.

Writing Activities

The following section will go into detail on the various writing activities that I have conducted with my Teen Writing Group. As I stated earlier, the goal of these activities are to encourage creative thinking, rather than to be primarily instructional on how to write. As the teens in your group spend more time with each other and with you and trust is established, they may feel comfortable enough for feedback after each of these activities.

Word Sprints, Song Sprints and Word Wars

A word sprint is a writing activity where the writer tries to get as many words as possible on the page. In a sprint, the writers race only themselves, trying to do better than their last sprint. This activity can be done with a shared prompt, or each person can work on their own piece. When the time is up, I generally let everyone finish the sentence they were writing, even though it goes into an overtime, because no one likes to leave a thought unfinished.

Similar to the word sprint is a song sprint. Instead of writing for a specific amount of time, a song is chosen, and everyone writes as much as they can for the length of the song. The song can determine the subject matter of what is written during the sprint, such as writing a scene of science fiction to Elton John's "Rocketman." You may also choose a song to inspire a certain mood in what is being written, such as using heavy metal to inspire a fight scene or argument between characters. Because everyone may not be familiar with the song, I suggest letting them listen to it without writing anything the first time but for a few notes about the feeling the music invokes. The second time you play the song is when they will try to write as much of their scene as they can.

Word wars are similar to sprints in that each person tries to write as much as they can in a given amount of time, but unlike a sprint, a war is competitive. Each person can compete as an individual or in teams, and if you choose to reward the winning individual or team, small items like a bookmark or a pen are inexpensive and not likely to cause hurt feelings among those who didn't win. I suggest waiting to have a word war until you know your group better as some teens do not respond well to competition.

Round Robin/Exquisite Corpse

A round robin story is one where each person begins writing to a prompt. After a set amount of time, they pass their story on to the next person, who continues it using the characters, setting, and plot established by the first person. The stories travel around to each person at the table until they return to the original author, and then each person reads the final outcome. Exquisite Corpse is very similar to a round robin story, except the first person folds over the paper so that only the last part is visible to the next writer. The story continues with each writer, folding the paper so that only the last part of what they have written is visible, until the story returns to the original author who reads it to the group. If time allows, you can try both of these methods during one program and talk about the difference between knowing and not knowing what came before in the story.

Word Crawl

The word crawl is an idea I took from the National Novel Writing Month forums. It combines prompts and sprints into something similar to a choose-your-own-adventure story or a role-playing game. There are many crawls on the NaNoWriMo forums, but you may decide to write your own in order to ensure that your teens can finish the crawl within the time constraints of your program. Many of the crawls use pop culture as a starting point, such as setting the story in the world of Star Wars or Harry Potter. Sometimes events are triggered or items are acquired by successfully writing a certain number of words during a sprint, and the writer uses that event or item in their story. Some crawls also use dice like a role-playing game, where the dice result is multiplied by a set factor to determine how many words must be written. If you are familiar with the interests of your teens, or know that they like to write fanfiction, you can tailor your crawl for an enjoyable writing exercise.

Truth or Dare

Truth or Dare can be played by itself with a prompt or as part of a word sprint or word war. I have used it as the consequence during a word war for the team that wrote fewer words. Again, I found this activity on the NaNoWriMo forums and adapted it for my use. The way we played had the losing team tell either a truth about their story, such as their character's greatest weakness or their favorite song, or take a writing dare, such as having their character reveal a big secret or making them have an argument with the next character they see. You can create the prompts for the truths and dares ahead of time and have a jar for each. I found that the truths allowed the writers to think about and understand their characters, while the dares encouraged them to stretch their imaginations.

Guess Who

In this activity, each person thinks of a character or actor that is extremely well-known. For example, the last time I did this activity, we had two people pick Thor, the movie version. Being as descriptive as they could about the character or person's appearance, personality, and demeanor, they had to write a scene without revealing their chosen person. After they read their scene, everyone tried to guess who the famous character or person was based on the descriptive words. For this activity, I gave them a printout from WriteShop and talked about using descriptive words, so it was more instructional than a normal program. Even though two people picked Thor, the words used for the descriptions were very different, so it was also an interesting lesson on perspective.

Storytelling Games

Ever since playing the storytelling game *Once Upon a Time*, I knew that it would be an excellent way to extend the writing experience. It has become a favorite game among my teens, and since I began Teen Writing Group, I have looked for other games to incorporate. The use of storytelling games fits well with the goal of my writing club, to encourage my teens to write without editing. The following section will describe the games I have played with the writing group and any adaptations that are required.

Once Upon a Time

Once Upon a Time by Atlas Games is a collaborative storytelling game for two to six players, though it is still playable with seven or eight people. Each player is given at least five Story Cards, depending on the number of players. Each card features one of the following elements: a character, a thing, a place, an aspect, or an event. Each element must be prominent in the story they tell, with the goal being to drive the story toward their own secret Ending card. They continue telling their story until they pass it on to the next player, either because they can't think of something to say next or because they don't have a card that they can logically use. One might think that an especially crafty storyteller could take over the whole game without ever passing it on, but some of the Story Cards have the ability to interrupt the current storyteller. The storyteller can also be forced to pass the story on if they are stuck, have said something that contradicts the story as it has been told so far, starts to ramble, have said something that the other players agree is too ridiculous and illogical, or if they are listing elements to get rid of cards without making them prominent in the story. Play continues until someone reaches their ending and wins.

Gloom

Gloom, also by Atlas Games, is a competitive storytelling game where each player is in control of a very strange family. The goal is to have as many tragic things happen to each of the characters as you can before you send them to their untimely, or perhaps timely, demise. While you want bad things to happen to your own family, giving you negative points, you also want good things to happen to your opponents, giving them positive points. Each player is in possession of modifier cards that make good or bad things happen. The game ends when a player kills off all of their characters, and the game is won by the person who has the least amount of points. It is possible to play Gloom without doing anything more than reading what is on the card, but the fun of Gloom is telling the story of all the terrible things that are happening. The challenge of Gloom is also weaving the stories of the families together and keeping up with what has happened to everyone. Gloom is only a four-person game, so my teens played in pairs, which allowed them to collaborate in their storytelling.

Superfight

Superfight is a game similar to Apples to Apples where each player chooses their cards and the best play is determined by a judge, winning the trick for that player. In Superfight, players choose a character and an attribute to fight another player's character. Some of these characters are very normal and expected, such as a zombie. The same is true for the attributes, such as super speed. The twist to Superfight is many of the cards are highly unusual, leading to character-attribute combinations like a mime who is constantly taking selfies, or a hippo with literal jazz hands. While the game is fun to play just as it is, I added a story element by having them write their fight scene. Each teen picked their character and their attribute to fight my villain. They were then helped or sabotaged by the person to their left who gave them an attribute that they had to incorporate into their character. After their scenes were written, they shared their stories and voting continued as in the normal game.

Rory's Story Cubes

Rory's Story Cubes is a set of nine dice with icons on each side. The most basic way to play is the player must roll the dice and use all of them to tell their story, starting with a traditional opener like "Once upon a time." The cubes may also be used to tell a round robin story by splitting the cubes between three people. The cubes can be used to break a writer's block or even inspire a prompt. There are different sets of cubes, and these can be used together or separately. Because the icons are open to interpretation, the cubes can be used in any way that you can imagine.

Dixit

Dixit from Asmodee Games is a game where each player uses a picture on a card to tell a story. When the storyteller is done, the other players must try to match one of their cards to the story that was told. The cards are then shuffled, and everyone but the storyteller must guess which was the correct card, earning points for being right. Typically, the storyteller can choose any method to give their clue, including singing or reciting a poem. I challenged my teens to a six-word story when we played. Their clue had to be exactly six words, and they had to feel that it told a complete story from start to finish. It made an excellent exercise in choosing words thoughtfully.

Publications

Once your writing group is well-established, you have consistent attendance, and your teens feel comfortable in the group, you may want to consider creating an anthology of their work. To begin, you must determine if the stories in your anthology will simply be the best work of each of your teens or if you will have them follow a theme. A consistent theme provides a means of tying all of the stories together, even when the plots and genres are completely different. Have the group brainstorm ideas for their theme together. If there are any ideas that any one of the members feels uncomfortable writing, strike it from the list. You do not want them to feel like it is too difficult to write their story because they do not fully understand or buy into the theme.

Another consideration is the length of each story. I hold an annual Scary Story Contest at my library, and I take entries between 1,000 and 5,000 words. This is based on the experience of other libraries that hold similar contests. Depending on the number of teens in your group and if you want to print your anthology, you may want to adjust the word limit for the stories in consideration of printing costs.

When it comes time to publish your anthology, there are several free and paid options. You may decide to save your anthology as a PDF and make it available on your Web site. If you host your own eBooks, that may also be an option for you. My library has a subscription to FastPencil, which my group uses to collaborate on the anthology. Once the anthology is complete, it can be published as an e-book and added to the OneClickDigital library for downloading, and a print version can also be purchased. Other online printers include CreateSpace, Blurb, and Bookbaby. Each has different prices based on trim size, number of pages, and other options, so comparison shopping is important to get the best price. You may also have a local printer to whom you can talk about the cost of printing your anthology and who may be willing to discount or donate their services.

Conclusion

It is so important for librarians working with teens to offer, to the best of their ability, what the teens in their communities want and need. Providing a time and space and being a positive role model all contribute to their development. When the teens in my community demonstrated that they wanted a club that would allow them to share their writing and help them improve, I knew that was something I could offer. You do not have to be an excellent writer yourself in order to share resources and provide a safe space for budding authors.

Writers Groups at the Library

Sarah Fisk

Establishing a writers' group is a great way for libraries to build a strong, dedicated writing community within their own walls. For large systems, it's an excellent addition to any writing workshop series or, for smaller systems, could be the entirety of programming for aspiring authors. The goal is for members to return to each meeting to read, critique, discuss topics, and ultimately take their writing to the next level.

Starting a writers' group can be overwhelming for anyone, especially if the organizer has never participated in a group or isn't a writer. There are many formats a writers' group could take and the chosen format may slowly evolve based on the changing needs and recommendations of the group members.

Start by determining what your potential members would want from a group. If you have contact information of people who regularly attend writing workshops at your library, contact them with a poll to determine what structure and schedule they would prefer. If contact information is not available, set the date and time of the first meeting and ask those who attend. It's important to remember that you may not be able to meet every person's needs, but attempt to come up with a format and schedule that works for as many patrons as possible.

Schedule

Writers' group schedules can vary widely. A group could meet twice a week, once a week, every other week, or monthly. When in doubt, start with fewer meetings and increase frequency if needed or requested.

Keep the schedule consistent with changes occurring only due to major holidays. For example, the Orange County Library System's (OCLS) Writers' Group meets on the second Sunday of every month, but will meet on the third Sunday of the month in May to avoid a conflict with Mother's Day.

The length of the meeting should be pre-set. Most groups usually meet one to two hours at a time. Group members should know the expected length of the meeting beforehand to avoid interruptions due to people needing to leave early.

Many writers' groups need to determine a meeting location. Consider hosting occasional or extra meetings at a nearby coffee or sandwich shop for a nice change of pace. OCLS hosted a group meeting at Panera Bread Company during the 2015 Outside the Lines project and the members really enjoyed the change.

For library writers' groups, it is probably best to allow rolling enrollment in the group. Some private groups don't allow new members to join unless another person leaves, but those are generally groups with a strict member limit policies.

Scope

Determine the scope of your writers' group first by asking these questions:

- What categories of writing are permitted?
- What genres are permitted?
- Are unpublished authors invited to join?
- Are published, experienced authors invited to join?
- What content is not permitted?

It's recommended to start with essentially allowing any interested author to participate. In the OCLS Writers' Group there are writers who write romance, children's picture books, non-fiction, screenplays, poetry, memoirs, and more.

Clearly define policies on sexual content up-front and make sure to let potential members know this policy. To prevent limiting free speech and creativity, many multi-genre critique groups ask writers with sexual content in their work to place a disclaimer at the beginning so that members uncomfortable with that subject matter can opt out of critiquing that particular piece.

Keep in mind that attendance will fluctuate, so do not lose heart if there are a couple of low-attendance meetings. Some members will attend one or two meetings and decide the group is not right for them and that is perfectly okay.

On the other hand, if you have a larger group than is manageable for your format, consider splitting the group into two or more groups based on category, genre, or publication goals. To maintain the networking benefits of a larger group, consider doing one meeting a month for everyone and a second per month for each subgroup.

If there is a small group of authors looking to workshop novels or novel-length works, consider an alternative format known as "limited-duration intensives." These are ten- or twelve-week sessions where a small group meets once or twice per week to workshop progressive chapters of their work. These smaller, more focused groups give those aggressively pursuing publication feedback on their entire novel in a shorter timeframe.

Some of the aspects of a writing group could include:

- Critiques
- Outside speakers
- Guided topic conversation
- Submission Club
- Writing prompts and other activities
- Networking

Critiques

Receiving critiques on their work is the top reason writers attend writers' groups, but it is one of the most potentially contentious aspects of writers' groups. Critique groups should be supportive, constructive, and attuned to improving the writers' work. Feedback should consist of honest, open, and patient dialogue.

There are many different ways to run critiques and many factors to consider. First, determine a maximum length for each submission, defined in words, not pages. The group may need to have a guideline on how many times the same piece can be resubmitted. In some groups, authors will resubmit the same material over and over again, reworking it each time, leaving the group members with fatigue over that piece. Some groups do not allow first drafts and some groups prefer them. The OCLS group allows a draft at any stage, but each writing group should decide what's right for their group.

Determine how the material to be critiqued will be shared. Some groups have the author read the material during the meeting, while some will have materials emailed out to the members four to seven days ahead of time. The former is logistically easier and favored by hobbyists, but the latter allows for better feedback and is favored by writers pursuing publication. When material is read aloud by the author, the other members don't get the true reader experience because the author can put inflection and emphasis that may be lacking in the actual text. Also, getting the material ahead of time allows for the person giving the critique to write their feedback and read more than once in order to provide a more detailed and thought-out response. If logistically possible, providing the pieces to be critiqued ahead of time so the group members can come prepared with their feedback is usually the most desirable format.

Once the format of submissions is finalized, the group must then determine what format the critique will take. Some groups will have verbal-only feedback or written-only feedback. In this author's experience, a combination of both gives the best results. Group members can mark up the draft with grammar, punctuation, and word-choice notes while giving more content-based feedback verbally. This can open up discussion about the story, plot, emotions, and atmosphere while not wasting meeting time on more technical copyedits.

Determine how pieces to be critiqued will be scheduled. Our group has a first-come-first served system where the first four pieces submitted will be critiqued. If more than four are submitted, the subsequent pieces will be first in the line for the following meeting. Some groups have a rotating schedule, but that requires every writer to submit regularly and some writers may not be in a place to do that. If you choose to add a limited-duration intensive, the rotating schedule might be a good format for those sessions.

Many writers' groups, including the OCLS group, have a requirement that a member attend at least one meeting before being able to submit a piece for critique. This is so that the writer can get an idea of how the group operates and how the critiques proceeds. The writer can then know what to expect and gauge his/her needs against what the group provides.

It is useful to have a policy regarding submission format. If submitted electronically, materials should be in a Word document so that those who prefer to make their comments electronically can do so. This also allows members who cannot attend a specific meeting to still provide their feedback via electronic comments and edits. If the excerpt to be critiqued isn't the beginning of the story, the writer should provide a short paragraph of background information to explain anything that might be needed to understand the scene. If a writer is looking for feedback of a specific kind, they may include questions to the reader at the beginning of the piece. This is generally not counted in the word count limit.

For fiction and narrative non-fiction, the standard manuscript format is:

- Double space (using the word processing software's settings, not by manually entering two line returns)
- First line of each paragraph indented 0.5 inches (again, by using the software's settings, not by manually entering a tab or spaces)
- 12 pt. Times New Roman, Arial, or Courier font
- One inch margins on all sides
- One space following a period, not two.

The formatting will be different for poetry or screenplays.

It is essential that your group has and implements established guidelines for the feedback provided to writers. Common critique guidelines include:

- Urging readers to give constructive feedback, providing suggestions for how to fix certain issues
- A "compliment sandwich," where critique begins and ends with positive notes to create a more supportive atmosphere
- Not allowing the author of the piece to respond to critique unless it is to answer a direct question. Many authors will get caught up in the act of defending their work and explaining why the person giving the critique is wrong. This is not productive. Asking the writer to remain quiet encourages them to listen and absorb the feedback, while not allowing them to give extra explanations that are not going to be available to the final audience: casual readers.
- Allowing or not allowing other group members to chime in while one person is giving feedback. This is generally a short interject indicating agreement or disagreement, but some groups prohibit this because strong personalities tend to dominate the conversation.

Outside Speakers

Many writing groups will regularly feature speakers who teach the group members about a particular topic. These are usually local authors, editors, or writing instructors who have volunteered their time. Generally, the speakers are permitted to spend a small amount of time promoting their own work in exchange for volunteering their time. For instance, most authors will share bookmarks and editors will distribute business cards.

This is a great component to have if your library doesn't host other writing workshops, but may be redundant if you do. Some writing groups will alternate critique sessions with learning sessions, while other groups focus on one or the other.

Guided Topic Conversation

When several members of the group ask advice on a similar topic, it can be helpful to have a guided conversation around that topic. The facilitator can bring in books from the library collection in case the members of the group would like to read more about the topic. Some examples of these topics include:

- Submission tips
- Character development
- Social media
- Agent and publisher discussion
- Plotting

Submission Club

Many writers' groups have regular sessions every couple of meetings for writers to share the steps they've made toward publication. This can be part of the regular meeting or an additional event. Announcements may include submissions only, but could also include other writing accomplishments such as: finishing a story, finishing an edit, writing a query letter, plotting a book, writing a synopsis, attending a conference, or any other step a writer may take on their journey to publication.

One of my former writing groups met monthly for dessert and drinks and only writers who had submitted work to agents or editors in the past month could attend.

No matter how you format it or schedule it, this is an opportunity for writers to share their goals and progress with other people who understand the business, with all its challenges and wonders.

Writing Prompts

Some writing groups will open or close a meeting with a writing prompt or another kind of writing activity. If done at the beginning of the meeting, this should last no longer than ten or fifteen minutes. If the members of the group are interested in this kind of activity, it may be best to wait until the end of the meeting and allow those who are not interested to leave before it begins.

Networking

Networking is a great secondary reason to join an in-person writing group. Meeting other authors in person can make a writer feel less alone in their endeavors, provide a supportive atmosphere, and increase the chances of a writer meeting their writing goals despite the long and challenging path to publication. Many writers find career-long friends and business partners in their local writing groups. Some of them will pair off to beta-read, which is when one writer will read another writer's entire manuscript quickly and provide feedback.

A great way to kick-start networking is by starting the first meeting and any meeting where a new member joins with round-robin introductions. Ask the writers to state their names, what genre(s) they write, and where they are in their publication path. For meetings with only repeat members in attendance, a shorter version of the Submission Club described above may serve this same purpose.

After the meeting, allow ample time for the writers to socialize and network.

Communication

No matter the scope of the writers' group, a facilitator is required to ensure smooth operation of the group. This can be an employee or a dedicated volunteer who checks in regularly with an employee. If your library doesn't have an employee or volunteer willing and comfortable to facilitate, solicit advice from an experienced writer in your community.

The facilitator should be responsible for group communication and in-meeting structure. During the meeting, the facilitator is responsible for gently reminding members of the guidelines and bringing the group back on topic when it strays—and it will! He or she will also ensure that the time during meetings remains professional and focused. Socializing should take place before and after the designated time, but not during the meeting.

Some groups add an online component to their activities. This may take the form of a private Facebook Group, Google Group, or online message board where authors can interact, ask advice, compare notes, and seek out beta-readers.

Potential Challenges

While writers' groups can be a valuable addition to your local writing community, they are not without their challenges.

Most open writers' groups, especially at the beginning and over the holidays and summer, will face fluctuating attendance. If attendance consistently declines, consider polling both the remaining and former members to find out if a different format or schedule would help increase attendance.

Nearly every writing group, at some point, has struggled with a challenging personality. This is a member whose behavior or attitude disrupts the group's operation or, less severely, makes members uncomfortable. Establishing submission and feedback guidelines right away and having the facilitator regularly implement them will go a long way toward heading off a disruptive personality.

Many writers, especially inexperienced ones, will be concerned with confidentiality and copyright. Some writers' groups have a written confidentiality statement that members sign, but this is not generally necessary. It's important to remember that anything, upon being put into writing, is thereby copyrighted. If someone writes a poem on a coffee-stained napkin, it is technically copyrighted. It does not have a registered copyright, however, which is what most people think about when using the word "copyright." Writers "stealing" other writers' work is much less common than beginning writers believe it is and hopefully further experience with writing groups will alleviate these worries. If writers in the group have more questions about copyright, you can refer them to one of many texts on the subject, *The Writer's Legal Guide: An Authors Guild Desk Reference.*

Anthologies

Dearborn Public Library, Pasadena California Public Library, and Flint Public Library are three of many libraries that have published anthologies of short pieces written by their writing groups. It is recommended to wait to consider this until after the writers' group has been established and is steadily operating. The process can teach writers about the publication process and provide them with publication credits. Generally, the library acts as the publisher and the proceeds go toward the library. As the publisher, the library will need to:

- Draft a fair publishing contract.
- Coordinate editing. This may be done through several rounds of editing within the group or through a generous volunteer editor.
- Design a cover.
- Format the eBook and print book interior.
- Distribute the eBook to sites such as Amazon, Barnes and Noble, Kobo, iBooks, and more.
- Arrange for print copies to be purchased. A print-on-demand service such as CreateSpace (www.createspace.com) is a great alternative to costly traditional print runs.

If your writers' group is interested in publishing an anthology, more research should be performed on the process. *Let's Get Digital* by David Gaughran does an excellent job of breaking down the steps of publishing a book. Dearborn Public Library recommends *The Librarian's Guide to Micropublishing* by Walt Crawford. If you have an experienced self-published author in the community, they can be a great resource for the more technical aspects.

Conclusion

A writers' group can be an incredible resource for writers in your community and a great asset to library programming. Imagine an author achieving their dream of publishing a book, thanks to your library!

Of the OCLS writers' group, aspiring author Peggy Stubblefield says, "I've tried a couple of on-line writing groups before, but the face-to-face nature of the OCLS group provides two things I couldn't find elsewhere. The encouragement to polish and submit has a greater intensity when someone looks you in the eye to nag you. That same eyeballing makes me more considerate in my own critiques. We don't all read/write the same genres, so it's amazing what a poet will make of a suspenseful moment of science fiction."

OCLS writers' group member Elizabeth Jenkins says, "The OCLS writers' group experience has already provided me with encouragement to take myself more seriously as a writer. I really enjoy how diverse the group is across many dimensions and the genuinely supportive atmosphere which manages to combine respect, appreciation, and honesty. The opportunity for friendship with others who like to write is invaluable to me."

Member Tracy Bowens says, "The OCLS writers' group experience has helped me in my writer's journey. The deadlines give me accountability. I have a goal and it forces me to show my work." She adds, "Critiquing the work of others also plays an important role. This task helps me see what works and doesn't." The final benefit for her "is learning that I'm not the only one. Seeing how others cope with the publishing process is a valuable lesson."

Connecting and encouraging writers through hosting a writers' group is an excellent way for libraries to support and contribute to the writing community in their area.

Suggested Reading

Crawford, Walt. 2012. *The Librarian's Guide to Micropublishing.* Medford, NJ: Information Today.
Gaughran, David. 2014. *Let's Get Digital,* 2d ed. N.p.: Arriba.
Murray, Kay, and Tad Crawford. 2013. *The Writer's Legal Guide: An Authors Guild Desk Reference.* New York: Allworth.

Discovering the Personal and the Poetic Voice

Encouraging and Supporting Writers at the Public Library

DIANA J. LENNON

Writers

After observing patrons writing at the Greenburgh Public Library in Elmsford, New York, discussing their work, and receiving requests for books and guidance on how to become an author, I quickly realized that patrons needed a place to come together to learn and practice the art of writing. I recognized that the library, a symbol of literacy and the written word, would be the perfect place to hone their craft. A gathering place for community, the library would serve as a safe and inviting environment to share work, exchange ideas, and find one's creative energy. The original idea allowed the library to support potential authors with little investment of staff time and financial resources, two aspects of programming that were a constant concern. This straightforward approach would give writers a place and time to create with little pressure on a reduced staff to run a program or spend a great deal of time in planning and implementation—this would be an already formed group! The varying interpretations of this idea by the public, however, led to changes that required the administration's input, adjustments by participants and staff, and many difficult challenges.

To begin the new program, the library promoted a Writers' Gathering through social media and flyers, noting that both aspiring and published writers would find the library to be an appealing place to create their stories. As word spread, a core group of writers emerged and began to meet twice a month. I did not participate in the meetings, and the group initially appeared to be self-sufficient. Communication in between program meetings was through email, and I would check in with the group at the beginning or end of the sessions. As I had hoped and anticipated, a leader emerged and soon the group seemed to be moving in the desired direction of producing and editing their own work. The group participants offered comments on each other's work, and the library was pleased to host a seemingly successful program with little additional staff responsibility. The size of the group, in fact, steadily increased over the year and began to outgrow the designated meeting room. Finding a new space was difficult at best, as our two other program rooms were in constant use.

While I pondered this seemingly pleasant dilemma of a program being too popular, some newer members began to voice concerns over the quality of the meetings and the competency of the self-appointed leader. As these concerns grew and deepened in seriousness, I joined a few sessions unannounced and spoke privately with the leader as well as with the writers. It soon became apparent that not all of the members were pleased with the leader's style of directing the sessions. The writers noted that she was quite negative in her criticism of their work; that she did most of the talking; and that she presented herself as the only expert on writing in the room. This new information disheartened me, and caused unnecessary stress among the participants. I quickly realized that change was needed as soon as possible. Leaving this project to develop without structure had become the antithesis of the library's values of opportunity, diversity, relationships, and accountability. Perhaps most distressing was the fact that patrons were not feeling welcomed into this program. After several meetings and a number of difficult conversations, I decided that the writing program in its current form needed to come to an end. Although the director wrote a letter to explain why the library was terminating the writers' program, some unpleasant feelings remained within the group. As a result, a few patrons followed the former leader to a new location and writing group. Other patrons were not discouraged, however, and encouraged the library to re-invent the program. Despite the difficult situation, the fact remained that there was still a strong need and desire to develop, and even to broaden, the library's creative writing program.

With a new understanding of writers and group dynamics, I began to design a new program. I understood that initially a break was needed to allow participants and the library to reevaluate what a writers' group could and should be. Summer was a natural point to regroup, rethink, and plan for a new and improved approach towards supporting writers. I also discussed the situation with administration, who agreed that a writers' group did indeed reflect the library's mission to encourage lifelong learning, thus ensuring the group's continuation, albeit in a new form. I held an open meeting in late August to solicit input from writers interested in creating a new program. While some attendees were from the previous group, many were new faces, eager to form a successful and supportive group. But what would a new writers' forum look like?

At this and succeeding meetings, the new members and I decided on the necessary key components for each session:

1. Each writer fully participates in the sessions through critique and by producing written work to share.
2. All participants have equal opportunities to present their work.
3. I would facilitate each meeting.
4. I would coordinate the sharing of individuals' work.
5. All comments and criticism are based on a "two glow, two grow" system in which the one critiquing says two things she or he likes about the piece, and then offers two suggestions for change or improvement.
6. All comments are offered, and listened to, but accepting them is not required.

As the new sessions commenced, the participants seemed comfortable with this plan, and critiques were kind, thoughtful, and often quite helpful to the writers. It should be noted that I did not critique the patrons' work; I facilitated the readers' schedule, emailed copies of the work to each member, and was the timekeeper. Having a neutral person in the group enabled the participants to focus on their writing. It also eased the pressure on any one participant to lead, and soon a more supportive group emerged. Participants were no longer worrying about being judged harshly in front of their peers for sharing personal writing. As a result, they made helpful and thoughtful comments and deeper discussions ensued.

From this less restrictive and more open process emerged a variety of writers who willingly shared memoirs, short stories, poems, and novels in genres as diverse as science fiction, crime drama, flash fiction, non-fiction, and even chick lit! While many of the participants in their seventies and eighties were writing memoirs, others wrote fantasy, crime novels, teen trilogies, and poetry. They did not hesitate to point out to each other the areas that each needed to work on, but always critiqued with professionalism and fairness. Another pleasant surprise occurred when each session drew a diverse cross-section of ages and ethnic backgrounds, as well as an equal number of men and women joining the group. This rich mix of ages, personal backgrounds, beliefs and writing styles created a unique blend of work that the members reacted to with laughter, tears, and delight. The program truly reflected the community, and united the members through their shared writing process and collective creativity.

This new group needed a new name, and after brainstorming and voting, the GPL Writers' Community was born. A mission statement and informal policies soon followed. One guideline, for example, encouraged members to take turns and to volunteer to read their work aloud. Also, I would send electronic copies of their work via email and Drop-Box prior to meetings. Paper copies also were made available at the sessions. Many participants wrote their critiques of others' work, allowing the author to listen to comments and only take notes as needed. This provided a smooth and clear way for each voice at the table to be heard. The format was established and followed, but as issues inevitably arose, the group discussed and resolved them together. The members now had a personal stake in the writers' group, clearly a very important component needed for the success of the program. If they wanted help from others to improve their own writing, they had to actively participate and contribute to the group process.

An issue arose that revolved around regular participation in the group. Many people took a strong initial interest in the program, yet due to life's challenges and busy schedules, many also had to stop coming on a regular basis. While a core group attended routinely, a small percentage of the participants withdrew. In order to maintain an up to date participant roster, I would periodically ask the members who wanted to be removed from the email list because they were unable to attend the sessions due to other commitments. As people moved on, the list lost a few members each time. Still, only about one third of those on the list attended regularly. The group agreed to offer the option for members to email their critiques and thus participate virtually. A network within the larger group then shared their writing, and the critiques of each other's work, via email. This was convenient for some individuals and also provided writers with additional comments about their work.

A long email list, however, also created the issue of having one's writing shared among people who did not attend nor asked to be removed from the email list. One writer stopped coming to the group sessions because she did not want her writing to be shared with people who were not actively participating in the group's work. This was a valid concern and the members realized that they must make decisions about their own level of participation while also feeling comfortable about how much others will participate, as this affected the amount of feedback they received. Currently the group members and

I are researching the options for online platforms to find and assess alternative ways to share work that would be acceptable to all members and to the library. The group also is developing guidelines for presenting their work to the public via the library website.

Another issue with the feedback process was that not all participants were making oral or written comments, yet they expected a critique of their own work. The group agreed that each person at the table would be required to critique the work being shared. This format has improved the sessions in the following strategic ways:

1. Everyone participates in evaluating others' work, ensuring a more dynamic discussion.
2. Comments are offered in a safe and supportive setting.
3. Commenters disagree with, or piggyback onto, others' comments. Peer to peer feedback is essential to a successful analysis of the writers' work.
4. Authors refrain from explaining or justifying their writings. They must listen and thus better absorb the comments, guidance, and opinions of others.
5. Any and all advice can be taken or ignored, as long as it is listened to and considered.

Additionally, I have been able to offer writing workshops that focus on improving the participants' techniques and styles. The Friends of the Greenburgh Library committed to providing funds to engage professional teachers willing to share their talent, nurture writers, and to assist in the development of a robust writing program at the library. This has attracted the attention of people new to writing as well as seasoned authors, consequently adding new members to the GPL Writers' Community. The group has forged a rich balance of peer support, criticism, creativity, and learning from established writers. The GPL Writers' Community has emerged from a challenging and difficult situation and is now a strong and successful library program with prospects for continued success in the future. Even more important, the members have had an opportunity to explore and to find their voices, to write their words, and to create their stories.

Poets

The Brenda Connor-Bey Learning to See Legacy Workshop Series focuses on ekphrastic poetry and explorations of all art forms as well as other ways to "see" that are reflected in their poems. The workshop series was created by Connor-Bey, who was the town of Greenburgh's first poet laureate from 2006 to 2010. After she passed away in 2012, the Town's Arts and Culture Director continued this important legacy and led this unique program. As she was an author, poet, and librarian herself, it was a natural progression for the Arts and Culture Director to eventually bring the program into the public library. She has the honor of selecting from a list of trained and vibrant teachers to lead academic year workshops. I coordinate the spring and fall workshops by registering participants, scheduling program rooms, and assisting the teachers as needed.

All workshop leaders are successful poets with extensive teaching experience who have varied backgrounds. Their talent forms the core of the program's success. Their expertise ranges from Shakespeare to slam poetry, classical stage to improvisation. One teacher is trained in the Amherst Writers & Artist Method, and creates an environment that reflects their philosophy that "every person is a writer, and every writer deserves a safe environment in which to experiment, learn, and develop craft" (AWA 2016). Recently, there was an unfortunate situation when a teacher was unable to participate due to an emergency. The Arts and Culture Director selected one of the advanced students to fill in and teach the already scheduled workshop. Her style and approach to ekphrastic poetry were well received and she is now part of the regular teaching roster.

The student poets learn techniques, compose poetry, share their work, and receive feedback from the teacher and their peers. The writers' success is apparent as many publish their work, enter competitions and sometimes win prizes. Most importantly, they improve their writing and hone their own poetic style. Their love of poetry is apparent and contagious, and in response the library has increased its poetry collection over the years to meet the students' requests for a broad and diverse representation of authors and poetic styles. The collection includes published work by the Learning to See teachers and other local poets, including workshop participants.

Each workshop consists of three sessions of two hours each that span a three week period. The workshops are limited to fifteen students and frequently fill up so quickly that the library finds that little publicity is required. This has created a need to limit participation so students may sign up for no more than three workshops at a time. Otherwise, many would attend all of the workshops every year! Clearly, the sessions are very popular due to the amazing professionals that bring together creative ideas and instruction in a way that inspires their students.

Workshops are free and open to the public as mandated by the library's charter. The only significant cost is the teachers' fees. They are paid for six hours of instruction and numerous hours of preparation and review of the poets' work. I make any needed copies, and provide space for each workshop. The Friends of the Greenburgh Library and the Town's Arts and Culture Department share the funding of the program. Grant money from *Poets & Writers* also has supplemented the costs of the series.

Steps to Success

1. Formulate the poetry series' structure. How many workshops will the library offer? What is the length of each? Over how many days/weeks will they occur?
2. Reserve a room at the library once the schedule is developed.
3. Research how much poetry teachers are paid in your area.
4. Create a budget that includes teachers' fees, publicity, supplies, copies, etc.
5. Research funding sources. Is the program within the library's programming budget? Does a request need to be made to the Friends of the Library or other donors? Should the library apply for grants?
6. Recruit instructors by identifying established poets who also teach well. Create guidelines for the series in consultation with the teachers. Will they all teach ekphrastic poetry, for example, or is any poetic style acceptable?
7. Decide on a class size limit and how many workshops a student may take each season.
8. Publicize the program. Choose a method of enrollment (phone, email, online, in person). Recruit and enroll students. Request a commitment to all parts of the series, e.g. they must attend all three sessions.

9. Follow up with post-workshop evaluations.
10. Be sure to share library print and online resources about poetry with students and teachers at each workshop. Set up book displays about poets and writing poetry.
11. Promote the work produced by workshop participants during National Poetry Month in April.
12. Honor the year of poetry with a fun event after the completion all workshops.

The Learning to See Potluck celebrates the poetry written by students and teachers throughout the year. This enjoyable dinner and fun annual event brings together all the teachers and participants and showcases their creativity. They read aloud their work to share it with the public and their peers. Additionally, we now offer an Annual Poetry Contest with monetary prizes donated by the Friends of the Greenburgh Library. It is very popular and the library receives numerous teen and adult entries. The winning poems are announced at a National Poetry Month celebration in April, and also shared with the community via the library's website, social media, and on posters and displays.

Currently, I am considering expanding the poetry series to offer workshops to teen writers and to those who speak and write in Spanish. I hope that bringing these two large constituencies into the library and into the creative process will broaden the community circle of creativity. I would like to further develop our patrons' passion for writing that the library has seen emerge over recent years. By using the established Learning to See format, students will be able to learn together, share their work, and also receive professional feedback about their poetry.

Conclusion

Both the Learning to See model and the GPL Writers' Community offer an example of peer to peer writing programs in a supportive environment. They value authors' commitments to write and edit their work on an ongoing basis. Each program builds a sense of belonging to a creative and vibrant community while also recognizing individual endeavors. They allow community members to share their personal writing and poetry with one another and with their readers while gaining the library's admiration and support. The peer to peer component is critical to their confidence as writers and poets, and allows them to hone their craft in a helpful and encouraging library setting.

These two programs make the library an active center for creative expression. The Greenburgh Library's mission to be "a source for learning, literacy, discovery and delight that enriches lives and strengthens our community" (Greenburgh Public Library 2016) is brought to life through these inspiring programs that engage the public. They are a core component of the library's overall success.

As a public library develops effective programs focused on writers, it will find itself privileged to use the participants' stories—both their creative writing and their personal narratives—to show funders and donors the far-reaching impact of the library. While usage statistics frequently drove library budget decisions in the past, the American Library Association's current Libraries Transform campaign was established "to increase public awareness of the value, impact and services provided by libraries and library professionals." (ALA 2015) This statement clearly identifies library patrons' roles in promoting libraries' continued financial, programmatic, and community-based success. The library's writers and poets will tell stories that represent the importance of libraries in their lives and communities. They will have greater impact than statistics in attracting the municipal, academic, and school district funding sources that libraries require. Libraries can take their own first steps to success by encouraging and supporting writers who in turn will tell the story of how the library has improved and changed their lives.

Works Cited

American Library Association (ALA). 2015. "Libraries Transform." http://www.ilovelibraries.org/libraries transform (accessed May 26, 2016).

Amherst Writers & Artists (AWA). 2016. "The AWA Method." http://www.amherstwriters.com/about/awa-method (accessed May 30, 2016).

Greenburgh Public Library. 2016. "Greenburgh Library Strategic Plan 2016–2019." http://www.greenburgh library.org/wp-content/uploads/2016/04/2016-19-GPL-Strategic-Plan.pdf (accessed May 27, 2016).

Poets & Writers. 2016. "Funding for Readings and Workshops." http://www.pw.org/funding/funding_readings workshops (accessed May 30, 2016).

The Power of Words

Drawing Authors and the College Community Together Through Author Talks

LAUREL ERIN FENNELL *and*
ALDA NORONHA-NIMMO

This chapter is a case study involving a college setting. We, a faculty librarian and a reading/English professor, are both part of a committee that plans a campus-based arts festival each year. This case study focuses on how we have incorporated literature into the festival and how this has evolved over time.

In our primary event, called the Power of Words, we bring published author(s) to speak to college students. Each year we have had 150 to 200 students attend talks by writers and poets, ranging from published faculty at our college, to a *New York Times* and *USA Today* bestselling author. Last year we began a second literature-related event, Writing by the Lake, which is a writing workshop for students. In addition, the librarian had previously created a mobile library program called Library on the Fly. This mobile library visits the literary events during the arts festival as one of its yearly stops, further enfolding literature into the annual festival.

This chapter details how we plan and design our Power of Words event and also includes information about our two related initiatives, Writing by the Lake and Library on the Fly.

In the Beginning

At a time when the arts are being squeezed out of schools across the country, our campus administration had a different philosophy. We work at a large college campus in an urban area which has a campus administration that was admirably looking to find ways to infuse the arts into students' lives. Many of our students may not have the opportunity to experience the arts in their daily lives, so this potential exposure to the arts was especially valuable. For instance, one campus arts initiative was a sculpture garden. Through the donation of sculptures, a sculpture garden was created with 69 sculptures installed around the campus grounds. A map of the sculptures and audio tour can be checked out from the library.

Another initiative, the one focused on in this chapter, is a yearly arts festival which would expose students to a variety of arts. Events include such activities as choral performances, theatre improvisation, a student photography exhibit, tours of the sculpture park, faculty/staff music and dance performances, film screenings and question and answer with the directors, and a student competition to design the festival poster. The yearly arts festival is planned by a committee of faculty, staff, and administrators from various departments on campus including philosophy, theatre, photography, film, English, math, etc. Due to a background in dance, the librarian co-author of this article was included on the committee. Events grew organically to fill the week-long calendar of events for the festival each year with one or two committee members usually responsible for each event. Music, dance, theatre, and the visual arts were well represented. However, the reading/English professor and the librarian, noticed a problem—literature was not represented at all! Thus began our collaboration to bring literature into the festival.

On our campus, we already had the occasional student writing contest, and a yearly spoken word café, so we wanted to do something different. We decided that author talks would benefit our campus. Authors would talk about their own works, the publishing industry, and the writing process. Listening to published authors would provide real world exposure for students and would present them with role models of people who have succeeded in the field. Writing is an essential way of expressing oneself and a skill with which many students have difficulty. We felt that bringing in published authors could lead our students to not just learn about new topics and contemporary writings, but to consider the power of the written word and how each of them could also harness that power. Our author event was born and branded, the Power of Words.

Bringing Forth the Power of Words

Our first consideration when planning the event was our audience, including their interests, demographics, and needs. Our primary audience is college students and the college community. However, we work at a large college with eight campuses and each campus has its own unique ethos and student profile. Our goal was to match our students' interests when deciding which authors to contact. There are many accomplished authors whom we would not pursue if we did not think that their particular talks or books would capture the attention of our student population. With our location in Miami, and with many students who are recent immigrants or who have roots in the Caribbean, we felt that authors speaking about books set in these locations would be popular with our students. Knowing that many of our students have children, we have also not shied away from hosting authors of children's books.

The first year, we chose to invite faculty and staff from our college who were published authors. They ranged from an award winning poet to an author/illustrator of a graphic novel. Having our own faculty and administrators speak as published authors put the spotlight on talent within our college that the students and the rest of the college community may otherwise not have known. It was exciting and enlightening for our students to discover, for example, that their professor had published a book on a topic of interest; that an administrator published a novel set in a certain location and had a similar background to them; or that their librarian had published a book of poetry. Having speakers who were already familiar to students and the rest of the college community made the author talks especially meaningful for the audience. Much of the writing was about

South Florida, Cuba, and other islands in the Caribbean, which served to make the works accessible and interesting to our student body.

We were constrained by class times of 50 minutes or one hour and fifteen minutes, depending on the day of the week. We chose to use the hour and fifteen minute sessions and to have three authors speak at each event. If by chance one author did not show up, we still had presenters for the event. However, we found that having three authors made the event rushed and we wanted students to be able to ask all their questions and get the most out of the presentations.

The schedule of the event consisted of the following: we welcomed the audience and introduced each author who then spoke, reading a selection from the book and discussing his/her writing. After all the authors spoke, we had a Q&A session where the audience could ask questions. We wrapped up the event by raffling off the authors' books and presenting the authors with a framed certificate of appreciation along with a small gift.

We were fortunate to be able to choose from several rooms on campus for our event. We chose a spacious conference room where we could determine the seating arrangement. We used the maximum number of seats (200) and organized them in rows with a middle aisle for easy access. The room was arranged with a podium and table at the front and a big screen to project a PowerPoint presentation or picture, etc. Authors took turns going to the podium to speak and sat together at the table to answer audience questions at the end of the session. We also arranged a microphone on a stand in the aisle for student/audience questions.

It was extremely important to ensure that we had an audience for our event. Email blasts about the festival events went out to all faculty and staff on campus. Electronic signs on campus also advertised the festival events. We sent e-mails about our event to department chairpersons personally and requested that they pass the information on to their faculty. Most importantly, we contacted some faculty members directly, inviting them to bring their classes to the author event and asking them to RSVP with the estimated number of students attending. These classes made up the bulk of the audience and allowed us to be confident that the event would be well-attended. We provided biographical and additional information about the authors to the professors in advance so they could find ways to work the event into the content of their classes. Linking the author reading to the course content made the session more relevant and meaningful for students. For example, one journalism professor provided information about the author to his students prior to the event. Later, the students had to write a press release. In addition, social media sites such as Facebook, are one avenue we have used to publicize our events to the general public. Attendance exceeded our expectations the first year with two sessions of 200 seats each, filled to capacity with standing room only.

The next year we branched out, contacting local university English departments to see if any of their published faculty members were interested in speaking at our event. Through this effort, we have had several published authors from local universities speak at our event. During the second year, our Power of Words event paired an award-winning poet (professor) from one university with an adjunct from another university who had published a novel set in Cuba. The juxtaposition of these two authors worked well, as some students were intrigued by the novel while others really appreciated the poetry. We realized that having two authors speak during an event can provide contrast and draw different crowds. This particular year, we tried holding the event in a different room. We used a special event room with amphitheater-style seating. The room was newly renovated and seated over 100 people, but it just did not have the intimate feel that we prefer for our author talk. Though the conference room we used the year before was large enough to hold up to 200 seats, it still felt much more intimate than the amphitheater-style room.

In subsequent years, we went on to utilize local writers groups and personal networks to recruit published authors to speak at our event. For instance, our local Society of Children's Book Writers and Illustrators (SCBWI) critique groups include published authors, so we have invited a couple of them to speak at the Power of Words event. Recently, one children's book author spoke about the micropublishing company she created and her newly published picture book which includes themes of gender identity. Our students and faculty learned about the structure of a picture book, and discussed issues (such as how race is depicted) with the author.

Besides local writers groups, we also mined personal networks to find local authors. For example, during small talk before a work meeting at another campus, one of the authors of this article discovered that a staff member's aunt is a popular *New York Times* bestselling author who has written over a hundred novels. Last year we hosted this best-selling author and for the first time we planned the event with one author/speaker and it worked well. We had a separate event with our other speaker (a university professor/poet) who is popular with our faculty. Due to this success, in the future we will focus on having only one or two authors speak at each event.

The conference room was not available for the event with the *New York Times* best-selling author; therefore, we decided to try having the event in the campus library. One side of the library used to have bookshelves but these were removed a couple of years ago so that space is open to accommodate tables for student group study. This makes a cozy space for an author reading event. We asked our campus facilities team to hang curtains to partition off the area. We had seating for up to 150 audience members. We had a low stage set up against the back wall with a podium. This setting was a little more restricted in terms of space as compared to the conference room, but the advantage was that we got people into the library for the event. It was an intimate setting and the library felt like the perfect place to have an author reading.

As our primary audience is the college community, we focus on them when we plan our events; however, we do also invite the public. All our events are free and open to the public. We hope to build more connections with the public in the future, positioning the author talks as a bridge between the college and the community. This is important to us as community involvement enriches our event and also the community members it touches. We are fortunate to have a college culture which encourages and takes pride in community engagement.

Nuts and Bolts

The following are some issues, ideas, and recommendations relevant to those who may be planning similar events:

Branding the Event. Our first year, we named our event the Power of Words, and we have kept this name every year for continuity. The Power of Words title is broad enough to be suitable for various author or poet talks, and at the same time it has profound implications that appeal to our students. Consider branding your event with a catchy title.

More Ways to Locate Authors. We used several different avenues to locate authors such as contacting published authors internal to our organization, reaching out to local university English departments, pursuing local writers groups, and mining personal networks. Other avenues to pursue when looking for authors would be to contact local organizations and independent (indie) bookstores. Some local writers' institutes may bring in authors year-round and may agree to partner with you. Some indie bookstores host many author talks, have great networks, and have staff who can be valuable resources. Authors in town for a book fair or conference may be willing to speak at your event, and you may be able to save on travel fees in these cases.

Honorariums. Honorariums and speaking fees for authors can vary widely. Some authors may be willing to speak for a small honorarium or basic travel costs, while others may have a set fee of thousands of dollars. If budget is a concern, grants can be pursued or fundraisers can be held to pay for the author visit.

Selling Books. It is important to let authors know if they will be able to sell and sign books at your event. We were able to secure permission from our campus administration to allow the authors to sell books. If you are going to let authors sell books, determine the parameters. For example, do the authors need to make arrangements with your campus bookstore or handle all the details of selling independent of your institution? In addition, we suggest that authors bring a copy of their book to raffle off during the event.

Getting Creative with Location. We have experimented with a variety of locations for our event. If you have difficulty finding an appropriate location for the event, try thinking outside the box. Peet (2015) gives some examples of creative library programming, such as the New York Public Library's (NYPL) Books at Noon series. Jessica Strand, NYPL associate director of public programs and events, holds the event in a public entryway which allows room for 200 people standing. For limited seating capacity, one could utilize an overflow room with monitors where people could watch the event in real time or stream the event over the Internet to those at a distance.

Handling Technical Issues. We always have someone from our campus media services department present in case there is a malfunction with microphones, computers, or other equipment. This plan certainly came in handy one year when the usual podium with computer and monitor was missing from the room on the day of the event. If possible, have someone present during the entire presentation to take care of any technical issues. Also, make sure to check with authors in advance to determine what technology they need available for their presentations along with any other assistance they may require.

Outreach. An option to consider for growing your audience would be to reach out to student groups, other universities, and community organizations that may have an interest in a particular speaker you are hosting. One issue when inviting the community, however, is that locating the event room and appropriate parking on the college campus can be confusing for community members. Therefore, we make prior parking arrangements and provide a campus map.

Survey. We like to collect audience feedback to use for evaluating an event and for planning the next event. Consider distributing a survey to the audience members at the conclusion of the author talk.

Refreshments. We always offer refreshments such as coffee, tea, and cookies for the audience after the author talk. This serves as an incentive for people to attend so we recommend mentioning refreshments in the advertisements for the event.

Expanding

The college has a five-year mission that focuses on writing across the disciplines. In keeping with this goal and incorporating it into the literary theme of the festival, Writing by the Lake was an ancillary event conceived by the Reading/English professor two years ago. Writing by the Lake is a hands-on writing workshop where students practice their writing skills using a picture as a writing prompt. This event is by invitation only as it requires a hands-on activity and small and large group instruction/demonstration.

Many students do not like to write; others feel that they are incapable of producing any significant written work. It is important, therefore, to tap into their innate ability to produce language and then guide them to organize it in written format. This can be done through the use of a step-book, which serves as a three-dimensional representation of a graphic organizer. A step-book consists of three or more pages of blank paper folded—like steps—and stapled to look like a booklet. During the workshop, each student receives a step-book and selects one picture to write about (from a variety of pictures cut out from recycled magazines). The professor demonstrates how this information can be organized when planning a written draft on the booklet. The process ends with students having a written outline of an essay. The kinesthetic nature of the activity along with the ability to choose one's own picture—in essence one's own prompt/topic—frees the mind to engage in creating language.

Tables with chairs for no more than five students per table are set up by the picturesque lake. There is a portable dry-erase board for the professor to explain the lesson. The professor walks around and engages in meaningful communication with students who may require additional explanations or who may have difficulty harnessing their innate imaginations. Ideally, at least two hours should be set aside to address this activity, but because the professor has to comply with the standard timeframes set for classes, this activity is assigned a time block of one hour and fifteen minutes. This event is designed for one class (20 to 25 students). In the two years that this event has taken place, the classes that have participated were from the college's Continuing Education Department which meets one important goal of the festival (reaching a diverse audience). Students have voiced their gratitude for this activity, and the instructors have expressed interest in implementing this lesson in their own courses.

As a way of expanding our literary offerings, we incorporated Library on the Fly into our annual literary events for the arts festival. Library on the Fly is a library program which brings books to events around campus; this program was started by the librarian author of this article. This is a way to 'bring the library' to students and the campus community. From bookmobiles to biblioburros, many different types of mobile libraries have been successful in different parts of the world, and this is our campus version. Sometimes a special tall cart is used to transport and display the books and DVDs. Other times, a typical library book cart is used to transport materials to an event, and then the books are displayed at tables set up at the event. Library on the Fly increases student awareness of the library, and how to use it, along with increasing student access to books. This convenient service allows students to browse and check out books and DVDs to take home. Therefore, they become more familiar with the kinds of resources that are available through the library. The Library on the Fly program aims to help improve student core skills in reading, writing, and algebra (as many of our students need remedial help), along with helping students gain information seeking/information literacy skills.

This year we brought Library on the Fly outside to the Writing by the Lake event. After the event's writing activity, the librarian discussed some library services, gave out bookmarks, and invited students to take a look at the books. The students were surprised to see the variety of books that the library offered, from books about writing and grammar to popular books and graphic novels. Attending the event was one class of about 25 students, and over 20 books were checked out by these students. We have also brought Library on the Fly to other events during this arts festival, where we highlighted books on the various arts.

We have found Library on the Fly to be a valuable way to market our collection. We also use Library on the Fly to advertise our other library services and resources by, for example, providing handouts about our e-books and online databases of articles and streaming video. When we have some discarded books or donations we will not add to our collection, we bring these books to give away. In addition, we often use this interaction with students to provide reference help and collect surveys or other written feedback from students. Below are a couple written comments we have received from students:

- "It's wonderful, this campaign for students. We need to know that the library gives us this service."
- "The free books are a great idea and I appreciate the concern for reading."

As we look to the future, we are constantly in communication about adding new events to our cache of activities. For example, next year we are considering a storytelling event at the college daycare and a workshop for parents on puppet-making and bringing storybook characters to life. Our diverse festival of the arts committee plans events which enrich the campus and the wider community. We believe it is imperative that festivals like this continue to highlight the importance of the arts in contemporary times.

Works Cited

Peet, Lisa. 2015. "Author! Author!" *Library Journal* 140 (8): 26–29.

The *Latino Americans: 500 Years of History* Grant Experience

A Case Study in Cooperation

Alyssa Martin *and* Christopher Shaffer

In 2015, Troy University Libraries in Troy, Alabama, received the *Latino Americans: 500 Years of History* grant, a public programming initiative for libraries and other cultural organizations made possible by the National Endowment for the Humanities and the American Library Association. The project featured the PBS documentary series *Latino Americans: The 500-Year Legacy That Shaped a Nation* (2013). In addition to public screenings of the film, Troy University Libraries hosted additional programs on all three Troy campuses including a variety of speakers and an art exhibit during National Hispanic Month.

Librarians at Troy University felt that the cultural life of Troy communities would benefit from the university highlighting Latino American histories and cultures and encouraging a tradition of having speakers and events to celebrate National Hispanic Heritage Month. During this grant experience, Troy University Libraries engaged the community in examining the histories of Latino Americans during film discussions and by listening to Latino Americans talking about their own past and present experiences.

This chapter will explore the *Latino Americans: 500 Years of History* grant experience as a case study in cooperation between librarians at Troy University Libraries and one of the grant participants, author Lila Quintero Weaver. Ms. Weaver spoke as a guest lecturer and exhibited her artwork at Troy University as part of the grant activities.

Troy University Demographics

Three Troy University Libraries were involved in this programming grant: Troy University Rosa Parks Library in Montgomery, Troy University Library in Dothan, and the Troy University Library in Troy. Through the programming events at Troy University Libraries, three communities in Alabama (Montgomery, Dothan, and Troy) were educated on the histories and cultures of Latino Americans and the ways they have shaped the United States we know today. With this programming, Troy University Libraries brought scholarship on Latino American histories and cultures to new audiences, engaged people in examining the histories of Latino Americans in their communities, and fostered understanding of local histories in regional, national, and international contexts.

The Troy University Rosa Parks Library, located in downtown Montgomery on the Troy University Montgomery Campus, sits above the nationally recognized Rosa Parks Museum. The Troy University Montgomery Campus has a population of over 1,700 non-traditional students with the average age being 29. Montgomery is the capital city of Alabama. According to the 2010 census the city had a population of over 205,000 people and the Montgomery metro area had an estimated population of over 370,000 people. This central Alabama "River Region" community includes the surrounding cities of Prattville, Wetumpka, and Millbrook. The residents of the city of Montgomery include: 56.6 percent African-American, 37.3 percent Caucasian, and 3.9 percent Hispanic or Latino.

The Troy University Dothan Library is located in Dothan on the Troy University Dothan Campus. Troy University in Dothan has a population of over 1,200 students. Dothan, according to the 2010 U.S. Census, had a population of over 68,000; however, the Dothan metro area had over 145,000 people and is a significant hub for Southeastern Alabama, Southwest Georgia, and a portion of the Florida panhandle. The residents of the city of Dothan include: 63.1 percent Caucasian, 32.5 percent African-American, and 2.9 percent Hispanic or Latino.

The University Library is located on the main Troy campus in Troy. Troy University is a residential campus with over 7,000 traditional age students (18–25). Troy is a rural, college town with a population of over 19,000 people. The residents of the city of Troy include: 55 percent Caucasian, 39 percent African-American and 2 percent Hispanic/ Latino.

A Culture of Community Programming

Community programming is a priority at Troy University Libraries. According to the Dean of Troy University Libraries, Dr. Christopher Shaffer, "The role of the academic library is evolving. Not only do libraries continue to provide traditional services, but they also conduct outreach to students, faculty and surrounding communities."

Both internal and external partnerships are crucial for successful programs. For example, the Office of Sponsored Programs at Troy University has been instrumental in helping the library find and implement grants. Academic colleges and departments are also beneficial. Forging these ties will lead to faculty promoting library events and possibly to future collaborations.

External partnerships are extremely important. External partnerships promote attendance and allow for exposure within the community for the library and the university at large. Examples of past external partnerships with Troy University Libraries include public libraries, churches, local government and local arts organizations.

The benefits of library programming include better relationships and increased exposure of the library to the campus administration, faculty and staff, and potential donors. As a result of the emphasis on library programming, campus administrators have praised the Troy University Libraries for their efforts to help the community. This increased exposure has translated into increased library usage by faculty, staff and students and has attracted donors. For example, one local Montgomery, AL resident recently donated a significant collection of Civil Rights books to the Troy University Rosa Parks Library.

Library programming brings library faculty and other university departments together to work on projects. As a result of the Pragda film series, the Tournees French film festival, and the Southern Circuit of Independent Filmmakers grant, the Troy University Library has cultivated relationships with the Spanish department, the French department, the First Year Studies Department and the College of Communication and Fine Arts. These partners support programs hosted by Troy University Libraries by promoting the events in the community and encouraging their students to attend these events.

Since 2010, Troy University Libraries have received numerous programming grants including film and lecture series, book talks, exhibits and concerts. In addition to the *Latino Americans: 500 Years of History* grant, other grant-funded programming by Troy University Libraries includes:

- December 2015: The Wiregrass Common Heritage Project, a grant from the National Endowment for the Humanities, provided workshops on African American genealogical sources in Alabama and other public programming intended to engage residents of this region and enable the digitization of materials in the Wiregrass region, which spans southeast Alabama, southwest Georgia, and northwest Florida.
- November 2015 and November 2014: The Pragda Spanish Film Festival involved film screenings and discussions related to Spanish history and Latino culture.
- March 2015: The South Arts, Southern Circuit-Civic Engagement through the Arts grant provided a six film series that is aimed at raising awareness about critical issues and events through the use of various films. As part of this series, filmmakers travel to campus to screen their films and interact with the audience.
- October 2014: The French American Cultural Exchange Tournees Film Festival involved film screenings and discussions relating to French history and culture.
- May 2014: The Wiregrass Blues Project, funded by the Alabama Humanities Foundation, educated participants about the role blues music played in the history of the Wiregrass region. Activities included a community-wide concert, an educational panel discussion, and public school visits by performers.
- March 2014: The National Endowment for the Humanities (NEH) and the American Library Association's (ALA) Let's Talk About It: Muslim Journeys Round 2 funded a follow-up to the original Let's Talk About It grant. Students and faculty participated in a series of five book discussions relating to Muslim history and culture.
- December 2013: The Alabama Humanities Foundation's They Had No Voice grant partially supported lectures by Mr. Denny Abbott, who exposed the abuses at the Mount Meigs Youth Detention facility in Montgomery.
- September 2013: The Alabama Humanities Foundation Let's Talk About It: Muslim Journeys provided funds to support four lectures by Dr. Matt Malczycki, an expert on Middle Eastern history.
- June 2013: The National Endowment for the Humanities and Gilder Lehrman Institute of American History's Created Equal: America's Civil Rights Struggle provided a set of documentaries on the civil rights era along for a teacher workshop.
- February 2012: The Alabama Humanities Foundation funded two lecturers. The first speaker, Mr. Ed Wood, is the subject of a documentary on the civil rights era

in Anniston, AL. The second speaker was Rachel Hawkins, *New York Times* best-selling author for Disney-Hyperion who discussed her books, the creative writing process, and how to become a published author.

- Summer of 2011: The Alabama Humanities Foundation provided support for Dr. Thomas Nadar and Rabbi Kenneth Kantor to speak on topics related to an American Library Association exhibit, "A Fine Romance: Jewish Songwriters, American Songs, 1910–1965."
- February 2011: The Alabama Humanities Foundation provided funds to support Mike Searles, a professor from Augusta State University, to discuss black cowboys in the American West.
- April 2010: The Alabama Humanities Foundation provided funds to bring Ann Rosenheck, a Holocaust survivor, to discuss her story. Mrs. Rosenheck, a survivor of three concentration camps, spoke at Troy University Libraries and at two public schools.

Latino Americans: 500 Years of History

As part of the *Latino Americans: 500 Years of History* grant, Troy University Libraries hosted a total of nine scholar-led film screenings, seven book talks, and an art exhibit. At the Troy University Rosa Parks Library in Montgomery and the Troy University Library in Troy one professor discussed her book about her experiences in Cuba. At the Troy University Library in Troy, another speaker talked about his military experience in the U.S. as a Latino American, and Latino author and illustrator Lila Quintero Weaver presented at three Troy University Libraries.

Lila Quintero Weaver spoke about her graphic novel *Darkroom: A Memoir in Black & White.* (2012).Select illustrations from Ms. Weaver's book, *Darkroom,* were on display for almost two months in the exhibit hall of the Troy University Rosa Parks Library and Museum.

Troy University Libraries showed several episodes of the *Latino Americans: The 500-Year Legacy that Shaped a Nation* (2013) film series including the episode "Prejudice and Pride." This episode corresponded with the time period of Lila Quintero Weaver's memoir about life in Alabama after her immigration from Argentina in the 1960s, during the civil rights period. Lila's book talks and illustrations from *Darkroom* explored humanities questions such as "How can literature and art serve as vehicles for social change?" and "How are prejudice and bias created and how can we overcome them?"

A Conversation with Lila Quintero Weaver: Her Life, Her Book and Her Illustrations

Lila was born in Buenos Aires, Argentina and immigrated to the U.S. with her family in 1961. Her book *Darkroom: A Memoir in Black & White,* is graphic novel that explores the connections between immigration and race. It is the story of her family's immigration to the American South from Argentina. *Darkroom* is both an immigration story and a first-hand account of the racial tension and violence that Lila's family witnessed in their adopted hometown in Alabama's Black Belt region. Lila's arrival in Alabama coincided with significant developments in the civil rights movement; she has an illustrated middle-grade novel forthcoming from Candlewick Press.

During her book discussions, Ms. Weaver talked about writing and illustrating *Darkroom* and how her life experiences influenced her growing up in America. Reflecting on her life experiences: "My family immigrated to the United States in 1961, when I was five. We settled in Marion, Alabama, which is situated in the heart of the Black Belt region. Our arrival coincided with major events in the Civil Rights Movement: the closing years of Jim Crow law, the voter-registration drive, and the desegregation of public schools. On February 18, 1965, my father was an eyewitness to portions of a bloody protest that ended in the shooting death of Jimmie Lee Jackson" (Weaver, January 2016).

Regarding her book, Weaver (January 2016) explained: "In *Darkroom*, I relate my immigration journey, both as an outsider during a deeply conflicted and consequential decade, and as a young child anxious to erase the cultural obstacles that kept me from feeling that I belonged." Lila drew all of the illustrations in *Darkroom*, which took her four years to complete. In the "artist statement" for the Rosa Parks Museum exhibition of her artwork in September 2015, she stated:

> The drawings in this exhibit appear in my graphic novel, *Darkroom: A Memoir in Black & White*. The book contains over 500 similar images that range in subject matter from immigrant life, reflections on Argentine culture, racial identity and conflict, and other aspects of growing up as a minority Latina in a small Alabama town during the 1960s.
>
> The book resembles an album of family photographs. This concept originates from a central artistic influence: my father's passion for photography. As a child, I spent time in his makeshift darkroom where the magic of images manifesting on blank paper captivated my interest.
>
> I employ elements of the darkroom and other photographic motifs throughout the book. My intent is to engage the reader's visual curiosity through themes of black, white and gray. Using images of the camera and the human eye, I explore aspects of life in the South that the dominant culture often prefers to hide. I reflect on what it means to be looked upon dismissively as a Latina and how I grew past my own racial blindness. I also pay homage to the critical role of photojournalism in the forward march to obtain justice and civil rights for all people.

Librarians Reflect on a Successful Experience

The *Latino Americans: 500 Years of History* programs at Troy University positively impacted Troy University and the surrounding communities. Over 225 people attended the *Latino Americans: 500 Years of History* film screenings and other program events including Lila Quintero Weaver's book talks. The illustrations from *Darkroom* were viewed by over 2,100 people as they toured the Rosa Parks Museum.

At the end of each program, participants were asked to fill out an evaluation sheet that asked what they liked best and least about the program and whether they would want to participate in a similar program in the future. Most of the participants said they would want to have similar programs in the future and very few had negative comments. When they did have negative comments, it usually had to do with technical problems related to presentation such as sound issues and problems with equipment.

When asked "What did you like best about the program?" participants overwhelmingly had positive comments. The program attendees found Lila Quintero Weaver's book talk and illustrations about her experiences with the civil rights struggle very informative and interesting. One person said what they liked best about her talk was that it was a "personal experience of a challenging time."

Participants felt a connection with the author and her work. One person said "I really enjoyed the personal connection with all the historical facts." Another said "She made history come alive with her book and illustrations." In the Rosa Parks Museum exhibit hall, guests who viewed the illustrations from *Darkroom* left comments like "very inspiring" and "Beautiful depiction on the power of vision and the double-consciousness of race relations in America."

People also felt Lila was genuine and creative: "she was honest and her art was very unique." When talking about her presentation, one person stated that they "liked that it contained excerpts from her book and that the speaker (Lila) not only addressed the book, but also her influences."

Troy University Libraries plan to use comments and other feedback from the programs to analyze strengths and weaknesses to learn for future programs. Listed below are some best practices for successful programming grants, including both tips for authors and librarians.

Lila Quintero Weaver Tips for authors:

- Authors need to understand what type of program the hosting library prefers. Possibilities include a traditional book talk, a behind-the-scenes look at the book's creation, a talk that focuses on particular thematic elements within the book, an interview format with a moderator, or a hands-on workshop with audience participants.
- It is important to know who the audience will be, for example: community, academic, young people, retired persons, writers or artists. Establishing this as clearly as possible will help the author adjust the presentation's focus, length, tone, vocabulary level and other matters.
- The author should clearly communicate in advance any physical accommodations or technical devices required for a successful presentation.
- The library and author should agree on whether books for sale will be available following the presentation, and whether the organization of the sale is up to the author, or if this will be a function of the host.
- It is helpful if all parties understand their role in promoting the event. The author should comply with requests for biographical materials and photographs. He or she should have a clear understanding about the presence of media outlets. (Weaver, February 12, 2016)

Tips for Librarians prior to the program:

- When asking the author to speak, be clear about what you want them to do.
- Develop a relationship with the author throughout the process, answering any questions and addressing concerns.
- Reply promptly to e-mails/phone calls.
- If the author is paid, make sure the contract is clear to both the author and the university. Get all paperwork signed and completed as soon as possible. For example, talent release forms, documents requiring signatures for payment etc.
- Give the author all of your contact information and make sure you have the author's contact information.
- Give the author an itinerary for the program, including locations, directions and times so that the author knows where they are going on campus and who they will meet and at what time.

During the program

- Make the author feel welcome when they arrive. Ask them if they need anything (i.e. water, etc.).
- Introduce the author before his or her presentation.
- Provide the author with technical support—both before and during their program.
- Expect the unexpected—technical problems with computer; sound system not working, etc. Be prepared ahead of time with a backup plan in case something goes wrong.

After the program

- Immediately following the program, hand out program evaluation forms. These forms will provide feedback that will be useful for future programs and may be required by grant agencies.
- Thank the author for speaking and ask if they need anything else before they leave (i.e. directions, etc.).
- Pay the author in a timely manner!
- Later, follow-up with a thank you note. You may end up working together again on other projects/programming activities.

Above all else, the key to successful programming is communication! Make sure to keep in contact with the author throughout the entire process.

Conclusion

The *Latino Americans: 500 Years of History* grant experience was a successful case study in cooperation between librarians and authors, highlighting the importance of libraries and community programming. The grant programs were able to get the community and program participants talking about issues such as civil rights that they may not have otherwise discussed. Troy University Libraries successfully brought scholarship on Latino American histories and cultures to the community and engaged people in examining the histories of Latino Americans.

Works Cited

Latino Americans: The 500-Year Legacy That Shaped a Nation. 2013. Directed by David Belton and Sonia Fritz. 2013. Washington, DC: WETA, Bosch, and Latino Public Broadcasting. DVD.

Weaver, Lila Q. (2012). *Darkroom: A Memoir in Black & White*. Tuscaloosa: University of Alabama Press.

_____. Discussion with author. January 2016.

_____. E-mail to author. February 12, 2016.

The Hugh C. Hyde Living Writers Series at San Diego State University

How One of the Nation's Oldest Reading Series Found a Home in the Library

MARKEL TUMLIN *and* MEAGAN MARSHALL

Background and Context

The Hugh C. Hyde Living Writers Series (HCHLWS) at San Diego State University (SDSU) has a deep and varied history. Often touted as one of the nation's longest continuously running reading series, its beginnings can be traced back to the SDSU English Department in the late 1970s. The series, originally known as simply the Living Writers Series, has been part of SDSU's campus life since then, and every semester several readings are presented. Since fall 2000, almost all of the readings have been held in the SDSU Library. This chapter discusses how the partnership between the HCHLWS and the SDSU Library evolved and also the roles each partner plays in keeping the series successful.

Since its beginning, the series has promoted stylistic inclusiveness. Prose writers and poets of all kinds have read; the series has welcomed formal, academic poets as well as slam poets, experimental writers as well as more traditional ones. Past readers have included such literary luminaries as Derek Walcott and Tillie Olsen, as well as many local and regional writers. SDSU MFA graduates such as the Newbery Award-winning author Matt de la Peña have also returned to read. Each semester the series includes one special event sub-titled the Laurie Okuma Memorial Reading that features a woman writer from an underrepresented group. It is named in honor of the SDSU MFA in Creative Writing student whose family endowed the reading after she tragically passed away at a young age. The series seems to have fulfilled the vision of early series director Dawn Kolokithas; a February 19, 1980, article in the *Daily Aztec* (SDSU's student newspaper) reveals that she had been interested "in setting up a series of varied, but talented, literary figures." Students who regularly attend the readings are exposed to an embarrassment of stylistic riches.

Perusing the series' newspaper listings during the two decades before it found a home in the library might lead one to think that a diversity of performance venues was also a goal. Events were advertised at locations all over the SDSU campus. Some took place in regular classrooms, some were held in various locations in the Aztec Center (SDSU's student union), and many—at Scripps Cottage, a small stand-alone building located in a garden area with a turtle pond. People who were regular attendees had to pay especially close attention to a specific event's location, since the series utilized so many different campus spaces.

A Mutually Beneficial Partnership

Around the turn of the century, two events occurred that enhanced the series while allowing it to maintain its aesthetic sensibilities. First, it received a generous endowment from Hugh C. Hyde, which brought greater stability to its funding; the series was renamed at that time to honor his contribution. Second, it found a long-term home in the SDSU library. Unlike the other campus venues the series had been using, space in the library was available free of charge. The library simply asked that it be given credit for co-sponsorship and that its policy of making all events free and open to the public be followed. Since HCHLWS events were already free, this was not a problem. Saving the room rental fees enabled more of the series' limited funds to be spent on writers. Another benefit was logistical simplification. Holding readings in a consistent location was easier for regular attendees as well as for the organizers.

The partnership between the library and the HCHLWS resulted from some key developments in the library. A new library dean was hired in 1999, and her initial strategic plan included a goal of making the library a campus center for lectures and creative activities. She asked the library faculty and staff for ideas that could help achieve that goal. A staff member who was an alumna of the university's creative writing master's program suggested to the library's liaison to the English Department that the HCHLWS might be receptive to holding readings in the library. The liaison, who had also been just recently hired, contacted the English Department chair who put him in touch with the people running the series. The liaison viewed this as a great opportunity for multiple benefits: to bring writers into the library for public readings, to strengthen his fledgling relationships with English Department faculty, and to make connections with the local writers' community. When the HCHLWS discovered that the library could provide a free room as well as promotional and logistical assistance, they were willing to try out a partnership. It made economic sense for them to move the series into the library, and the fall 2000 semester marked the first time it was held there.

The library had little prior experience hosting public events, and there were growing pains. An immediate concern was where to hold them. The library did not then have and still does not have a theater space. But there were multipurpose rooms. In 2000 there was a quiet study room located near the library entrance that was occasionally converted for other purposes. For example, library-wide staff meetings were sometimes held there. That room became the initial library home for the series, although a larger space located elsewhere in the library was infrequently used when a larger audience was anticipated. When readings were scheduled, the room was closed an hour prior to the reading so that it could be prepared. This turned out to be a great location for raising visibility, because patrons entering the library could see events as they happened. Of course, there was also a down side to using a room that was usually a study space. Students who studied there regularly were sometimes resentful when the room was converted. A few of them would even pitch in after events to help transform the room back into a study space as quickly as possible.

In addition to needing a dedicated space, the library initially lacked some other necessary items. Perhaps the most obvious was a podium or lectern. There was also no microphone, nor was the room equipped for audiovisual needs. The only way those early readings were possible was by borrowing equipment from the university's Information Technology Services (ITS) Department, located in another building. A fold-up plastic podium with an attached microphone was wheeled to the library on an as-needed basis. The library eventually purchased a wooden podium on wheels with a built-in speaker. It was used for Living Writers Series readings but could be easily moved to other spaces as needed.

Rolling with the Punches

During the economic downturn of 2008, the university was in dire need of classroom space and decided to convert the room where the series was held into a regular classroom. It would no longer be available for library events. The library had by this time cohosted dozens of readings and was interested in continuing. As a result, another multipurpose room with a capacity of eighty was identified, and that is where the series is still held today. A disadvantage of the current location is that it is less visible; it is located on the fourth floor. However, since so many of the series' regular attendees had already become accustomed to attending events at the library, re-directing them after the initial move was easy.

In spite of the less desirable location, the current room also has some significant advantages. Chief amongst those are the following:

1. When not being used for public events, it is dedicated to internal library use (e.g., meetings, workshops, etc.). It is never necessary to chase studying students out.
2. It is adjacent to another room with a capacity of forty, separated by an accordion room divider. Both rooms can be set up in advance, but the accordion divider allows the adjacent room to be opened only if needed.
3. It is equipped for audiovisual needs.

The larger space located elsewhere in the library continues to be used when anticipated demand justifies it. However, that space is usually a study room, and scheduling events there has become increasingly infrequent.

From Independent Author Series to Academic Course Offering

In 2011, with staunch support from SDSU's Department of English and Comparative Literature and the MFA Program in Creative Writing, the HCHLWS became the foundation for a new SDSU academic course offering, English 579: Living Writers. The professor who teaches the course also coordinates the series. Students enrolled in this course have the unique opportunity to read the work of and interact directly with each visiting author, attend the author's public reading in the library, pose questions about the author's aesthetic, publications, affinities, and experience in the publishing world, and compose analytical/creative texts based on knowledge gained during this interaction. This process is built into the course format so that all readings and question-and-answer sessions are scheduled during the normal course meeting day/time. Occasionally featured writers will generously schedule visits to additional writing and/or literature classes.

The scheduling process for guest authors depends on the individual needs and schedules of visiting authors and varies each semester. Generally, the HCHLWS invites between six and ten authors each semester and schedules readings on a biweekly basis. The series will occasionally book multiple authors for one reading event to highlight a specific theme (e.g. International Writers or National Poetry Month) or aesthetic/style (e.g., Performance Poets or Flash Fiction Writers). Class sessions that are not occupied by author visits are dedicated to studying the work of each visiting author and/or other related concepts (e.g., genre, literary theory, craft, and aesthetics).

There is no substitute for direct contact with poets and writers who read and discuss their work, their creative process, and their experience in the publishing world. Comments from students who have completed the related course component are consistently favorable. Guest authors alike enjoy the experience of speaking to an informed group of students and discussing their work in an academic setting. The conversion of the HCHLWS from independent guest author series to academic course offering demonstrates its role as an integral part of the cultural and literary fabric at San Diego State University.

The partnership between the library and the HCHLWS has proven beneficial to both. The series has maintained its reputation for presenting an outstanding assortment of writers while becoming an academic course, and the library has become a hub of creative and scholarly presentations. This success is the result of contributions by both partners. The following "how-to" guides describe how each role is delineated.

The Role of the HCHLWS Coordinator: A How-to Guide

Coordinating a reading series or event can be difficult and time-consuming. However, the results are very rewarding. It is imperative to have a team to assist with the process. The scope of each event may be varied, but the following steps have proven to be necessary.

Determine the Goal and Target Audience of the Series or Event

Defining these aspects will help in deciding which speakers to invite. The goal of the HCHLWS is to bring a culturally and stylistically diverse group of contemporary writers, poets, and artists to San Diego State University for student/faculty/staff-attended readings, classroom visits, workshops, and discussion forums. The series emphasizes diversity, both in terms of writing styles as well as multicultural and multigenerational perspectives and backgrounds. As a result, the HCHLWS provides an opportunity for students and members of the community to meet and hear from writers whose experience and expression represent a broad range of stylistic, cultural, and ethnic diversities.

Procure Necessary Funding Sources

In order to attract authors and poets whose work is defined by excellence, it's important to offer competitive honorariums and fees. Currently, the average fee for mid-range (or second-tier) authors is $800 to $4,000. High-end (or top-tier) authors command fees of $5,000 to $12,000 and higher. These figures do not include per diem expenses, accommodations, and transportation. Some academic institutions may offer opportunities for procuring funds such as grants or stipends. There are other organizations that accept applications for event funding such as Poets and Writers, the Harriet Monroe Poetry Institute, and the National Endowment for the Arts. Although the endowment from Hugh C. Hyde helped stabilize funding for this series, it has been necessary to pursue supplementary funding sources.

It is easiest to offer a "flat-fee" honorarium: one inclusive sum that covers airfare, accommodations, and per diem expenses like meals. Under this arrangement, authors can book their own travel and hotel based on personal preferences. They are then 'reimbursed' for these expenses when they receive the inclusive honorarium. Authors who are represented by literary agencies or specific publishers (e.g., Blue Flower Arts, Steven Barclay Agency, etc.) will have more specific contractual obligations and may require that the hosting entity cover airfare, accommodations, and meals separately. Once an author's agent has been contacted, the agent will negotiate the terms of the event.

Schedule Speakers

Scheduling for an event or series can take place anywhere between two months to two years prior to the desired date(s). Many authors have comprehensive websites that provide a current schedule of upcoming events and contact information for booking purposes. Many literary agencies and publishers also have websites that feature the authors they represent and contact information for booking. These sites can be helpful when attempting to contact an author. If an author has just released a book, there may be a promotional tour planned. Booking a touring author and/or an author with previously scheduled readings in your area can be cost-effective.

Prepare for the Event

Find a space that suits the needs of your specific event. The designated reading room for HCHLWS is an essential component of its collaboration with the library. The room(s) seats 80–120 guests. It is equipped with a podium and microphone as well as additional audiovisual equipment. This supplemental equipment can be used to project images, slide presentations, and/or any additional presentation components that guests might have.

If possible, arrange for book sales at the event. If there is not an onsite coordinator for book sales, the author or the author's literary agent or publisher may want to bring copies of books to sell at the reading. For well-known authors, a signing table and chair should be provided. This will assure that both guests and the signing author are comfortable. Books sales at almost all SDSU readings are provided by Aztec Shops, SDSU's on-campus bookstore.

Provide authors and/or their agents with a detailed itinerary at least two weeks prior to the event. Include all relevant information for the author's visit, such as flight and hotel information (if necessary), specific date(s) and time(s) for the event, duration of the reading, location of the event space, and contact information for the coordinators/hosts.

Designate someone to introduce the author and host the event. One or more individuals should prepare to give a general welcome to the audience and introduce the guest author. If a question and answer session is included in the event, someone should be designated to facilitate this process (e.g., field questions for the author, bring a wireless microphone around to the audience if needed, manage time, etc.).

Promote the Event

Promotion should begin at least one month prior to the event. The unique partnership between the HCHLWS and the library facilitates collaboration between the HCHLWS Coordinator and the library's Marketing & Communications Specialist to develop promotional materials for each event. These include informative posters and flyers and related media. Events are promoted in local periodicals as well as through multiple social media outlets, including Facebook and Twitter. Events are also listed on several campus websites. Over the years email addresses have been collected from attendees, and electronic invitations are sent for each event. Please note that email addresses were provided voluntarily, and invitations are sent using the bcc privacy tool so that no private information is shared in the process.

Execute the Event

On the day of the event, the author must be provided with adequate transportation. A designee can arrange transportation or a taxi service can be used. If the author's own car is being used, detailed driving directions and a parking permit (if need be) must be provided. Though meals might be included in the "flat-fee" honorarium, it is nice to treat the guest to a meal either before or after the event. Be sure to determine the dietary preferences and needs of guest authors before deciding on an appropriate restaurant.

Videotaping and audiotaping events may be desirable. The recordings can be used to promote additional events or for other purposes. However, it is necessary to get signed permission from an author for any public use (e.g., YouTube) of the recordings.

The Role of the Library: A How-to Guide

The HCHLWS procedures described above were largely in place prior to the partnership that was begun in 2000, and the library has not tried to influence programming decisions. Rather, it has seen its role as one that supports the series by providing space for it and by contributing to the logistics that are essential to its success. While the partnership was initiated by the library's liaison to the English Department, several other library staff members have become involved in carrying out the various tasks. Those tasks include the following steps.

Schedule the Room

Once the HCHLWS Coordinator has a list of writers prepared for an approaching semester, she forwards it to the liaison librarian and to the library's Administrative Office

Coordinator. The Administrative Office Coordinator at SDSU is responsible for all room scheduling. In addition to scheduling time for the readings, she also schedules time beforehand for room set-up. Since the room is used for a variety of purposes, it oftentimes needs to be reconfigured into a theater-style seating arrangement appropriate for a reading. It is important to schedule the room as early as possible, since it is so heavily used. Luckily, the schedule is generally known well before the beginning of any semester, and few conflicts have been encountered.

Notify the Other Participants

The Administrative Office Coordinator also sends an email with the listed reading dates to other library staff members who have a role. That list includes the Marketing and Communications Specialist, the Web Designer, the staff members responsible for room set-up, and technical support staff. Notifying all participants simultaneously facilitates coordination.

Promote the Event

The Marketing & Communications Specialist is the primary library staff person tasked with promotion. In addition to working jointly with the HCHLWS Coordinator as mentioned earlier, she also promotes the event through the library's usual promotional apparatuses. That includes preparing poster-sized versions of event flyers for the library entrance and placing notices of events in the library newsletter. She also works with the Art Librarian, who is the person currently charged with managing the library's events calendar. The Art Librarian ensures that all readings are posted as soon as possible and that approaching events are given increased prominence on the library's web page. The library's web designer assists her by creating appropriate web graphics and by posting ads for readings on the digital signage located throughout the library.

Execute the Event

A number of things must be done in the library on the day of a reading to ensure its success. The liaison to the English Department coordinates day-of-reading tasks to ensure they are completed. The most important of these is room setup. A number of different staff members have been assigned this responsibility over the years; the administrator who assigns this duty considers workloads and staff schedules in making the assignment. The main reading room as well as the adjacent room are set up theater-style. The accordion divider that separates them is then shut, only to be reopened if attendance warrants it. The podium is positioned in the front of the main room, and the microphone is tested. A table is set up in the rear of the room for book sales. The general condition of the room must also be inspected to ensure that there isn't any trash or other messes that might interfere with the reading. If a reading includes an audio/visual component, the liaison ensures that the technical support person tests the equipment ahead of time and is available if needed during the reading. The library also provides one bottle of water per reader; these are placed in advance on or near the podium. The liaison is usually the only library employee who attends the readings, and, in addition to coordinating the aforementioned logistics, the liaison ensures that the room is unlocked before events and locked after they are over.

Conclusion

The Hugh C. Hyde Living Writers Series has been a successful and welcome enhancement to the SDSU Library and has helped the library achieve the goal set by its former dean. Moving the series into the library has benefitted both the library and HCHLWS in a number of ways. It provided a way for the liaison to the English Department to strengthen his relationship with that department, which has led to opportunities for additional collaborations. For example, the library (and its liaison) have been utilized by other English Department faculty members for events not associated with the HCHLWS. These have included additional literary readings as well as scholarly presentations. The liaison librarian has also been able to establish relationships with the local writing community and individual writers, many of whom are graduates of the SDSU MFA Program in Creative Writing. Recently, the library has begun hosting "electronic reading" events with writers invited by the Digital Humanities Coordinator. In addition, a partnership has formed between the library, the HCHLWS, and the KPBS One Book, One San Diego program, and a joint event is currently being planned. The conversion of the Hugh C. Hyde Living Writers Series from independent guest authors' series to academic course offering demonstrated its role as an integral part of the cultural and literary fabric at SDSU. If anything, that role continues to grow and to excite interest.

Perhaps the greatest benefit for attendees and participants is the strong sense of community that has grown up around the series. In *Poetry: A Survivor's Guide*, Mark Yakich (2016) writes that "A reading often feels like a little convention of loners who believe they should get out at least once a month" (p. 103). That does *not* accurately describe the atmosphere at HCHLWS events, which display a lively spirit of comradery. Conversations continue long after an event has finished. There are undoubtedly many reasons why there is such a spirit surrounding the series, but presenting events regularly in the same space as part of an academic course offering is likely a major one. It provides a level of comfort and familiarity in which intellectual and creative pursuits can thrive. In the end, the faculty and staff whose teamwork keeps the series going can get some satisfaction from knowing that the students and others who attend have been able to enjoy enriching experiences while being a part of a vibrant literary community.

Works Cited

Yakich, Mark. 2016. *Poetry: A Survivor's Guide.* New York: Bloomsbury.

Literary Events at Your Library

Best-Practice Tips for Happy Writers and Patrons

TINA M. METZGER *and* MEG KING-SLOAN

The Chesterfield County Public Library is a ten-branch system just south of Richmond, Virginia. It serves over 235,000 cardholders among 337,000 county residents, as well as users from neighboring localities. CCPL libraries logged over 1.1 million visits in 2015 and presented over 2,500 programs between July 2014 and July 2015. In 2015, CCPL held literary-themed events at several branches. With careful planning, we enjoyed successful outcomes for the library, the authors, and the community.

The Festival of the Written Word took place on a Saturday in November at the Midlothian Library, a 15,000-square-foot branch in an affluent, highly educated area of the county. Twenty-one local authors shared their craft with more than 700 attendees in four hours of readings, panels, presentations and workshops for all ages.

The Clover Hill Library held "Murder at the Library" on Friday evening, October 30. Branch manager Margaret Howard got the idea from another library that had held a similar event. She contacted them and used the information to create her own program. Clover Hill Library is CCPL's branch with the highest circulation of children's materials, highest attendance for children's programs and serves the most elementary schools. As a result, the branch usually does children's events and she viewed this as a "date night" opportunity for parents. The event would be held in the evening, with dinner, an interactive performance and a panel discussion. It featured library staff actors engaging with patrons to use planted clues to help them solve a murder mystery. The event was a fundraiser for the Friends of the Library. Tickets sold out two weeks before the big night.

The North Courthouse Road Library celebrated Valentine's Day by inviting romance writers, editors and booksellers to a panel discussion of their craft. The event was proposed by local bestselling romance author Cathy Maxwell, also a Festival of the Written Word participant. CCPL also offers traditional author talks with book signings, but uses unique ways to expand them into more engaging experiences. Jarrett Krosoczka, author of the juvenile graphic novel series Lunch Lady, was a hit and will always remember CCPL for having him introduced by actual "lunch ladies" from county schools. While CCPL hosts several author events annually, the rest of this chapter focuses on the Festival of the Written Word and "Murder at the Library," with details and helpful tips for planning literary events at your own library.

Pep Talk

If you've never planned anything larger than a birthday party, planning a literary festival can be, well, terrifying. It helps to be passionate about writing and authors. Event planning skills can be learned. As librarians, we are often called upon to be fearless about learning new things, with very little instruction from anyone about how to proceed. This is one of the most truly rewarding things about the profession. Librarian Kate Miller describes her first time planning an author program for her library: "There were times when I felt engulfed, but I was also proud of all that was accomplished, and, along the way, I gained a sense of ownership of the process" (Miller, 2014). "Becoming an author event coordinator has been a highlight of my library career," says librarian and author Jennifer Johnston. "If I had one last piece of advice to offer, it would be only this: Enjoy yourself! Though planning and arranging author visits can be stressful and overwhelming at times, it's absolutely worth it. Not only are you attracting people to the library, but you're also making the written word come alive for them" (Johnston, 2008).

Likewise, organizers of "Murder at the Library" created the outcomes of partnerships with the community, a fun opportunity for the library to engage with its local neighborhood, and an influx of new library users.

First Steps: Name, Date, Authors and Content

To create a name for Midlothian's event, we had to decide what the event would and would not be. If you're holding an event for readers and writers, a name like the Festival of the Written Word will cover both. If, however, you are just focusing your event on writers or on readers, you can use a specific name, like "writer's festival," or "(Your City Name Here) Reads." The decision to hold our Festival in November was partially driven by the mandate that each library branch commit to holding its signature event in a particular quarter of each year. We had very unscientific reasons for choosing November: not only is it National Novel Writing Month, but the weather is cooler, people curl up with books at fireplaces, and the dying autumn light and the smell of decomposing leaves conjure the writing muse. It's appealing to envision creative people in dark turtlenecks gathering at the library, holding cups of coffee and enjoying learning about local authors and writing. At the Festival, not everyone sported a turtleneck, but many gave positive, detailed feedback, including the opinion that November was a good choice. We suggest starting your event at library opening time. Ours began an hour later; consequently, by event time many regular patrons already occupied spaces meant for the program. Duration-wise, one survey respondent remarked that there was so much going on that the event should have been spread out over several days. Consider how many elements your day will include, and how much time they require. This is challenging your first time out, as with our Festival. A four-hour event with a feature lecture, two poetry workshops, four children's readings, five panel discussions, three walk-in writing activities and two crafts was a bit dizzying.

At the Clover Hill Library, major event planning began nine months in advance. The team reached out to the Central Virginia chapter of Sisters in Crime, a national organization of women mystery writers. One was already a library patron. Manager Margaret Howard used Twitter to locate others. The Sisters in Crime not only wrote the event's script, but also presented a mystery writing panel discussion on being a writer involved in the local community. Three of them also participated in the Festival of the Written Word. "I was fortunate to be able to attend both signature events," says writer Heather Weidner. "We enjoyed writing the mystery for the signature event and working with the library staff and Friends of the Library. It was a wonderful event for local authors."

As you plan the day, begin inviting author participants. For the Festival of the Written Word, we chose local writers and authors, with great success. We had a limited budget of $1,000 plus $500 for publicity. That ruled out any big-name authors with high speaking fees who would have to travel in from other locales. In June, we selected local creative nonfiction writer Dean King, author of the bestselling book *Skeletons on the Zahara*, as our featured presenter. When his agent found out we were a public library, she politely advised that we probably couldn't afford his regular speaking fee. But we were welcome to contact him by email directly, she said. We took the plunge and asked him if he would appear at the library pro bono. He graciously agreed. Now we had the centerpiece for the event. In July, about 27 other local authors received invitations, some of them friends and acquaintances who happened to be local writing teachers and/or published authors.

There are many ways to find local authors. Librarians have noted that libraries planning small events with small budgets should consider local writers, including self-published ones (Peet, 2015). Two self-published authors participated in the Festival of the Written Word, and at least one other had originally been self-published. "If your local authors are yet to be famous and you worry about drawing a crowd, that's a great time to consider hosting several authors at once," said library manager Chapple Langemack in her 2007 book about planning author events. "Who can resist a panel of up-and-coming mystery writers, for example, or a showcase of local literary talent?" (Langemack, 2007).

Does your library hold copies of local authors' works? Ours had just created a local author collection. CCPL currently has 170 different items in its local author collection. We consulted the website of James River Writers, the premier association for writers in the Richmond area. We then checked to see which ones had books in the CCPL collection, and how well they circulated. A web search for Richmond authors revealed the Richmond Children's Writers group. Several members had books already in the CCPL collection, and members Lana Krumwiede and Brian Rock participated in the Festival, reading their work and leading a panel discussion on writing kids' books.

Reach out to local colleges and universities. Search online for authors published in their literary magazines. If your city has institutions offering adult writing classes, contact those who teach them and ask if they can participate. Scan the books section of your local Sunday paper for author names, as well as any free local arts publications. Some writers publish columns or articles in your daily newspaper, but may also be published book authors. One of the participants in the Festival of the Written Word, for example, has a parenting column in our Sunday paper but also writes and publishes inspirational fiction. Finally, review your meeting room users. Some may be writing groups.

All of the Festival authors were excited about the event, with only a few regretting that they had prior commitments and would not be able to participate. Several asked to be included on the next year's list. Authors at both signature events expressed how much they appreciated the opportunity to connect with readers in the local community. In choosing authors, decide how you would like to plan, namely whether you'll sketch out specific programs like "Murder at the Library" requiring certain types of authors and then find them, or cast a wide net and then form the accepting authors into panels and workshops that suit their particular talents. We had no idea so many of the authors invited to the Festival of the Written Word would accept. Set a limit on your number, leaving a small cushion to possibly let in authors who inquire after they hear about the upcoming event. At one point, we had 20 authors scheduled to participate, and considered that number final. Then, one day an author new to the area came into the library, saw the event publicity, and asked to participate. She happened to be a published romance author, and it happened that we could use another one on the "Romance Meets Mystery" panel. Every week, a few more writers and authors emerged, but I did cut the event off at 21 authors. The fact that so many local writers were asking about the event was encouraging. It confirmed that we were on the right track in choosing to hold an author festival.

Once you have a name, date and time for your event, it's time to plan what you'll offer. Provide food if your event occurs over mealtimes. That way, patrons won't leave the event to eat and never return for the rest of your wonderful programs. We hired two food trucks. One challenge was estimating for the vendors the attendance we expected at this first-ever event. Also, your library might be like ours and have limited eating space inside the building. We erected two tents in the parking lot, but still people commented that there should have been more places to eat inside. In addition to the food trucks, we offered free coffee. Our Friends funded this, using a local independent cafe that was kind enough to sell them the coffee at cost. Our event planning coordinator suggested inviting the vendor to sell pastries. This was quite popular. "Murder at the Library" included a silent auction of donated items. Food vendors granted discounts and their names were listed in the event program.

Will you sell authors' books at your event, and have book signings? For the Festival of the Written Word, we engaged a local independent bookstore. This was a bit challenging. We had several self-publishing authors, whom the bookseller did end up accommodating, as well as a couple of other conventionally published works the bookseller did not want to stock for fear of losing money on unsold books. He offered sixty percent of each sale back to the accepted authors. They gave mixed reviews of the book signings. Some enjoyed being at the signing tables, but others saw little value in it. Several mentioned that we had them scheduled to sign before they had actually participated in a panel discussion, so people didn't yet know their work.

The Event Schedule

We offered the printed Festival schedule in the branch for several weeks before the event. Despite this, attendees commented that they wished there had been a schedule available beforehand, including on the library website, especially since there were so many tightly scheduled programs to choose from. We did not distribute the more attractively formatted event program until Festival day. People also wanted an event map of the building, though we had signs everywhere and guides escorting customers to program areas. The schedule was jam-packed. You'll want to make sure you schedule time for the authors to have lunch, and at least ten or 15 minutes between each program in a room. Many authors commented that panels should include no more than three or four authors, so that all have time to speak and answer questions. You might designate one long lunch break for authors and patrons in the middle of the day, perhaps engaging a guitarist to play coffeehouse-type music.

Festival manager Tina M. Metzger named each program, drafting the panel discussions and letting the authors review them. She appointed one member of each panel as a moderator. Several stepped up right away and gave constructive suggestions, emailing their fellow panelists and planning the programs. Dean King titled his feature presentation. Bios collected from each author helped introduce them at the event. Dean King suggested we share these with all of the authors beforehand, which they appreciated. Many authors gave feedback on panel construction and titles. Some worried that what they were being billed to present was not actually their area of expertise. Poet and writing teacher Susan Hankla was apprehensive about being on the "Turning History Into Stories" panel. "I don't write memoir," she told Tina M. Metzger. "Yes," Metzger said, "but you teach it, and well!" Then, she mentioned that she was publishing a collection of poetry based on her childhood in Appalachia. We told her this made her perfect for the panel. After the event, she said, "I would tell other local authors that the librarian knows her stuff in putting together such a thorough program, because she is well-organized and because she is a terrific writer herself, so that makes her care deeply about such an event … what a benefit to us all."

Funding

Will your authors be compensated? A local creative writing teacher advised that it was customary to offer authors a small honorarium in lieu of a fee. Carefully consider your own plan for this. For our Festival, some simple but regrettably belated mathematical calculations proved, after 20 authors had been offered honoraria, that this would be difficult given our $1,000 event budget. It was late August when we realized we'd need sponsors.

We took a few days to brainstorm about possible sponsors. A neighboring concierge medicine practice had already partnered with us on free quarterly wellness lectures given by one of their doctors. We gathered up our Festival manager and event coordinator, and the two of us presented the letter in person. We did our best to show how the Festival might serve the company's neighborhood marketing goals. They contributed $500, in exchange for having their logo on promotional materials and having a table at the event. In seeking sponsors for your event, try to involve someone with fundraising expertise. Our sponsor, an experienced fundraiser, walked us outside and introduced us to another potential sponsor from the building, from an orthodontist's office. This raised another $500. A few authors opted out of the $75 honorarium, so we compensated our featured presenter at a much higher level.

Marketing

For signature events, CCPL provides a $500 publicity budget. Your library may be part of a county or city government with an in-house print shop, like ours, or you may need a private printer. Your in-house shop may be cheaper than others. For example, 100 11 × 17 posters for the Festival of the Written Word cost $30.00. We spent the rest of the budget on a four-foot by eight-foot outdoor banner, an indoor banner with reusable stand, 100 yard signs, and three-to-a-page bookmarks. All featured the same festival image. CCPL's talented graphic artist, Kate Denwiddie, designed the publicity. Many authors remarked on its quality. We created a rough mockup illustrating our vision for the poster, and she made it happen. Contact any sponsors well in advance for camera-ready logos to include on publicity. You also may be able to produce some items in the library, as we did.

Get the Word Out

"It's easier to market to groups than to individuals," says Denwiddie. "It's more effective to send an email to a group of writers than to hand out flyers on the street and hope that some of them are interested in writing. Authors and publishers know a lot of people interested in the written word. Ask them to reach out to their colleagues and customers." We also have a media relations specialist, who got "Murder at the Library" and the Festival of the Written Word into the local daily newspaper, and in local media calendars including the public radio station's calendar. If your event serves children and teens, contact teachers and get them to advertise the event and offer it as extra credit. To create event buzz, the "Murder at the Library" team created the mannequin murder victim, librarian Elsa Leadbottom, and displayed her in the library. They also created a video for the library's Facebook page. Take posters to:

- coffee shops
- grocery stores
- libraries
- colleges
- schools
- gyms
- apartment complexes
- churches
- arts centers
- festivals
- museums
- bookstores
- library programs

Equipment

Work well in advance with those who will provide special equipment for your event. For one thing, unless you're expecting a population the size of Manhattan, you will not need two cases of 48-count toilet paper for your literary event. Our county's event equipment manager pointed this out, and his calm demeanor and invaluable suggestions were crucial to our events' success. Here are some of the special supplies to request:

- restroom supplies
- large trash and recycle cans

- extension cords, power strips, cord covers for floors
- microphones/sound system
- sandwich boards
- bright vests for directing parking staff
- cones
- duct tape
- tablecloths
- tables, folding chairs
- tents
- easels
- podiums
- port-a-potty

Staffing the Event

A well-conceived plan is crucial. Make a list of library staff, Friends and other volunteers. Think about each person's talents and interests and assign suitable duties. The Clover Hill Library emphasized staff buy-in for its event. Margaret Howard notes that the murder mystery succeeded because staff actors stayed in character, and guests interacted with them and asked questions. Teen volunteers and Friends can run craft activities. Librarians can help regular patrons. If your library is open for regular business during the event, you need to staff the circulation desk. Appoint an author host for welcoming and hospitality. "You want to do a lot of planning," says Jennifer Shepley, CCPL's community services manager. You don't want your authors to have to do anything other than what they're there to do. Arrange accommodations if they're from out of town, and plan dinners and outings to entertain them if they are in town early. Assign staff to each program "venue" in the library. They maintain that area all day, introducing presenters, ushering audiences, answering questions, etc. Distribute a list of everyone's duties. Remember important duties like timekeeping, door counts, emptying trash and restocking restrooms. Consider physical limitations. Some of our older Friends volunteers are not in top health and in retrospect should not have been lifting tables or hoisting trash bags.

Reviews, Rave and Otherwise

Many hoped we'd hold the two signature events again. We'll conclude this chapter with compliments and critiques from patrons and authors:

"The poetry talk was great!"

"Love this event!"

"Awesome event for the community! Well organized, fun, informative. Will be back next year!"

"Wonderful event—very inspiring. Great job!"

"Great event! Something for everyone-me and kids."

"Fascinating and informative. Please do it again!"

"Glad there will be another one next year."

"I would like each presentation to have some sort of handout."

"I didn't see the full schedule on the website and would have liked to have known what events were happening at what times beforehand so I could have arrived earlier."

"Young adult area is a bit crowded."

"It would be nice for all panel authors to have a copy of their book up on the table with them so we can connect them with their work."

"Parking was tight."

"It would have been nice to have a space for people to eat inside."

"You always want there to be large attendance for the authors," Jennifer Shepley says, but the 20- to 30-member panel discussion audiences at both of the signature events in this chapter best facilitated community engagement. "People were definitely able to be engaged with the authors," she says.

Festival authors also provided helpful feedback. Vivian Lawry said she got energy from the event as a writer. "It's a fun event, with lots of variety, and responsive audiences," she said.

Others said:

"From the audience questions at the two panels I was on, you could see you were successful in attracting people who are writing and want to publish."

"More than anything, going to the Festival of the Written Word provided an opportunity to connect with readers and writers I might not meet anywhere else."

"FOTWW gave me a chance to better connect with people in the very place where I live."

"I had the pleasure of moderating a romance/mystery fiction panel. It was great to network with other authors and have the opportunity to talk to readers at the panel and at the book signing."

"The first thing I got out of this experience was a chance to connect with other writers in our community. We have a diversity of experience and knowledge in the greater Richmond area. Also, I got a chance to share my experiences as a self-published author and as an indie publisher."

"The event gave me a topic for press releases, blog entries and social media posts. The honorarium was fair and very much appreciated. Meeting other local authors was also meaningful."

Works Cited

Campbell, Edith, and Ashley Hope Perez. 2014. "Twelve Tips for Author Event Success: Win-Win Partnerships Between Authors and Librarians." *Voice of Youth Advocates*, June, 26. Accessed March 2, 2016. voya.com.

"Festival of the Written Word Coming to Chesterfield Library." 2015. *Richmond Times-Dispatch*, October 31. Accessed March 15, 2016. richmond.com.

Gilbert, Lauren. 2014. "Author Author! Programs That Pop." *Library Journal*, August 5. Accessed March 2, 2016. libraryjournal.com.

Hughes, Korey. 2015. "Writers, Readers Gather for Festival of the Written Word." *Richmond Times-Dispatch*, October 29.

Langemack, Chapple. 2012. "Author Events Made Easy." Programming Librarian. January 12. Accessed March 7, 2016. programminglibrarian.org.

Miller, Kate. 2014. "Creating a Forum: Planning Author Events at the Tigard Public Library." *The Heart of a Librarian*, July, 11–17. Accessed March 3, 2016. scholar.google.com.

Peet, Lisa. 2015. "Author! Author! Hosting Writer Events at the Library Takes Networking, Creativity, Solid Logistics, a Grasp of Community Interests—and a Little Money Doesn't Hurt." *Library Journal*, May, 26. Accessed March 3, 2016. Information Sciences and Library Issues Collection.

Cents and Sensibility

Planning the 14th Georgia Literary Festival

MELISSA E. JOHNSON, ANNA CAROLINE HARRIS, KARIN GILLESPIE *and* ERIN PRENTISS

History

The turn of the century brought a renewed interest in the written word with the creation of many literary festivals. Throughout the late 1990s and early 2000s, many statewide literary festivals were established. Oftentimes, these statewide festivals grew out of local book fairs. One example of this is the Georgia Literary Festival which grew from the Eatonton Literary Festival. Eatonton, Georgia, was the home of Alice Walker, Joel Chandler Harris, and Flannery O'Connor. For several years, the city hosted its own book festival that had several hundred people in attendance. Then in 2001, the local event grew into the statewide literary festival. The first year of the Georgia Literary Festival highlighted local writers Walker, Harris, and O'Connor.

As with most states, Georgia has a rich literary history that frequently goes unnoticed. In addition to the Eatonton natives, other authors including Conrad Aiken, Toni Cade Bambara, Judith Ortiz Cofer, Pat Conroy, Carson McCullers, the Rev. Martin Luther King, Jr., and, of course, Jimmy Carter, all hail from Georgia. As the festival grew, so did its focus. When the festival moved to Sparta, Georgia, during its second year, it highlighted Jean Toomer and other writers from the local area of Hancock County. In addition to the novelists and poets, screenwriters have been honored at the festival as well. In its third year, when the festival was held in Madison, Buddy Atkinson, a screenwriter for *The Beverly Hillbillies* and *Green Acres*, was honored.

Since its inception, the Georgia Literary Festival has been hosted in various cities across the state including Sparta, Rome, Macon, and Statesboro. One of the intriguing aspects is the focus on the "hometown" authors and the fact that any surplus monies raised for the festival are donated to local libraries or literacy centers. Although the festival moved from city to city, one of the locations that had not previously hosted the Georgia Literary Festival was Augusta, home of the Masters Golf Tournament and the Southern National Drag Boat Races. The Georgia Center for the Book approached members of the Augusta literary community to gauge interest in hosting the statewide event.

Committee

Planning a large scale literary event requires a lot of help: because you need people with different kinds of experience and expertise, and because some people will never return after your initial meeting. When Augusta was selected as the host city for the fourteenth Georgia Literary Festival, the person who applied on behalf of the city was responsible for putting together a steering committee. Initially, that group included public school and university teachers, librarians, a bookseller, a jazz musician, a local artist, and two members of the city's convention and visitors' bureau. As time progressed, we discovered that a wider net needed to be cast. As new members were recruited, our steering committee became increasingly strategic and purposeful in extending invitations—seeking a variety of talent, and carefully avoiding asking too many people to perform the same tasks. Eventually, our steering committee grew to also include writers, marketing and public relations experts, retirees, and nonprofit workers.

Once you establish a dependable, core group, you need to delegate roles and specify duties in writing to ensure tasks are completed, but not overdone. Rather than establishing subcommittees, we decided to designate individuals or pairs to lead various efforts: fundraising, volunteers, vendors, advertising, authors, and venues. For grant writing purposes, it became necessary and beneficial to assign officers: president, vice president, secretary, and treasurer. Officers also served as key contacts in the community to answer questions and accept donations. Finally, our steering committee designated several members as "generalists"—people who could not consistently attend meetings or commit to prolonged tasks, but who remained connected to the planning process and proved invaluable the week and day of the big event for unanticipated errands and tasks.

It is important to initiate a regular meeting schedule for accountability. We met every two weeks for the first fifteen months, then every week for the remaining three months in our case. Our steering committee also utilized email and Dropbox, which proved especially helpful for sharing everything from meeting agendas and minutes to sponsor, vendor, and venue agreements. Dropbox was efficient for those of us who already knew how to use it; however, it created problems for less tech-savvy members who occasionally changed, copied, deleted, or moved files. In retrospect, Google Drive would have been a wiser choice, given its more user-friendly options for document ownership and settings: commenting, editing, and viewing.

Budget

Literary festival budgets can vary widely, depending on how many authors you want to invite, what author expenses you agree to pay, and the venue you choose for your event. The local university provided our event space at no cost to the festival except for some labor and set-up fees. This resulted in a savings of several thousand dollars which enabled the committee to dedicate more funds to other areas as well as the most important item on any literary festival budget: authors.

Author costs will vary widely from festival to festival. We set a $700 budget for our keynote speaker and planned to pay a $150 honorarium to all of our out-of-town authors, in addition to covering their overnight accommodations. The committee negotiated a $106 rate with a local boutique hotel that was close to our venue. We also invited a number of local authors and paid them each a $50 honorarium.

Additionally, we agreed to fund an authors' reception at the hotel. The reception, which included two drinks and heavy hors d'oeuvres, cost approximately $60 per author, not including $1,000 for the ballroom rental. We also sold tickets to committee members and author guests. The reception was one of our largest expenses, and we likely could have paid less with another caterer, but we appreciated the convenience of having it at the host hotel.

Our author budget also included a designated hospitality room at the hotel, stocked with snacks and drinks, and an additional hospitality room at the festival site where breakfast and lunch were served. We asked our visitors' bureau to prepare welcome bags for all of our out-of-town authors, but we supplemented with swag of our own. Some other items on our budget included name tags, programs, signage, volunteer costs (t-shirts and lunches), and social media advertising. Naturally, you should seek as many in-kind donations as possible to provide the above items.

Funding Your Program

After you have established your tentative budget, you face the most challenging aspect of putting on a literary festival: drumming up funds to support it. No one on our steering committee was a professional fundraiser, but our community connections and passion for the cause compensated for our lack of experience. Our goal was to raise twenty thousand dollars.

Investigating available grants should be the first step in your fundraising efforts, as they must be applied for well in advance of the date of your festival. Grants that support art events are usually available at the state and city levels; it's simply a matter of research. Our fundraising team consulted area art groups to discover what grants they've pursued in the past. None of our fundraisers had grant writing experience, but they found the process fairly straightforward with one caveat: in order to qualify for most grants, your organization must have a tax-exempt status, i.e., 501(c) (3).

If you're planning a literary festival for the first time, consider applying for tax-exempt status. Be mindful that it can take as long as a year to be approved, and the process is time-consuming and onerous. It may be worthwhile to pair up with an existing non-profit organization in your community, like an arts council, to piggyback on their tax-exempt status. The Georgia Literary Festival is under the umbrella of the Georgia Center for the Book, so we were able to use their tax-exempt status. This allowed us to apply for a regional grant that awarded the festival $15,000, which greatly simplified our fundraising efforts.

After you research grants, you'll want to seek out in-kind media sponsors, i.e., radio, print and television stations, who will publicize your event at no cost. It pays to secure your in-kind media sponsorships as early as possible because you'll want to use them as an incentive when approaching local businesses to help sponsor your festival. Businesses are more apt to offer their support if they know their logos will be highly visible in the media during promotion time.

Most media outlets are agreeable to supporting nonprofit events, but it's wise to offer them incentives. We promised media sponsors tickets to the authors' reception, reserved seating at panels, free vendor space in a prominent location, inclusion of logos in the program, and gift bags that contained a signed copy of a book from a festival author. In all, we secured $30,000 in in-kind media sponsorships. It's important to note that it's the festival's responsibility to design TV ads, write copy for radio spots, and prepare camera-ready ads. Media sponsors don't generally provide that service. This is another opportunity to network with people in local art organizations to find out what marketing and design businesses they rely on to prepare media material.

In-kind donations are not just limited to the media. Some businesses may be willing to donate food or other services in exchange for recognition in your program or in your media materials. Along with securing our venue through an in-kind donation, we negotiated in-kind sponsorship with a marketing firm that designed our media materials and with a printer who provided us with free posters and rack cards.

The final phase of fundraising is asking for gifts from the community. Everyone on our committee generated a list of business leads and personal connections to assist our fundraisers. The fundraisers prepared sponsorship proposals which included the same incentives offered to in-kind media sponsors. Admittedly, our festival was a hard sell because it was our first year, and many business owners weren't familiar with concept of a literary festival. In fact, the majority of our donations came from individuals. All individual donors were promised recognition in the program, and we also offered the popular option of making a donation in the name of two late local authors for $100 each.

Another way to generate funds is to set up an online fundraising campaign through a service like GoFundMe. A GoFundMe campaign takes only minutes to set up on Facebook, but be aware the service takes eight percent of your donations. Our committee's campaign raised a little over $1,000.

In all, our donations totaled over $31,000, eleven thousand more than we'd projected.

The Care and Handling of Authors

You can't throw a festival without authors, but they are usually the most expensive item of your budget. One of our strategies for author selection was to include as much local talent as possible. Using local writers keeps costs down because they don't require lodging or reimbursement of travel expenses. Also, if you feature local presenters at your festival, your community becomes more invested in the event, and local writers will generally help with promotion on social media or their personal websites.

Not all presenters have to be authors of books; they simply need some sort of literary connection. At our festival, we had a panel of academics discussing our city's literary heritage, and we also featured a roundtable of local print columnists. The literary community tends to be close-knit, so ask your local talent to suggest authors who've recently published a book and live nearby. Authors are more apt to participate in your festival if they're within driving distance. Also confer with nearby university presses. They are often a source of interesting and diverse authors.

To attract patrons, you'll want to invite a well-known keynote speaker, as well as some brand name authors. Bestselling authors are most likely to accept your invitation if they're promoting a book and you offer them a featured slot on the schedule. It pays to contact the publicity departments of major publishers to see if they can suggest authors who'll be touring during the month of your festival. Keep in mind that many touring schedules are made up to a year in advance.

Once you've assembled a group of authors, look for commonalities among them to create compelling panels. Some of the popular panels at the Georgia Literary Festival were those that featured authors of Civil War books, Georgia history books, young adult novels, mysteries, memoirs, debut novels, and Southern literature. The festival also featured an area devoted exclusively to children's activities and several panels aimed at aspiring writers. Typically, we had four activities running concurrently to offer a variety of entertainment for patrons to attend.

When the panels are established, the next step is to select moderators who will read the authors' books and prepare questions to keep the discussions lively. Moderators also typically contact authors before the event to let them know what types of questions will be asked.

Venue

When you look for a venue, you need to find an affordable facility with plenty of parking, enough rooms of variable size to accommodate simultaneous sessions, and an area for authors' signings, booksellers, and vendors. Several members of our steering committee were faculty at the local university which meant that we could utilize the school's facilities; we chose the Student Activities Center (SAC) and the attached green areas as our venue.

The SAC was a fairly new facility on campus attached to the library via an indoor breezeway. It contains several meeting rooms and ample restroom facilities. The SAC was reserved for the authors' sessions and panel discussions. Writers were arranged in the rooms according to the anticipated audience. Most rooms held 40 to 75 people; the ballroom accommodated 338 and was designated as the room for the keynote speaker and brand name writers.

Early on, you will need to map your festival layout. We wanted to use the breezeway for the bookseller and the authors' signings. Originally, we planned to host the vendors and food trucks in a nearby green area. The facilities personnel created a diagram with a covered food area near the parking lot and the vendors under tents along the sidewalk.

It was also necessary to ensure that electricity was available for select vendors, as well as enough trash receptacles for the anticipated crowd. Several workers from the university's facilities department were hired to see that trash was picked up and the grounds and restrooms were kept clean. We also hired several off-duty public safety officers for crowd and traffic control and ensured with their department that parking would not be an issue on the day of the festival.

Be sure to create an alternate festival layout in case of inclement weather well in advance. At the committee's final meeting and walk-through three days prior to the event, we met with the campus facilities director who said it was supposed to thunderstorm on the day of the festival—a contingency we did not expect. At that point, we had to figure out how to fit the entire festival indoors. The various panels and speakers were left in the rooms where they were originally scheduled. Our bookseller moved into the library along with some vendors who also filled the breezeway. Despite re-routing the crowds, the new arrangement worked out well.

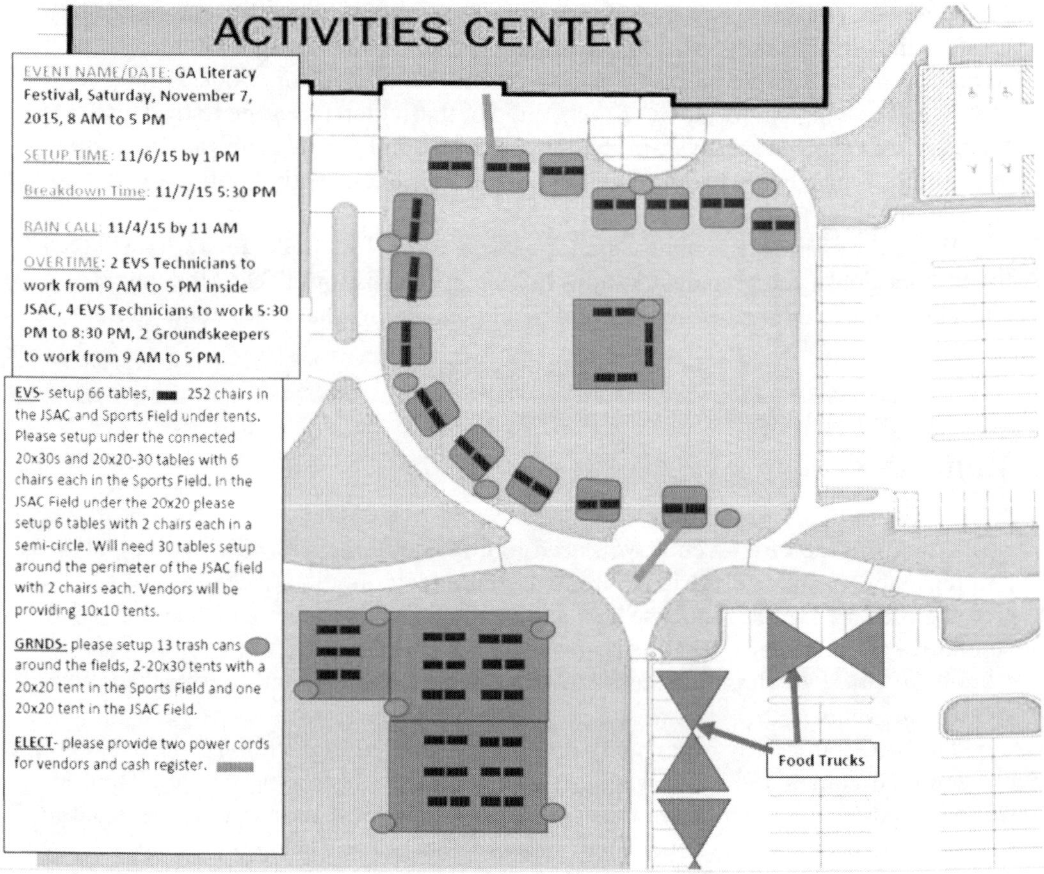

Map of the festival layout.

Volunteers

When you have almost 100 presenters and vendors at your literary festival, you absolutely need to recruit volunteers to ensure that everything will run smoothly. We strongly suggest selecting a committee member or two to serve as volunteer coordinators. These people should be very dedicated to the festival's success and have the time, energy, and people skills needed to successfully coordinate volunteers.

Pre-planning is essential before sending out a call for volunteers. First, you should define your volunteer duties. Basic positions include greeters, ushers, bookseller and vendor assistants, and panel monitors. The number of volunteers needed will vary depending on the size of the festival. Ask yourself these questions: How long can you reasonably expect a volunteer to commit his or her time? How many spaces need to be staffed? How many people do you need to accomplish a particular task? We decided to have approximately 30 total volunteers split between morning and afternoon shifts.

It is helpful to create a volunteer manual and provide training, particularly for more complicated volunteer tasks. Our volunteer manual included the position descriptions, festival maps, a FAQ section, and contact information. The training plan was simple and involved walking the festival layout and explaining different positions as we went along.

Once these steps are accomplished, you will be ready to send out your call for volunteers. We used our personal networks to contact potential volunteers, but a larger festival might need to put out a public call. Our call included a description of the volunteer positions, an online sign-up sheet for shifts, and information about training dates. Potential volunteers will still have questions, but with all the preparation that you have done, you will be able to respond to the majority of their concerns.

Be prepared to make a lot of calls, e-mails, and even text messages to your volunteers. Some people provided all of the information the volunteer coordinators requested. Others did not, so we contacted them again (sometimes repeatedly). We also sent phone and email reminders about the trainings and their shifts at the festival.

Festival day will be extremely busy for your volunteer coordinators and volunteers. You will need to tell your volunteers where to check in in advance. At check in, we also provided each volunteer with a copy of the volunteer manual and any additional supplies that they needed for their duties, e.g., attendance sheets. To address the unexpected (which will happen), the coordinators checked in with volunteers at their stations. This allowed the coordinators to proactively solve issues that came up, particularly those that the volunteers were not able to handle on their own, such as microphone problems.

Planning

12+ months:

- Assemble a core planning committee.
- Determine the festival's focus (e.g., local/regional authors, children's authors, self-published authors).
- Draft a preliminary budget.
- Research and contact potential major donors, giving careful consideration to ways in which your festival correlates with their giving priorities or mission.
- Establish a fundraising strategy (e.g., letter campaign, phone-a-thon, raffle) and set it in motion. It helps to prepare a sponsorship package.
- Identify and invite your keynote speaker(s) and any bestselling authors.

9 months:

- Identify and secure festival site(s).
- Compile a list of desired authors and invite them.
- Solicit vendor applications.

6 months:

- Commission the design of necessary artwork and logos.
- Design and distribute first wave of promotional materials (e.g., press releases, posters, rack cards).
- Revisit author list and invite additional authors, if necessary.

3 months:

- Draft a complete schedule of events and map festival layout.
- Secure moderators for panel discussions and readings.
- Recruit volunteers for pre-festival and day-of activities.

1 month:

- Design and order programs.
- Enter event information into online and print community calendars.
- Launch your social media campaign (e.g., via Facebook, Twitter, Instagram, and EventBrite).

2 weeks:

- Follow-up with venue contact(s).
- Rent/purchase decorations.
- Host volunteer training sessions.
- Order name tags for authors, committee members, and moderators.

1 week:

- Schedule a final walkthrough with committee members and necessary venue personnel.
- Contact volunteers with important reminders.

Day of Festival:

- Assign someone to take attendance at various readings and panel discussions.
- Designate someone to distribute checks to authors and presenters.
- Remember to attend and enjoy festival sessions.

Post-Festival:

- Follow-up with authors and presenters. Let them know you appreciate their participation.
- Collect and pay bills as they come in.
- Share any positive festival press or testimonials with the committee.
- Schedule a post-festival debriefing with your committee one to two weeks after your event.

Conclusion

Finding the funding, using common sense, and a bit of sensibility will make your festival a success. While there were a few difficulties along the path to the 14th Georgia Literary Festival, we were able to hold the festival on November 7, 2015. The committee had to handle some last minute cancellations from food vendors and the rearrangement of furniture, vendors, and panels; but despite the glitches, the festival went on as planned. Between 800 and 1,000 literature lovers attended and expressed their profound appreciation for bringing the festival to Augusta.

Hosting an Author Festival

Sarah Fisk

Hosting an author festival is an excellent way for libraries to connect with their local writer and reader communities. They help a library build recognition, goodwill, and a reputation as a place where literature lives and thrives.

Once your library decides to host an author festival, give yourself plenty of time to plan the event. Rushing a large-scale event leaves too much room for mistakes or errors of oversight. Planning of large-scale events should begin ten to twelve months prior, but smaller events can be planned in approximately four months.

Size and Scope

Author festivals come in many shapes and sizes and the first step in planning one is deciding exactly what kind of event to host. An event can consist of a couple local authors signing their books in a library space or be as large as a multi-day event featuring authors from all over the world participating in panels and workshops.

Some possible elements of author festivals include:

- An author's fair, defined as a period of time where authors sit at a table and sign books purchased and/or brought in by readers, i.e., a multi-author book signing.
- A keynote speaker, usually an author who opens or closes the event with a pre-written speech.
- Workshop sessions taught by an instructor on a specific topic, usually a writing-related topic.
- Panels consisting of three to eight authors answering questions posed by a moderator and/or the audience, usually loosely centered around a specific topic.
- Character appearances from someone dressed as a popular book or comic character, possibly with photo opportunities for attendees.
- Cooking demonstrations featuring cookbook authors.
- Story time for children, read by a library staff member or a picture book author.
- Vendors who sell items for book lovers.

Libraries can incorporate one or more of these elements into their festivals, based on their goals, available resources, and service area demographics. The Orange County Library System hosts three signing-only Local Author Festivals per year plus the Orlando

Book Festival, which is an all-day event with multiple activities. OCLS also hosts special author festivals revolving around themes. For example: a romance-only author festival in conjunction with a screening of *Love Between the Covers* in February 2016 and a "Festival de Literatura Hispana," or a Hispanic Literature Festival during Hispanic Heritage Month.

Budget

The first step is to determine your budget for the event. This will help you plan the size and scope of your author festival. In addition to the amount of money to spend on the event, the budget should also include any other resources that may be used during its planning and facilitation. Staff time, space allowance, and physical resources such as tables and chairs must be assessed and allocated prior to determining what the author festival is going to entail. Do not forget to estimate the money and effort required to promote your event.

Depending on the size and structure of your library, staff time can be a considerable issue when planning a larger program. Systems with dedicated programming/event staff will have an easier time running an author festival, but systems without such staff can still host a great event with careful planning and budgeting of hours.

When looking at budgeting financial resources, consider seeking sponsors to pay for larger expenses such as author travel costs, equipment rental, and speaking fees. Potential sponsors could include your Friends of the Library organization, local bookstores, local restaurants, literary organizations, and local civic organizations. Consider offering sponsors who donate over a certain amount the opportunity to have their logo on the event posters and programs, or to have a table or promotional materials at the event. Some larger events sell advertisements in their program to authors, publishers, and local businesses.

When budgeting physical resources, evaluate your library's parking situation. Not only should you be able to offer the participating authors parking near the venue, public parking for attendees can frequently become an issue for larger programs. If your library doesn't have adequate parking, look at neighboring businesses and property owners that would be willing to allow parking in their lots. If your event is in a congested downtown area, offer as much information as possible to attendees on parking availability.

Book Sales

Another aspect that needs to be decided upon early in the planning stages is how book sales will be handled. Many libraries have a policy against goods being sold inside their building, but since the primary reason authors attend book festivals is to promote and sell books—and one of the primary reasons people attend book festivals is to buy signed books—any library with this policy may want to consider making an exception when hosting an author festival.

If the library has a bookstore that can order and return copies, that is a great advantage. If not, your library can partner with a local bookstore to handle book sales. Major chains, such as Barnes and Noble or Books-a-Million, will usually participate if a certain sales threshold is expected, but independent booksellers can be a great partner for these types of events. Use the phonebook, Google.com, or indiebound.org to find your local independent bookstores.

Independent stores are usually capable of handling sales for authors published through small presses or published independently, due to established consignment agreements or other programs. If your event features independent authors, a bookstore may not be able to order their books and, most likely, won't be able to return unsold books. Unless a bookstore has a consignment option, these authors will need to sell their own books. A consignment agreement allows the bookstore to act as the author's sales agent for a defined number of books. Unsold books are returned to the author at the end of the agreement and payment for sold books is issued, minus the bookstore's agreed-upon percentage.

The procedure for buying books will depend on your space and preferences. Some events will have the books on the tables with the authors. In this case the reader picks out a book, the author signs it, and then the readers pay on their way out the door. If an event doesn't have limited entry and exit points, the books will be available for sale at the bookseller's table and they must be purchased before the reader carries them to the author(s) for signature.

The simplest option for the library is to have all the authors sell their own books. Authors who attend many events are accustomed to this practice. However, some traditionally published authors will not be able and/or willing to sell their own books. Providing access to Wi-Fi is useful for the authors selling books, because they frequently use applications like Square Register and PayPal to take credit card payments.

For larger author festivals, OCLS usually has a hybrid book selling arrangement. We work with an independent bookseller who orders the books for the traditionally published authors and offers consignment for the small-press or independent authors. Independent authors also have the option of selling their own books. For smaller, local-author events at OCLS, we require authors to sell their own books.

Author Participation

Before sending invites to authors, determine if there is a cost to the author to participate. Most book festivals held at libraries don't charge authors anything, but some ask for the author to donate a book either for the collection or for a door prize. Have this requirement decided upon and let authors know their obligations up-front.

Once you're ready to invite authors to participate in your festival, you may find that you already know of a few in your community and they will be a great starting point for you. When inviting them, ask them to let you know if they know of other authors who might be willing to participate. Based on my experience, word of mouth can be the best way to discover new authors in any community. Your library can post on its social media channels and ask for followers to share the call for authors.

If you don't know any local authors, or would like to find more, start contacting local writing groups and chapters of larger organizations. Local writing groups can be found via social media sites like Meetup.com or Facebook. Check for local chapters of national organizations like Romance Writers of America, Society of Children's Book Writers and Illustrators, Mystery Writers of America, Science Fiction and Fantasy Writers of America, and also state-wide writing organizations, such as the Florida Writers Association.

If there is a university nearby, take a look at their professors' publications; some will have broad public appeal. If the university has a thriving creative writing department, consider partnering with them to plan, recruit authors, and promote your event.

If you are looking to host a larger-scale event and would like to invite non-local authors, find out who your patrons would be excited to meet. Poll your staff for author suggestions.

For popular authors, you should expect to pay for their travel costs, at minimum. Finding out how much an author charges for visits usually requires contacting the author or their representative and asking directly. Some authors may make this information available on their website, but most do not. Bestselling authors can cost approximately $20,000 to $45,000 per appearance. Mid-list authors tend to charge a smaller fee plus travel and accommodations.

Remember, it never hurts to ask. You never know if your dream author has been waiting for the perfect opportunity to travel to your area and some authors are extremely supportive of public libraries.

Schedule

The larger is an event, the more complicated is its schedule. In addition to planning author schedules, you need to balance them with each individual author's preferences, and also consider event staff schedules. If scheduling software isn't available, simple Excel spreadsheets can be powerful tools.

Ensure there is abundant time for author load-in and pack-out, especially if authors are selling their own books. If your location has limited or restricted parking, you may need to establish an unloading area and timeframe, with ample staff on hand to watch the authors' belongings while the author finds parking.

If there are multiple events happening at the same time, those events should appeal to different audiences, if possible. For example: schedule a writing workshop opposite a children's story time, instead of planning two writing workshops at the same time.

Give authors, staff, and attendees plenty of time to move from one aspect to another, including small breaks. When planning event staffing, remember that overstaffing an event is always better than understaffing. One useful tip is to have someone at all times who is not assigned to a particular function, but can fill in wherever there is a need or pop-up task.

Advertising and Promotion

Once an event is planned, authors are confirmed, and the schedule is set, focus on promoting the event. To start with, it is a great idea to have one website to serve as your "home base" on the Internet. All of your promotional material should direct people to this website, where interested persons can acquire more details and find a way to contact the library for more information. On the website include information such as: location map, driving directions, parking directions, a list of featured authors, featured author bios, panel moderator information, event schedule, dining information, and anything else an attendee might need to know. The URL should be reasonably short and easy to remember. If your library's website doesn't allow for you to create a short link, consider using a service like bit.ly or tiny.cc to create a custom short link. If your website doesn't allow you to easily create pages like this, consider using a Facebook event page as your "home base."

Contact local newspapers, magazines, radio stations, and television stations to see if they would be interested in featuring your event. Many authors are willing to appear on local programs to help you promote your event. Most local newspapers and news stations have community calendars to which you can add your event.

Use social media and Google search to find bloggers who write about local events and books, then ask them to feature the event in a post and on social media. For author festivals that feature panels, consider asking book and local interest bloggers to moderate one panel. This gives them exposure and they exhibit more excitement and enthusiasm when talking about the event.

Promote on the library's social media accounts and ask the attending authors to promote on theirs, as well. If you create a Facebook event, the authors can then directly invite their friends and family to the event. In the weeks leading up to the event, post the book covers and headshots of the featured authors with a short note explaining how the public can meet this author at your event, making sure to include a link to the your "home base" website. Creating an eye-catching, professional-looking graphic can help increase your social media exposure because images are more likely to gain someone's attention than simple text. Keep in mind, that others may share your image without your corresponding text, so the image should have all the pertinent information on it, or a link to where they can find all of the information. This includes: date, time, location name, and location address.

Create an attention-grabbing poster to be used both inside the library and around the community. Posters used outside of the library should include the location name and address. It is also a good idea to include the "home base" website mentioned earlier. Ask local restaurants, coffee shops, and more if you can tape the poster in their window or on their bulletin board.

Invite local reader and aspiring author groups to attend your event by contacting the organizer. These groups can be found via social media and websites like Meetup.com and Goodreads. If your event includes authors who write books for children or teens, invite local schools and home school groups to attend. If you have nonfiction authors who write on special interest topics, such as cooking or gardening, invite appropriate groups by featuring the relevant author in your communications with them.

Author Treatment

One of the best ways to ensure that your event continues to have a great reputation and expand is by treating the featured authors and moderators well and providing them with all the information they will need well in advance. Authors all talk to each other about events they attend and one of the biggest complaints is bad communication.

About one month before the event, send a reminder email with all the promotional information you'd like them to share, including the link to your "home base" website, the Facebook event link, promotional posters and images. Let them know what their schedule will be like during the event and when you will be contacting them next.

One week before the event, contact them again to provide directions and logistical details, such as preferred unloading and entry points, arrival times, parking information, and anything else they might need to know before arriving. Give them a phone number they can call on the day of the event in the case they are running late or need directions.

Once the authors arrive, provide them with a welcome package including: a welcome letter, their name badge, and any small gifts you may want to provide. The written welcome letter should answer any frequently asked questions, such as wireless Internet information, bathroom locations, and their individual schedule. Not only is it great for them to have the information so readily available, it will reduce the amount of time your event staff spends answering the same basic questions. You should have a name badge for every participating author, or a simple sign on their table if your event only features an authors' fair. For a special touch, provide each author with a small gift, such as a pen or bookmark featuring your library's branding, if you have those on hand.

If you have a longer event with multiple activities, consider hosting an author green room. This is an area only the participating authors and your staff can access, providing a stress-free space for authors to take a break. Provide the authors with bottled water and light snacks.

Before the event starts, ensure the authors know whom to ask if they have questions or need something. It is helpful to have your event staff identified by special badges or t-shirts. If books are being sold by a bookseller, make sure the authors know the seller's location and procedure. If you have plenty of volunteers, have a few roam the author's fair area, offering to watch the author's table in case they need to go to the bathroom or to a panel.

Day of Execution

When an author festival is well-planned, the day of the event will proceed relatively smoothly. There are bound to be pop-up surprises, but if the authors and staff are well-prepared, these should be easily handled.

Perform as much of the event setup as you can in the days leading up to the event. Test all audio-visual equipment and connections.

If the event has multiple activities, post the schedule in several visible places throughout the event venue. At the minimum, ensure every author and staff member has a printed copy of the schedule. If you have the resources, a printed program can be offered with activity schedules, author listings, panel descriptions, lunch options, event layouts, and anything else attendees may need to know. It's also a great keepsake if attendees ask each author to sign the program.

Prior to the event, determine how attendance is to be recorded. For larger events with multiple activities, OCLS counts the attendance at each individual activity to help determine which activities were the most popular.

At the event, have special surveys and encourage attendees to fill them out. Use these surveys to discover how the attendees found out about the event so that you can adjust your advertising and promotion efforts for the next event. Ask readers which authors and types of activities they would most like to see at next year's festival. You could also poll the authors, asking them if you could have done anything differently to make the event go more smoothly from their perspective.

Hosting great author events can help libraries contribute to and gain respect from their local literary communities. A well-planned and well-executed author festival of any size is an excellent addition to library programming.

Papers and Prose

Touring Literary History with Students

JENNIFER V. MITCHELL

Researchers often find inspiration in the archives. That is one of the things that makes Special Collections so special. In recent years academic libraries have placed an increased emphasis on highlighting the unique holdings of Special Collections, which were in the past relegated to proverbial dusty basements. The Louisiana State University Libraries Special Collections department has been no stranger to this trend. Our response has led to an effort to showcase rare books and manuscript material through a growing number of outreach events, exhibitions, and instruction sessions conducted by the personnel of LSU Libraries Special Collections. Advertising these events through social media outlets has helped grow our audience, demystify our processes, and reduce the anxiety students have about the use of Special Collections materials.

In addition to increasing the number of courses and events Special Collections instructors have also sought to move away from the more traditional one-shot show-and-tell sessions that characterized the early teaching efforts of archivists. These show-and-tell sessions present archival materials as little more than curiosities and do little to connect collections to course content. Through the use of in-class assignments, class holds, and hands-on exercises instructors are able to build stronger connections with students and increase their comfort level with the use of primary source material. There also has been an effort to build stronger relationships with faculty by partnering with them for specific types of instructional sessions. These partnerships ensure that the session meets the learning objectives of the course and increase the buy-in of faculty outside the libraries. One successful partnership which has reached a number of diverse audiences has been the LSU Literary Tour.

The first literary tour was conducted in fall 2014. LSU English professor Nolde Alexius, co-author of *Best of LSU Fiction* was interested in putting together a tour of LSU highlighting the landmarks significant to the literary history of LSU. Alexius was inspired to include Special Collections and the materials in Hill Memorial Library as a stop on the tour when she learned about the richness of our holdings. Since its inception the tour has been given to several different groups of varied backgrounds and interests. The literary tour presents Special Collections with an opportunity to demonstrate the versatility of our materials while enriching the classroom instruction happening on campus. The stops on the tour and the material shown in Special Collections help connect the students to the literary figures that they are studying in class and teach them about the rich literary history that once thrived under the stately oaks of LSU. The tour also presents Special Collections with an opportunity to highlight the literary papers in our manuscript collections.

Literary History of LSU

Before the selection of materials commenced, a little background information had to be gathered on the history of the LSU English Department and the illustrious figures that had occupied Allen Hall. The literary history of LSU would not be complete without an examination of the reign of the Kingfish. Huey Long utilized a firm hand in the running of Louisiana State University. Long was interested in seeing the University grow as a prestige project for the state of Louisiana. A period of prosperity for LSU began with the appointment of James Monroe Smith as President of the University. As one of Long's chosen few, Smith was given carte-blanche to hire the best and brightest professors and build up the physical plant of the University. At a time when jobs all across the country were drying up along with funding for state programs LSU was growing: increasing the student population from 1500 students in 1928 to 6000 students by 1935 (Cutrer, 13).

One of the first tasks that President James Monroe Smith set about to turn LSU into a "real" University was to create a new program for graduate education and hire Charles Pipkin, a top-notch scholar as the dean of the newly formed Graduate School. In addition to Pipkin, Robert Penn Warren and Cleanth Brooks were hired for the LSU English Department. Pipkin, Warren, and Brooks began campaigning for shared publication rights for the Southwest Review but it became apparent that the identity of the "Southwest" did not extend all the way to Baton Rouge, Louisiana. Brooks and Warren were encouraged to start their own journal; thus the *Southern Review* was born. It was at this time in 1935 that LSU also established the LSU Press. With the *Southern Review*, emphasis was placed on literary merit, not status. Authors published included: Katherine Anne Porter, Aldous Huxley, John Crowe Ransom, Eudora Welty, Jean Stafford, and Robert Lowell. Within its first year, *Southern Review* gained an international reputation for being of the highest quality in the United States. The reputation of the *Southern Review* helped the growth of a literary community in Baton Rouge which left an indelible mark in the Southern literary landscape (Cutrer, 36–49)

The growth of this community was not without its detractors. Many groups had their own ideas about the direction the University should be taking. But the fight against the Long political machine was a difficult one; all of those obstacles were removed with the assassination of Huey Long in September 1935. In 1939, president James Monroe Smith was indicted for using bond money, both real and imagined, to enhance the endowment for LSU. General Campbell Hodges (a member of an Anti-Long family) was appointed as President of the University and began to undo much of what had been built up including closing the *Southern Review* as a "wartime economy measure" in 1942 (Cutrer, 242).

The *Southern Review* remained dormant until Donald Stanford and Lewis Simpson succeeded in reviving the publication to much fanfare from the literary community. Amongst the holdings of Special Collections are letters of congratulations from Cleanth Brooks, Walker Percy, and Katherine Anne Porter. From that point forward the *Southern*

Review continued its reign as one of the premier literary magazines in the South. It is the people mentioned who are highlighted by the stops on the tour which includes Allen Hall, the historic home of the English Department. The tour begins there with a discussion of the works of Robert Penn Warren, continuing towards the historic quad highlighting the frescoes of muralist, Conrad Albrizio, and discussing other notable authors who have made their mark on LSU and the literary world including Andrei Codrescu and John Ed Bradley.

Materials on Display

The selection of materials in Special Collections started with materials which had so inspired the faculty member in the first place: a rare, first edition of Edmund Spenser's *Faerie Queen* and the correspondence between Walker Percy and Lewis Simpson regarding Simpson's repeated efforts to entice Percy to come and teach, present, or do just about anything for the LSU English Department. It is important when planning instruction sessions to establish clear lines of communication with course instructors. This is an important step to ensure that the course objectives are met and also to guarantee that the instructors' expectations are clear as well. Inclusion of instructors in materials selection can help ensure that there is buy-in for the instruction session by the faculty. In addition to seeking requests for specific materials it is also good to get a general overview of the course objectives that are being served by the instruction session. If possible, a review of the course syllabus should shed light on course content and bring the instruction session in line with other material covered in the course. It can also help to see if any course assignments will be impacted or directly relate to the materials covered in the session in Special Collections.

For the initial offering of the literary tour the theme for the course was meant to explore the literary influences of the writers who were represented in our collections. For the stop at Special Collections a small amount of material was selected to augment the things discussed on the tour and highlight the contents of our collection. Here are a few of the most important materials displayed:

- First edition of Edmund Spenser's *Faerie Queene*, a copy *All the King's Men*, and a letter by Robert Penn Warren. In the letter, Warren is responding to a request to discuss his experiences in the LSU English Department and he shares his opinions of Huey Long's role in the beginnings of the *Southern Review*. *Faerie Queene* also had a special impact on the composition of *All the King's Men*. In an introduction to a 1953 edition of *All the King's Men*, Robert Penn Warren writes:

  > For better or for worse, Willie Stark was not Huey Long.... Certainly, it was the career of Long and the atmosphere of Louisiana that suggested the play that would become the novel ... may be indicated by the fact that in the verse play the name of the politician was Talos—the name of the brutal, blank-eyed "iron groom" in Spenser's *Faerie Queen*, the pitiless servant of the knight of justice. My conception grew wider, but the element always remained, and Willie Stark remained, in one way, Willie Talos. In other words, Talos is the kind of doom that democracy may invite upon itself.

- Eudora Welty Papers: The correspondence in our holdings is with her close friend and confidant, John Robinson to whom she dedicated *Delta Wedding*. It was the diary of Robinson's grandmother that inspired the novel. These letters stimulate great discussions of the literary relationships discussed during the tour as they include discussions of her relationship with Katherine Anne Porter, a mentions of Welty's first meeting with Robert Penn Warren (a relationship which evolves to the point where in her letters she begins to refer to him by his nickname of "Red" Warren), and her thoughts and opinions of the writing of Jean Stafford in which she mentions the torment that Stafford suffered at the hands of her husband Cal Lowell while living in Baton Rouge.

- *Southern Review* Records: The authors' correspondence from these records includes a particularly interesting letter from Katherine Anne Porter in which she expresses her opinions about the demise of the *Southern Review* (she does not have nice things to say about Campbell Hodges). Another highlight are the letters between Lewis Simpson and Walker Percy as Simpson endlessly asks Percy to visit or teach at LSU. Simpson's requests are continually rebuffed until in 1974, Percy relents admitting that he could, perhaps use the money. Though his tenure as a visiting professor was short-lived, Percy is credited with the publication of LSU Press's most famous works: John Kennedy Toole's *A Confederacy of Dunces*, the first of four books at the Press to win the Pulitzer Prize.
- Walker Percy Interview: Included with a transcription of the interview are notes and corrections made in Percy's own hand. The interview demonstrates Percy's literary influences and includes discussions of his writing process.

Narrative Focus of Each Tour

The first tour was conducted in the fall of 2014 and has since been given to 7 groups mainly consisting of English classes taught by Professor Alexius. The initial offering was for a writing course. This course placed an emphasis on the writing process and finding inspiration in the archives. For this group special emphasis was placed on the introduction of *All the King's Men* in which Warren discusses *Faerie Queene* and Talus. The relationship between Eudora Welty and her correspondent, John Robinson, was also emphasized with special attention to her usage of a diary to inspire a work of fiction; a feat which could easily be repeated with any number of the diaries or letters present in our collections. Finally, a discussion was conducted about the interview with Walker Percy in which he talks of his writing process and literary inspirations. For subsequent tours, Professor Alexius has brought in different English courses which have placed a greater emphasis on the relationships between the authors highlighted on the tour. In this case, I emphasized the Eudora Welty correspondence and her discussions of meetings with Robert Penn Warren and her friendship with Katherine Anne Porter and her familiarity with Jean Stafford. The author's correspondence within the *Southern Review* records and Lewis Simpson's letters written to Walker Percy provide a glimpse into the inner workings of the journal and the professional relationships that developed between the editors and writers. These letters really help illustrate those relationships and bring home the point about the literary community that was fostered by the *Southern Review* and the atmosphere in the South during the time of its initial publication.

In addition to the English classes, Professor Alexius was asked to give the tour to a group of history classes that were visiting from a local high school. With only days' notice to prepare there was not much time to select new and different materials for the tour so the same material was selected again. But in this instance the professor moved away from literary relationships and influences and spent a greater amount of time on a discussion of the history of the *Southern Review* and LSU English department. All of the same resources provide evidence of the atmosphere created at that time and help illustrate the history for the tour. And finally, though Professor Alexius was not teaching any courses over the summer she still called to do the tour and asked to bring in her local book club. The book for the month was *The Movie Goer* by Walker Percy. I still selected the same materials although de-emphasized the Robert Penn Warren connections and Eudora Welty correspondence and focused more attention on the interview with Walker Percy where he discusses his writing process and literary influences including the characters in *The Movie Goer.* For this tour, we had a special guest speaker from the LSU English department who spoke in greater depth about the significance of Edmund Spenser's *Faerie Queene* and how it came to be an influence in the life of Robert Penn Warren which proved to be a tremendously valuable learning experience.

Instruction and Primary Source Literacy

The literary tour represents a perfect example of the value of the hands-on usage of primary source materials in instruction. The materials held in archives provide the evidence of human experience and are an inspiration. Though the primary audience is generally thought to be historians doing serious research it is important to note that these materials in our collection were not created for a specific grade level or course. Nor were these materials created with a specific discipline in mind. Each time regardless of the group that was coming in the materials selected did not change a great deal. But in order to meet the instructional goals of the course the discussion and activities of each session could be altered. Each of the collections selected was useful in illustrating the narrative approach of the different versions of the tour and meet the objectives of each course.

This type of event is not only useful in highlighting the richness and versatility of our collections at LSU but also in emphasizing a strength of teaching with archival materials. The trans-disciplinary nature of primary sources allows for the instruction given in conjunction with the materials shown to be tailored to fit the structure and aims of the courses being offered. With these primary source materials we are able to provide the evidence for the points made on the tour and bring the literary history of LSU to life. The students taken on this tour could possibly walk by the same buildings every day never realizing the significance of the place or importance of the people that once occupied the offices and classrooms. While the tour serves as a useful tool to point out the significance of people and places, the letters and interviews introduced send the point home. Allowing the students to see and touch and read the words helps bring the history to life while also serving to demystify the work and holdings of Special Collections. This literary tour and similar outreach events offer archivists the unique opportunity to showcase the versatility of archival collections and reach different groups of students from across disciplines. The tour also represents one more opportunity for us to promote the availability of these resources to students who have never been in this building before and emphasize that they have the ability to access materials that could have an impact upon their own research and help enrich their writing.

We hope that further development of the tour will include greater involvement in the assignments and courses that are directly impacted. To that end, additional materials have been introduced from recently processed collections that will help explore in more depth the literary history of LSU. For example, a recent project has included the processing of the papers of John Hazard Wildman, an LSU English professor. Wildman used the correspondence of his Civil War ancestor, John Boylston Hazard, to compose a short story called "The Sword" which was published in the *Southern Review* in 1968. These types of examples can contribute to discussion of literary influences. Additional improvement in outcomes could also be achieved through increasing student engagement with the material in the form of specific assignments which utilizes specific documents from the collections. Evidence has shown that attaching a more hands-on assignment to the course provides a much more valuable experience for the students and increases their critical thinking skills. It would be very simple in a discussion of literary influences to ask the students to select something from our holdings in order to derive a short story or essay from it. There are plenty of stories to be told and inspiration to be found in the archives. The story of the literary history of LSU is definitely worth telling.

Works Cited

Cutrer, Thomas. 1984. *Parnassus on the Mississippi: The Southern Review and the Baton Rouge Literary Community, 1935–1942.* Baton Rouge: LSU Press.

Warren, Robert Penn. 1953. *All the King's Men.* New York: Modern Library.

The South Carolina Poetry Archives

A Case Study in Collection Development, Outreach and Collaborative Growth

Jeffrey Makala

The South Carolina Poetry Archives is housed in the department of Special Collections and Archives in James B. Duke Library at Furman University in Greenville, South Carolina. Furman is an independent, selective liberal arts university with a student body of 2700 undergraduates and small graduate programs. Founded in 1826, Furman's library collections reflect its liberal arts heritage. Librarians make special efforts to meet the curricular and research needs of its faculty and student body. The department of Special Collections and Archives is the repository for the official records of the university and maintains rare book and manuscript collections ranging from medieval manuscripts to contemporary artists' books. The department also maintains an interest in collecting materials related to the Upstate region of South Carolina and has special collections in music and Baptist history as well.

Focused collecting of South Carolina poetry and adding the papers of South Carolina poets has been a relatively new area of focus for the department. Following an extensive library renovation that was completed in 2004, the newly redesigned Special Collections and Archives department had as its focal point a large reading room. It was named the William Gilmore Simms Research Room after South Carolina's most notable antebellum poet and novelist, following gifts from Mary Simms Oliphant Furman, Simms's great-granddaughter, and her husband Alester G. Furman III.

Using the renovation and the naming of the Simms Room as an opportunity for reflection, then Special Collections Librarian Debbielee Landi realized that there was no special collections library or archives in South Carolina actively collecting the work of living South Carolina poets. In what is a vibrant contemporary poetry scene throughout the state, the idea to comprehensively collect printed works and document the work of South Carolina poets by collecting their personal papers was decided upon as a new area of focus and a natural outgrowth of the department's mission and work. In choosing to collect the personal papers of South Carolina poets, the department was able to add manuscripts, corrected proofs, publisher correspondence and reviews that document each author's professional growth and development and the way in which a series of individual poems grew into a published book. It was also understood from the beginning that these authors were often quite active in their own communities as literary figures. They lead workshops, worked with young people in local schools, taught, and wrote and spoke widely about their art to a wide variety of groups. Their papers would therefore reflect this community "embeddedness" as well. So, in gaining a single author's personal papers and manuscripts, what was often gained were groups of documents that demonstrated the interconnectedness of that author with their community, to a larger literary world within and outside the boundaries of the state, together with manuscripts that documented their work publishing poems and books within a larger community of letters across the country, and occasionally around the world.

The resulting collections, all gifts, grew quickly. Using local connections at Furman University to announce our new collecting interests, many authors were pleased to be asked to house their papers in the newly formed South Carolina Poetry Archives (SCPA). Eleven years later, the manuscripts component of the collection currently houses the personal papers of twenty poets, among them the past poets laureate of South Carolina, Bennie Lee Sinclair and the current laureate, Marjory Wentworth. As most authors in the collection are still living and writing, the collections are regularly added to with new accessions, and the Special Collections Librarian has as one of their responsibilities the need to keep in touch with SCPA authors and their work. After the initial group of authors transferred their papers to the SCPA, they served as informal ambassadors for the Archives to other poets around the state, encouraging them to contact us about their books and papers as well. The SCPA has thus become a central point for contemporary poetry in South Carolina through its collecting and its connections with living writers across the state.

In addition to manuscript collections, the Archives contain at present over 500 volumes of poetry written by over 100 poets. The definition of who qualifies as a "South Carolina poet" for inclusion in the printed component of the SCPA is somewhat expansive and falls under the following general categories: individuals who were born and grew up in South Carolina, regardless of where they live at present (e.g., Pulitzer-Prize winning poet Terrance Hayes, who was born in Columbia); poets who lived or taught here for a substantial number of years (James Dickey; Kwame Dawes, editor of *Prairie Schooner*); and individuals who were born elsewhere but now make their homes in South Carolina (Gilbert Allen, William Aarnes) all qualified for inclusion. Some alumni/ae of South Carolina colleges and universities who are published poets and have additional ties to the state are also represented in the archive. In addition, anthologies of South Carolina poets and collections of poetry resulting from poetry initiatives, workshops, or special projects from around the state featuring new, emerging, or youth writers are also included. As a result, the print collections include all manner of single-authored monographs, anthologies, chapbooks, broadsides, and limited edition fine press books.

South Carolina's Poetic Heritage

South Carolina has a rich literary heritage stretching back to the colonial period, when poems by native authors regularly appeared in the *South-Carolina Gazette* and other newspapers beginning in the 1730s (Shields 162–164, Epps). Nineteenth century South

Carolina poets Henry Timrod ("the poet laureate of the Confederacy"), Paul Hamilton Hayne, and William Gilmore Simms were all active in the antebellum and immediate postbellum years. They published their works with Southern and Northern publishers alike before and after the Civil War, in newspapers and literary journals, and wrote extensively about the land and landscape of South Carolina. The Archives contains a substantial collection of their works and will grow as we begin to fill in eighteenth- and nineteenth-century gaps in the coming years. Archibald Rutledge (1883–1973), South Carolina's first poet laureate, served from 1934 to 1973 and was a prolific author during his long life. Rutledge is represented in the archive with a comprehensive collection of his works, including limited edition publications.

James Dickey, the Georgia-born former Poet Laureate Consultant in Poetry to the Library of Congress, took a teaching position at the University of South Carolina in Columbia after his term of office in Washington concluded in 1968. He taught at the university until his death in 1997. Dickey's influence on poetry and poets in South Carolina was substantial, as he was a well-known, active reader of his works throughout the South, and by all accounts a brilliant teacher who influenced and nurtured the talents of several generations of writers who came to the university to study with him, and subsequently became published authors (Greiner). Dickey's papers were acquired by Emory University in the 1990s.

South Carolina is often divided into three geographical regions which correspond with its major metropolitan areas: the coastal Lowcountry, which stretches from the Georgia border and Hilton Head Island through Charleston and Myrtle Beach to the North Carolina border; the Midlands, which includes the state capitol, Columbia, and is home to the University of South Carolina; and the Upstate, which includes the foothills of the Blue Ridge mountains as well as urban centers such as Greenville and Spartanburg, Clemson and Furman Universities, and some bedroom communities of Charlotte, North Carolina. In each of these three regions, which can often appear somewhat distinct in regional orientation, culture, and media outlets, there are literary networks, venues for readings and workshops, and universities that exist to support writers and provide places for them to read and publish their work. Though located in the Upstate, the South Carolina Poetry Archives strives to collect comprehensively from the poetry being written, published, and performed throughout the state. We are especially conscious toward working to maintain ties to areas, groups, and individuals outside our own poetic back yard.

There are a number of small presses currently operating in the state that publish literature and poetry, including the Muddy Ford Press in Columbia, the Hub City Writers Project in Spartanburg, and the Ninety-Six Press in Greenville. Together with an MFA program in poetry at the University of South Carolina and many small liberal arts colleges and universities throughout the state, there are substantial and vibrant communities of writers, teachers, and students studying and writing poetry in South Carolina.

Edgefield, a small town of 4700 near the Georgia border, appointed poet Laurel Blossom as its official poet laureate in 2015. Blossom maintains an active schedule of readings and working with children in the Edgefield schools, has placed a public poetry board outside the town library, and writes a column in the town's weekly paper in which she features poems and writes about poetry. Blossom has also edited an anthology of 20th century Edgefield poetry published by the local historical society (Blossom). Known for its pottery heritage and the enslaved master potter David Drake who often wrote verse couplets on his pots, Edgefield's first "Pots and Poetry" contest took place in 2016 (Todd). Authors were required to submit their own verse couplets on pots they had thrown and fired themselves. Blossom, who helped organize this event, has placed her papers in the SCPA, which will then have a complete documentary record of this event preserved.

Columbia, the state capitol, appointed poet Ed Madden as its first poet laureate in 2015. Madden was given a modest budget by the city to create initiatives to place poetry into everyday life in Columbia. The first round of his "Poetry on the Comet" project, placing printing poems on advertising signs on the local bus system, was successfully realized in 2015. A second round of poems, on the theme of "rivers," has been accepted for 2016. A chapbook of poems from the first round has been issued, and there is significant interest in including Spanish-language poems for the second round to appeal to bus riders whose first language is not English (Madden). An upcoming project of his will place poems by local writers on coffee cups and cardboard sleeves in many of the independent coffee shops in the city. Madden's papers are housed in the SCPA, which will also house the record of these activities.

South Carolina Poet Laureate Marjory Wentworth's poem, "Holy City," written as a response to the Charleston church shooting of June 17, 2015, appeared in the Charleston *Post and Courier* and was widely circulated in print and online during the aftermath of the event. Because the shooting had national and international attention from news media, there was also significant interest in Wentworth, a Lowcountry resident, and her poetic response to this traumatic event. Video footage of Wentworth reading this poem was broadcast by the BBC in the United Kingdom and was widely praised as a sensitive and necessary reflection on the city of Charleston, its citizens, and their ability to live through trauma and to heal. This horrific experience taught many that poetry has a place in speaking through trauma, or in articulating certain things that cannot easily be said, or worked through in other formats or media. As a result of these poets laureate actively performing their appointed roles in the state and in their communities, the SCPA will have extensive documentation of this work in each author's respective collections.

A further recent testament to the power, need, and relevance of poetry in everyday life can be seen in the media coverage given the poem "A New Day Dawns" by Columbia, SC, native author Nikki Finney, a National Book Award-winning poet and Professor of Literature at the University of South Carolina. Her poem appeared on the front page of *The State*, the capital city's daily newspaper, in July 2015, alongside a photograph of the Confederate battle flag being lowered for the final time and removed from the State House grounds. Long a source of contention in South Carolina, the flag formerly flew at the top of the State House dome. There was a renewed interest in removing it altogether from its place on a flagpole near the front entrance of the capitol building following the church shooting in Charleston in the summer of 2015. Finney wrote "A New Day Dawns" in the early morning hours after a groundbreaking vote in the state House of Representatives that passed a bill calling for the removal of the Confederate flag was sent to the governor for signing. Finney said, in response to questions about the poem and her thoughts on the flag coming down, "I have been writing these 230 words all my life" (Finney).

There are several other statewide organizations that help support literary arts and activities in South Carolina. The South Carolina Academy of Authors, an organization that recognizes high achievement in literature, and the Poetry Society of South Carolina, which promotes poetry throughout the state, have both provided networking assistance and publicity support for SCPA efforts through their board members, mailing lists, contacts , and activities throughout the state. The Humanities Council of South Carolina, part of the South Carolina state government, also provides support on occasion for literary initiatives throughout the state.

In Greenville, the Emrys Foundation, a local foundation that promotes excellence in the arts, especially literary, visual and musical works by women and minorities, has been a source of networking information, poetry publication, and the teaching of poetry in the Upstate region. Emrys grants, and its journal, have given many new poets a wider audience. More recently, new small presses have been founded in cities around the state to publish local or regional authors. In Spartanburg, the Hub City Writers Project is a model arts organization that combines a publishing arm, a bookstore, and a venue for readings, workshops, and classes. The Watering Hole is an online community for poets of color founded by South Carolina poets and headquartered in South Carolina. All evidence shows that we have a thriving arts scene across the state, and one in which poetry plays a significant role.

Outreach and Collaborative Growth

We see the South Carolina Poetry Archives as a center for literary activity, study, and research for poetry and poets in South Carolina. Having built relationships with the authors whose papers we house, we see it as part of our mission to support them and their work while making their manuscript collections available to researchers and for teaching and learning, to students at all levels. The SCPA serves as a reference and research center for its authors, being able to answer questions and supply them with information about their own prior activities, manuscripts, correspondence, and publications when needed for their own literary work or publishing activities. As a special collections repository, we are also happy to assist our authors by providing reference and research support for their projects.

As a research facility, we wish to encourage the SCPA to be used by classes and workshops for poetry education, teaching, and learning, on- and off-campus. Our printed and manuscript collections represent a wide range of writers creating poetry from across South Carolina from the eighteenth through the twenty-first centuries and are accessible for group instruction and workshops in our seminar room. The SCPA, partnering with the Friends of the Furman University Libraries and the Furman English department, sponsor programs each year, often featuring "our" poets, often during April, which is National Poetry Month, and that are free and open to the public.

In 2015, the South Carolina poet, griot, and musical performer Kurtis Lamkin gave a spirited performance to a packed audience, and in 2016 the SCPA hosted a "gathering of laureates" featuring the state poet laureate and city and town laureates from around the state. When the Greenville-based Ninety-Six Press published its two major South Carolina poetry anthologies, readings were scheduled around the state featuring many of the poets featured in the volumes. This ever-changing array of poets reading their work in multiple venues around the state to mark the publication of the anthologies is well-documented in the archives and is a model for other activities that the SCPA hopes to sponsor in the future.

Gathering of Laureates event poster, Furman University, April 2016.

Future Directions: Print and Digital

In 2015, the SCPA was given the complete records and assets of the Ninety-Six Press, a publisher of poetry monographs based in Greenville. The Press was founded by Furman English professors Gilbert Allen and William Rogers in 1991 with a mission to publish South Carolina poets. Named after the region of colonial South Carolina that eventually became the counties of the Upstate, the Ninety-Six Press published 21 books of poetry during Rogers and Allen's tenures as co-editors. The Press was known for offering book contracts to established poets who did not previously have a single-author monograph published.

In recent years, the Press partnered with Special Collections and Archives to offer the South Carolina Poetry Archives Book Prize. Working in conjunction with students from Allen's poetry and publishing classes at Furman, the annual prize offered was a book contract for a Ninety-Six Press monograph, given to a South Carolina poet without a monograph to their name. The submission process and much of the editing took place within the context of the Furman poetry class, and each book was then sent to press following this joint editorial process.

Upon Allen's retirement in 2015, the archives, backlist stock, and accounts of the Ninety-Six Press were transferred to the Furman Libraries for inclusion into the South Carolina Poetry Archives. The transfer agreement stipulates that the library will maintain the stock and website of the Ninety-Six Press and use the current and future assets of the Press for the benefit of South Carolina poetry and poets. As a result, the library has now assumed the role of bookseller (wholesale and retail) as well as potential publisher to carry on the Ninety-Six Press's name and mission. It was understood upon transfer that the library would not be expected to produce two single-author poetry monographs each year as the press had previously done, but that a reevaluation of the press's mission and activities was in order. This is the stage where we are at present.

In the fall of 2015, the library mounted an exhibition titled "Celebrating South Carolina Poetry: An Exhibition to Mark the Acquisition of the Ninety-Six Press Archives" and held an opening reception at which the transfer of the press archives was recognized and celebrated. At the opening, we made a public call to the assembled press authors and supporters of Allen's and Rogers' work to begin thinking about how we could jointly move forward with a new vision for the press, in print, online, or perhaps in both venues. The call for feedback and recommendations was also made via email and in conversation with other press authors and to the many stakeholders who supported the press and its work over the years.

We will continue to sell volumes from the press's backlist and maintain the press's website. Serious discussions are now being had to plan for a new wide-reaching anthology of contemporary South Carolina poets, to be published under the Ninety-Six Press imprint in 2017. Doing so would mark twelve years since the last anthology, *A Millennial Sampler of South Carolina Poetry* (Allen), which itself appeared a decade after the first anthology of South Carolina poetry to appear in several generations, *45/96: The Ninety-Six Sampler of South Carolina Poetry* (Allen). Based on the response from these two anthologies and the enthusiastic support they received, we feel there is a need for a taking stock of the state of poetry in the state on a somewhat regular basis. South Carolina itself has experienced significant demographic changes since the last anthology was published, and we hope they will be reflected in a new anthology of poets who accurately reflect the increased diversity of our home state. Publishing such a book will also entail a new series of joint readings and book signings around the state and the opportunity to further advocate for poetry, and the SCPA, to new and diverse audiences.

More than just a static archives focused exclusively on the past, we want the South Carolina Poetry Archives to be an active participant supporting the literary life and educational opportunities in South Carolina. The Archives is a cultural heritage institution

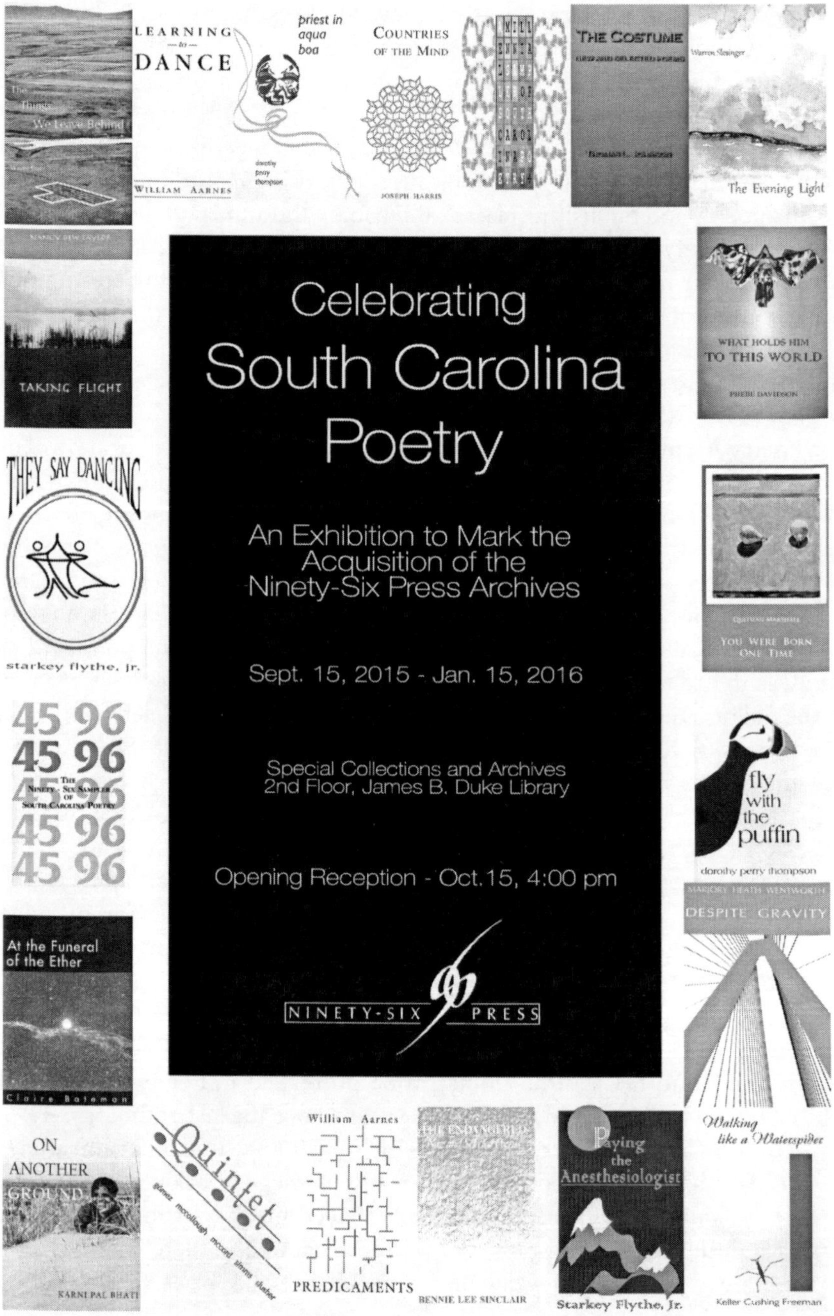

Exhibition poster for the Ninety-Six Press acquisition, Furman University, fall 2015.

that is very much alive, inclusive, and diverse. The collection is currently growing at a rate of 75 volumes and 10 cubic feet of archival material per year. Poetry initiatives in South Carolina cities and towns are active and growing, and we believe the future is promising for the continual support, encouragement, teaching, and learning activities that our archives can support to advance the cause of poetry in South Carolina.

Works Cited

Allen, Gilbert, and William E. Rogers, eds. 1994. *45:96: The Ninety-Six Sampler of South Carolina Poetry*. Greenville, SC: Ninety-Six.

_____. 2005. *A Millennial Sampler of South Carolina Poetry*. Greenville, SC: Ninety-Six.

Blossom, Laurel. 2006. *Lovely Village of the Hills: 20th Century Edgefield Poetry*. Edgefield, SC: Edgefield County Historical Society.

Dickey, James, and Donald J. Greiner, ed. 2004. *Classes on Modern Poets and the Art of Poetry*. Columbia: University of South Carolina Press.

Epps, Edwin C. 2004. *Literary South Carolina*. Spartanburg, SC: Hub City Writers Project.

Finney, Nikki. 2015. "A New Day Dawns." *The State* (Columbia, SC), July 9.

Madden, Ed. 2016. *Poetry on the Comet: A Project of the Poet Laureate of the City of Columbia*. Columbia, SC.

Shields, David S. 1997. *Civil Tongues and Polite Letters in British America*. Chapel Hill: University of North Carolina Press.

South Carolina Poetry Archives. 2016. http://library.furman.edu/specialcollections/poetry_archives/index.htm.

Todd, Leonard. 2008. *Carolina Clay: The Life and Legend of the Slave Potter, Dave*. New York: W. W. Norton. See also http://leonardtodd.com.

Cooperation Between University Librarians and Faculty Writers and Poets

Mantra Roy *and* Erin Vonnahme

Outreach librarians address the points of need in their liaison departments in order to successfully integrate library resources and services in faculty research and teaching. In this essay, we draw upon outreach agendas in our respective institutions to illustrate how we collaborate with faculty to develop creative writing collections. As recently hired Humanities Librarians at the University of Rochester, New York (Mantra Roy), and Miami University, Ohio, (Erin Vonnahme), we offer a study of the strategies, challenges, and successes we have encountered while working with Poetry and Creative Writing faculty members to build our institutions' collections in these areas. At the fore of our writing and planning strategies remains the core belief that collections serve as responsive, dynamic points of outreach, facilitating conversations beyond any single author or trend. As a flexible resource, the collection is a practical expression of librarians supporting scholarship, craft, and creativity.

We started our positions in the summer of 2015. We were friends from our MLIS program and our similar appointments have helped us identify overlapping trends, responsibilities, and possibilities in our current roles. Discussing and understanding the specific needs of the faculty members with regard to their crafts as practitioners and teachers was becoming an important part of our daily schedules. That is when we began sharing notes about our engagement with faculty members. This essay provides us with an excellent platform to discuss the strategies we employed (and continue to employ) in order to create collections that faculty members will find especially suited to the practice of their crafts.

Conversations with faculty have revealed the competing needs faced by creative writers and poets who are also teachers: what an artist seeks from a library collection and what a teacher requires may not always be the same. Meaningful, useful materials in the writing arts likely take different forms—from a more traditional anthology of a poet's collected works, for example, to technical craft manuals—especially if the needs of a writer's teaching load demand as much as his or her creative output. By beginning resource-based outreach conversations, we hope to build dynamic collections valuable to our users specifically and helpful and illustrative to other humanities librarians broadly.

In her article "Outreach Activities for Library Liaisons," Isabel Silver highlights many reasons why a liaison librarian today must engage with an "outreach-centered paradigm" including budget cuts, wider availability of e-resources, and a perceived sense of not requiring the library or a subject specialist (9). According to a 2013 Association of Research Libraries report, "engagement" is a core function of the evolving role of a liaison librarian's outreach model today. An essential aspect of engagement pertains to building strong relationships with students and faculty in order to employ a "user-centered" service model with an "outward focus" (Silver 9). The two critical features of the outreach model include empowering students with user-centered services and supporting scholarly productivity by understanding the needs of faculty members. Communication is key in the above processes so that students and faculty members become aware of the library resources and services that can aid their research and teaching. Silver lists collection development as an important aspect of the outreach workflow.

Becoming familiar with faculty members' research and teaching interests is an essential part of an outreach librarian's role because only then can the librarian understand what the library needs to procure (resources) and which services (workshops, library sessions, online tutorials) it needs to create and provide. Developing or building collections that respond to faculty members' interests will ensure their use. Outreach librarians should engage faculty members in two-way communication channels such that they hear directly from the faculty members about what they would like the library to purchase for their research. Creating an opportunity for faculty members to address their expectations from the library's collection is a primary responsibility of the outreach librarian.

As much as our respective job descriptions christen us "subject specialists," implying perhaps a solitary, deep-dive focus into our given field, we are also, out of necessity and preference, responsive and multidisciplinary collaborators. We want to share with and learn from our peers, faculty and librarians alike. Like Silver notes, the verbiage used to describe librarian liaisons (itself yet another term du jour) is fluid and recognizes the contextual nature of our positions (8). At Miami University, for example, undergraduate education takes the fore; as we recount conversations with Miami faculty and writer, Margaret Luongo, our focus turns toward a collection built to reflect instruction and learning goals. When we discuss poetry collection development at the University of Rochester, we highlight the specific scholarly needs of the faculty members as it is a research institution. Our conversational focus with these poets is the wide and deep collections they need to access in order to invest in their art form as well as to provide a rich collection of the best poetry written in English (and translation), from the earliest lyrics to contemporary times, for students to immerse themselves in the art form as a craft.

Likewise, in our meetings with the faculty members in our respective institutions, both of us have learned even more about the cycle of an English Department's needs in light of its own curricular, co-curricular, scholarly, and programming goals. In every conversation, whether meeting new faculty or supporting a speaker series, we ask a version of "Where are the Libraries in all of this?" Thankfully, we discovered in our conversations, we already are supporting our communities through established collections and services. Still, as our new collaborations reveal, each of us has fresh, site-specific ways we can further connect our collections to the work of poets and creative writers.

Here, and as we develop collections and relationships with our constituents, we consider questions of

- institutional focus and environment
- anticipated use considering, among other things, creative trends and location-specific plans (speaker series and the like)
- explicit requests (reactive) vs. proactive purchasing

In the following pages, we will present separate sections of individual projects before moving onto a third section, in which we share lessons learned from our own and each other's collection development strategies.

Poetry Collection and River Campus Libraries, University of Rochester

Drawing upon Peggy Johnson's book *Fundamentals of Collection Development and Management* and my conversations with my Head of Collections, I recognize that the essence of collection development is "choice" (135). However, it is arguable, that the faculty's teaching and creative needs inform the choice of titles so that I can build relevant, dynamic, and usable collections. Understanding the craft-based and teaching needs through regular conversations and interviews ensures an efficient way of doing outreach.

As a leading private research university, the University of Rochester hosts award-winning artists as faculty members in the English department. The historic Rush Rhees Library, as the main campus library, deems it a primary service to meet the research needs of faculty members. As such, it behooves the Humanities librarian to learn first-hand the perceptible gaps in the collection that need to be met to fulfill the research needs of the faculty members.

As part of my introduction to the English department, I made appointments with the two resident poets, Jennifer Grotz and James Longenbach during my first month at the University of Rochester. Professor Jennifer Grotz has published several collections of poetry. She is the recipient of the Pushcart Prize; the Translation Award, American Translators Association; a Writing Fellowship at the Camargo Foundation, Cassis, France; and the 2015 NEA Fellowship in Translation, among others. James Longenbach, the Joseph Henry Gilmore Professor of English, has published several collections of poetry and critical works such as *The Art of the Poetic Line* and *Wallace Stevens: The Plain Sense of Things*. He is also the recipient of an Award in Literature, American Academy of Arts and Letters; a Guggenheim Fellowship; a Mellon Fellowship; and a National Endowment for the Humanities Senior Fellowship, among others.

During my meetings I realized that certain gaps in our impressive poetry collection needed to be filled to meet their various artistic and teaching needs. I began with an open-ended question—what do you need from the library? The first round of conversations illustrated to me that engaging in longer subsequent discussions will be required to receive a more in-depth perspective of their ideal poetry collection. On returning to my desk I reviewed their responses and recognized that while the most noted publishers and poets were automatically listed in our library's Gobi profile, there were significant gaps. I followed up with the faculty members by seeking another set of individual appointments. Owing to her book tours and workshops in the semester, most of my correspondence with Professor Grotz was through email. But I was able to meet with Professor Longenbach.

Prior to meeting them (via email and in person) I researched several annual literary awards and winners for the last two decades and shared a detailed spreadsheet with Professor Grotz. She reverted with a positive response and suggested a list of publishers that should be essential candidates in our collection of poetry. I went through the list of publishers suggested by Grotz and Longenbach, agreed with all, and added some more to her list. Both poets emphasized the fact that while Prize winners must be included in the collection, it was equally important to buy titles from all the renowned publishers of poetry many of whom are very small independent houses. I developed a list of the significant publishers of poetry. In Gobi, I created separate folders for each publisher. An advanced search with each publisher's name revealed long lists of titles. I checked all titles Gobi listed against my library catalog and ordered the ones our collection was missing. As I continue to build this strategy of focusing on the publishers and acquiring their titles, I share the list of titles received with the faculty members periodically. This communication in essence is doing outreach because I keep the faculty members apprised of additions to a collection that matters most to them. Similarly, I have created another folder for the Prize winners and follow the same workflow of finding the titles we don't have, placing orders, and sharing the list of latest acquisitions with the faculty members. One of my follow-up questions to Professor Grotz involved the kinds of books that she had received through Interlibrary Loan. She sent me a record of her ILL orders. Perusing a list of titles that she had requested from consortia libraries indicated the books she required as an artist teaching her craft which we needed to make available through our collection. Once again, I followed (and still follow) the previously mentioned workflow to acquire books of poetry.

As a librarian I realize that for a genre like poetry I should figure out the best resources for poetry news. Based on Professor Grotz's response that "the best resource to track contemporary poetry is the Poetry Daily website (poems.com)" and that Publishers Weekly and Library Journal "acknowledge significant new books of poetry as well," I track these venues regularly to get the latest updates on new titles (Interview).

Professor Longenbach in an interview added that it is important to learn from the past—"the past (is) more important than the present" and therefore the "best, most up-to-date" editions of all major poets must be included in a world class poetry collection in an academic library. One can't "disregard" the contemporary poets but counts on the "structures of the poetic and publishing community. The "dependable" way to acquire poetry titles is to check the "reputable" poetry publishers or "finest presses" (discussed above) because they publish the best poetry being written. When I asked him about how the library can support his craft, he said that reading the stalwarts, such as Shakespeare and Yeats, is essential, for both his practice of the art as well as for his students. "You read other poets to learn how the greatest manipulators of the medium of language have made patterns" that one can learn from. Longenbach doesn't want to "diminish the importance of the present." Just as the present will hold little meaning if not experienced in relationship with the past, the past will hold no meaning if the art is not continued. We need both of these in a collection; it will "maintain that synergy" between the "history and the ongoing fact of the art."

While discussing the different ways the library can support the various poet and creative writer visits that the English department hosts every year, it emerged that a "thoughtful" collaboration would include availability of resources that have informed the visiting artists in close conjunction with the rigorous exposure to their work in classes in the English department.

My conversation with Longenbach eventually veered toward the possibility of making the library space an intellectually inviting environment where students, faculty, and staff can attend workshop sessions where practicing poets like Longenbach and Grotz can demonstrate the nuances of the art form by drawing on the library collection. It is a project I will be pursuing shortly.

Ultimately, learning from my constituencies what they need from the library's collection is key to successful outreach. The act of doing outreach, including making appointments with faculty members, listening to their library and research needs, their perceptions of library materials, and going back and forth with titles and suggestions, seamlessly blends with the collection building work of actually responding to users' library needs by purchasing the materials and updating the faculty members about the acquisitions.

Creative Writing and the Miami University Libraries

Founded in 1809, Miami University is a public university located in Oxford, Ohio. Since its inception, Miami has cultivated its environment to be one of stellar undergraduate education institutions. Because of Miami's institutional focus, any conversations regarding the Libraries find their way around to the goal of supporting instruction. The conversations that creative writer and faculty member, Margaret Luongo, and I shared were no different. Winner of the Pushcart Prize among other awards and a working writer and teacher for almost two decades, Luongo has been with Miami University since 2004. Here, she teaches undergraduate and graduate-level fiction writing workshops as well as seminars in contemporary fiction and American literature. Her forthcoming collection, *History of Art,* will be published in 2016 by LSU Press.

Professor Luongo and I met in December, both of us ready to enter a period of relative calm after a term full of teaching and creative output. At the local indie coffee house, we chatted about collections and craft, undergraduates and engagement. Before the day's conversation, I had worked with Professor Luongo and her classes already, building workshops to highlight library-based research skills and familiarity with Miami's holdings. Graciously (and thankfully), when I asked her what she thought about building library time into her courses, she responded instantly: "I think it's worth it." "Today we work here," she says to her students who visit. "The classroom" she recognizes, isn't always a creative space, but the library is a change of venue that is supportive and welcoming, conducive to creativity and critical thinking at once. I ask how the collection—the materials themselves and not just the physical space—fits into this creative and constructive paradigm. She replied that the collections could serve as a reminder of the permanence of research in our users' lives. Together, our resources can work alongside faculty and librarians in "convincing [students] that this [research] is not something they cross off their list and get done" once and for all, a necessary hurdle to suffer on their way to a semester's grade. Rather, research is a perennial presence, just as our collections will be, regardless of its specific shape or focus.

Yet, as librarians who cultivate literature-heavy collections, we know we must advocate for holdings that may look and feel different than other parts of what the library has to offer. As of academic year 2015–2016, the Literatures in English (LES) section of the Association of College & Research Libraries (ACRL) has articulated this larger idea—

that literary collections age and grow differently than others—into specific professional guidelines. According to the "Guidelines for Deselecting Literatures in English Collections in Academic Libraries" recently proposed by ACRL-LES, the group "does not endorse ... a strictly quantitative approach" to building or weeding a literature-centric collection. Raw circulation numbers and other "data-driven decision-making" criteria cannot reveal the whole story of such collections because sometimes, something from the 18th century is just as illustrative and contemporary as the hot new voice in fiction.

Plus sometimes a reader must stumble into something surprising, publication date aside. Repeatedly during our conversations, Professor Luongo and I considered the role of such serendipity and exploration. "The library is a space where [we] can expand on these little assignments," Luongo said, to build scholarship but also to provoke curiosity and creativity. The value of browsing in a supportive space can "give [students] some kind of grounding to immerse themselves" (and at this point, we joked about the juxtaposition of concepts like "immersion" and "finding ground," laughing and christening the idea "controlled drowning"). Luongo continues, in research sometimes "you stumble around. That's part of the fun." Careening into the collection is "all part of the creative process." My hope, as steward of the collection, is that such careening is joyful, well-supported, surprising, and provocative.

For creative writers like Professor Luongo and her students, then, an ideal collection could look like a sea of resources that supports craft and intellectual growth but also facilitates browsing and unexpected discovery (the serendipity factor). I recognize collections must evolve in content as much as they evolve over time, so my goal is to facilitate such experiences in both print and digital formats; in this way I can prioritize stability and agility. Certainly browsing physical stacks differs from browsing digital repositories. However, I can lead users into productive engagement with our materials despite impediments like format learning curves or technology fears. Miami's collection of literary journals, for example, is part analog, part digital. When I meet with Professor Luongo and her classes, I frame our sessions as discovery-centered, reassuring them that format is only one piece of a larger, layered learning process. This interactivity allows me to learn as much as I teach; every term there are new items to share and also new students, each with different interests and perspectives. Their ideas and questions offer me information about gaps in the collection. Their user behavior shows me what content seems to fare better in which format. Part of my own growth and fulfillment in my position at Miami has been this two-pronged approach to collection promotion: as I work with faculty and their students to navigate the collection, I learn how to develop it.

Likewise, a vibrant creative writing collection should support a writer-professor's twin goals: honing craft and teaching it. To that end, the collection needs to offer context-specific content—materials explicitly connected to class assignments and a given semester's author visits, for example—and to provide consistent access to relevant writers, whether canonical or avant-garde. Again, stability and agility are key. For example, Professor Luongo suggested building collections to offer users a broad look at authors for a better sense of how the trajectory of a writing career can form manifold shapes. She elaborates, "I would love for [students] to pick a writer they love with some history ... somebody who's had a good long career," so they can "do the research in between on [selected writers'] lives, their writing career, what they've written about writing, if anything, their philosophy and how that's changed, just to get a sense of how it works."

Considering "how it works"—a writing process, a writing life, a sustained career—

forces librarians to recognize that there is no single way to showcase these phenomena. What we can do, however, is use our collections to support a chorus of voices. Our holdings can offer the expected canonical writers, to be sure, but they should also prioritize the work of independent publishers and writers to create space for exciting new contributions. Our writing arts collection development should demonstrate a concerted effort to educate ourselves about the vast communities into which we are encouraging the writers on our campus to contribute.

Yet we must not expect to remain aware of this vast chorus on our own. Instead, we need to rely on our outreach and public service savvy. We talk. We listen. We read. As our conversation turned toward contemporary creative writing movements and trends, Professor Luongo shared with me that she, too, relies on collaboration to keep in the know. Certainly we must avoid an echo chamber that might keep us myopic and ignorant of voices different than our own, but that is why we must cultivate community across disciplinary and professional boundaries, like Professor Luongo, that is, like Margaret and I are doing over coffee.

In the end, Margaret's biggest hope was a version of my own: more of the last two hours. "I would love to have more of this," she said, "just making connections," talking about how we can work together as professionals to create cross-departmental relationships, as community members to support creative and intellectual curiosity, and as library users dedicated to voracious thinking, primed for discovery.

Converse, Collaborate, Collect and Repeat

As librarians who both build collections and do active outreach, we are in an enviable position today to advocate for effective and efficient use of our resources by engaging in conversations with users who shape the intellectual direction on an academic campus, our faculty members. An important lesson learned from our projects is that conversations with faculty members are key to finding out what they need from the collections for their research and teaching. Mantra heard from her faculty members that regular connection with the librarian helps them engage with collections more actively; Erin heard much of the same. Both of us heard the call for our collections to be part of an active and supportive library ecosystem.

As collections should serve scholarly and creative expectations, so, too, should they serve the fluctuating needs of an academic year and its instruction and programming? Since our creative writing faculty members necessarily engage with visiting speakers, for example, whose crafts in practice demonstrate the techniques and nuances of living art forms, we librarians realize that our collections should reflect the invited speakers' works. Thus our collections should speak both to the courses being taught and the overall terrain of a genre in current focus. What's more, our working closely with faculty is not just a lofty goal or hopeful ideal. Rather it is a pragmatic approach to building responsive collections while growing and cultivating creative scholarship. The professional relationship that Erin and Margaret have fostered speaks to the meaningful instructional collaboration that can spring from a handful of conversations just as Mantra's upcoming goals for creative outreach emerge directly from chats with Longenbach and Grotz. Ultimately, one-on-one conversations and regular communication with creative writing faculty are key to successful building of collections that will cover a wide and deep range of resources they need for their research and teaching.

Works Cited

Association for College & Research Libraries, Literatures in English Section. 2015. "Guidelines for Deselecting Literatures in English Collections in Academic Libraries." Accessed February 4, 2016. http://www.ala.org/acrl/sites/ala.org.acrl/files/content/aboutacrl/directoryofleadership/sections/les/GuidelinesforDeselectingLESCollectionsinAcademicLibraries-final.pdf.

Johnson, Peggy. 2014. *Fundamentals of Collection Development and Management*. London: ALA.

Silver, Isabel D. "Outreach Activities for Librarian Liaisons." *Reference & User Services Quarterly* 54.2 (2014): 8–14. *ProQuest*. Web. 22 Dec. 2015.

Poetry as the Scholar's Art

An Interview with Poet Amy Newman

JULIE L. MILLER

Amy Newman is the author of five collections of poetry, most recently *On This Day in Poetry History* (Persea Books, 2016). Her other books include *Dear Editor*, winner of the Lexi Rudnitsky Editor's Choice Award, *fall*, *Camera Lyrica*, winner of the Beatrice Hawley Award, and her first book, *Order, or Disorder*, which received the Cleveland State University Poetry Center Prize. She's won a fellowship to the MacDowell Arts Colony and recently was awarded the Friends of Literature Prize from *Poetry* for her poem "Howl." She is a board of trustees professor at Northern Illinois University.

Your new book On This Day in Poetry History *uses details from the lives of famous mid-20th century American poets such as Elizabeth Bishop, Robert Lowell, and Sylvia Plath. In his review for the* New York Times Book Review *David Kirby (2016,17) states, "This is the only poetry collection I can recall in recent years that has the same sort of 'Works Cited' page and notes you'd expect in a scholarly study." Did you begin this collection as a scholarly study? If so, when did you realize the research about these poets was finding its way into your poetry?*

It began as a study into T.S. Eliot's influences and ended as poetry. Like most poets, I've always got one ear open to the world hoping to be influenced by something that I can eventually explore in poetry. In this case I was doing research on Eliot for a class I was teaching. I'd just completed a collection of poetry that had, itself, begun with my decision to try to figure out what makes a poem a *poem*. I had wondered about that essential element that creates poetry: It isn't just the appearance on the page that defines what makes a poem poetic, is it? It can't be just the line break that separated poetry from everything else; there's something in poetry, a kind of energy, what R. P. Blackmur [(1987, 247)] calls its "animating presence." My wondering about this presence ultimately became *Dear Editor*, a book of cover letters to an imaginary editor in which the writer doesn't turn off the poetry mind when she turns to the task of writing the cover letters that accompany her submissions.

I was about to teach my usual survey course on poetry, and my mind was focusing on the Movement poets in England and the poets commonly referred to as "Confessional" in America. That poets of both schools responded to their time with a more personal tone—though distinct, of course, the British poets like Philip Larkin and Thom Gunn more inclined to work within restraint, the Americans more wildly personal—I could see as in part a strategy against Eliot's influence on the poetry of the time. To wildly oversimplify, Eliot's theory of impersonal poetry in part contributed to the idea that the poet's life was not a fit tool for reading the poetry: "Poetry is not a turning loose of emotion, but an escape from emotion; it is not the expression of personality, but an escape from personality" [(Eliot 1974, 58)]. Critics forwarded this idea, and we had a New Criticism that looked instead for a cold study of, say, tension and release of tension in poetry (and a number of New Critical readings that advanced the idea of the death of the author). But I've always felt that this theory of Eliot's was really a dissembling on Eliot's part, and that it's impossible to keep the writer out of the work. Just one look at "The Waste Land" or "The Love Song of J. Alfred Prufrock" in conjunction with any of Eliot's biographies knocks that pose down a bit. Further, my students blossom when we read, say, Sylvia Plath or Ted Hughes, with biographical information. The poetry is no longer a cold hard object to be studied for tensions but artifacts of lives lived by human beings made dimensional by the sources from which they grow. I had decided that bringing biography back to poetry would be my disruption.

I began to just marinate in the lives of these poets I'd be teaching the following semester; instead of the usual biographical details, I explored at a more atomic level. For some reason Eliot's power has always bothered me, and I focused on the poets whose response to Eliot was revolutionary. I was planning on teaching Robert Lowell's collection *Life Studies*, (of course even the title tells us that Lowell is craftily rejecting Eliot's dictum), and I began to enjoy this task I'd given myself to read all the biographical materials over, to spelunk into every poet's life. As I looked at these lives, at these people becoming poets, my mind returned to that open question: what makes poetry *poetry*?

Lowell writes in the shadow of Eliot; when does his tree limb, seeking light, twist out from under the bigger limb towards its way into its own way of seeing the world? I was studying for my class, but my mind started to wonder: Is there a way to note a moment in a person's life when he or she becomes a poet? What if we could see American poetry coming into being? In the midst of this thinking, I came across a minor detail in a biography of Elizabeth Bishop: as a child, after a major fire in her town, she picks up a stocking, diverted by it [(Miller 1993, 5). I came across a startling detail in a Lowell biography: he breaks Jean Stafford's nose not only the first famous time, but a second time [(Mariani 1994, 91)]. All these moments could be the moment when the poet *becomes*. No detail of a life is so trivial as to not have potentially widespread consequence, a kind of butterfly effect.

So, the shorter answer is the project began when, in studying for my upcoming class, I let my mind wander around, and it started to wonder: what if I explored these parts of American poetry happening, in poems? To consider writing about Lowell breaking Stafford's nose a second time, I'd have to read everything I could get my hands on; the biographies, the letters, Stafford's stories (my research taking me to her marvelous, essential short story about her post-broken nose surgery "The Interior Castle," for example [(Stafford 1986)]). And that's the first poem I tried to write. It went on from there.

I am interested in the mix of resources in the bibliography of On This Day in Poetry History. *You used primary resources such as correspondence, newspaper articles, a memoir, and the creative works of the writers. You also cite critical biographies and other secondary works. What are your go-to sources for finding the information you need? Are you on a first-name basis with the interlibrary loan staff at your library? Do you work with a reference (or liaison) librarian when you run into research problems?*

Interlibrary Loan wrote this book, mostly. I mean, they were a major supplier of necessary materials. I have never met a source I didn't like, so anytime I saw any reference anywhere, I wanted to have it in my hands and read it. Our library has some good materials, and those materials led me to others, so I would say the folks at my interlibrary loan know me very well.

Some of my favorite pieces were the obscure ones. I chased down a reference in a John Berryman biography to a nun who left the convent for the summer to take a writing workshop taught by a young John Berryman; this yielded a beautiful article about Berryman written by that nun, who turned out to be the poet Madeline DeFrees (1996). I mean, she wasn't the poet Madeline DeFrees at the time she took the class, and she wasn't cited as anyone but a nun in his class; that there would be a nun in a Berryman class was too interesting not to look into. I love big biographies, letter collections, all hard copy books that may be in any way related to my project; books are like fields with millions of seed in them, and though it's impossible to gather every seed, I am obsessed with trying. I am, further, happy for JSTOR and Project MUSE, databases I can access through Northern Illinois University's libraries, with which to locate some materials.

The reference librarians at the Harry Ransom Center at the University of Texas at Austin were great. I travelled there to study Anne's Sexton scrapbooks and correspondence, her personal effects. The reference librarians were patient with my obsessions. It's a revelation to see the actual materials and visualize, realize the correspondences: a ticket from the Ice Follies, a green swizzle stick, and then an ad for Librium a bit later; a brief clipping, with a page from a doctor's prescription pad attached, signed by the therapist with whom Sexton was having an affair, the note a little too professional and cold; the notes in her diary, in her lovely vulnerable script, in beautiful lines. And I was able to see some of her paintings. Did you know Sexton practiced painting? She did, a little, and they are very, let's say, of the period. The librarian at the Ransom Center set them out on a special room for me to study (but of course not to touch). I noted that the library had had to makes titles for the works I saw based on their subjects, like *[Landscape with purple mountains, water and trees]*; *[Still life with white penguin and deer figurines]*. Just being able to sit with these paintings and to study them was an experience that gave me insight into her days and her ways of seeing the world.

One of the jacket blurbs for your third book fall describes the book as "drunk on the dictionary" because it uses definitions of the word "fall" as a springboard for exploring the themes of grief and loss. How would you characterize a poet's relationship to her dictionary?

I would bet that most poets have a great affection for this room where they can find so many tools. But I have a complicated—a respectfully complicated—affection for the dictionary, a book that pretends to hold the meanings of words but is really just trying. Every definition of a word is an attempt to convey something, a kind of condensed sign for something other than what it is: a string of letters, little shapes made of ink on paper, unequal to what it represents. I get the feeling the dictionary is aware of its failure, of its inability to contain everything. But as a poet who is aware that it's impossible to effectively convey things with words, I appreciate the effort.

The idea that each word is trying to explain itself is actually what got me started on *fall*. I was interested in exploring the reason for grief in this world and, since many people use the word "fall" as a signifier for the fall of Eden and the loss of perfection—understanding grief as the result of our fall, say—I thought I'd look up the word "fall" to see its definition. I saw that this little word had 72 definitions, and that the definitions seemed to be trying to tell a story of how grief came into the world [(American 1976)]. It was striking, intriguing, and I thought I'd try to write a poem to explore each definition.

And I'm sure, too, that this idea of how the dictionary tries without success to tell each word's story carried over into *Dear Editor*, the book I wrote after *fall*. In *Dear Editor*, a collection of cover letters written to an unseen editor, the letter writer, an aspiring poet (who is also named Amy Newman) has her own complicated relationship to the dictionary which she describes as "a glum book disguised as enough language, within which I can't find one word to describe the look on the face of St. Anne de Beaupré…" [(Newman 2011, 56)]. I like the failure of words. It suggests that failure is a part of trying. That sounds like a downer, but it sustains me. Trying is everything.

Aside from writing poetry, you are also a prolific writer of book reviews, essays, and profiles of other writers, all of which are informed by research. Does the research process for this more scholarly writing differ substantially from the research process that informs your poetry? How does your participation in scholarly communication contribute to your creative writing practice?

In Wallace Stevens's *Adagia* (1997) he says, "Poetry is the scholar's art" [(1997, 906). This resonates with me. There are differences in degrees between and among the work that is not poetry that I produce, I don't think there is a marked difference in the amount of research, but there is a difference in the way I use the materials I find.

For me writing poetry is, at its heart, a process of learning; I think that's what separates poetry from verse. Verse says what you know, in clever ways; with poetry, the writer doesn't know everything beforehand. Wondering and exploration are part of the poem project. Scholarly work is pretty much part of the creative writing practice for me. Often, when I have found myself pursuing something because I'm about to teach it or I have a scholarly interest in it, I feel like I'm picking up Ariadne's thread and that eventually it's going to be attached to a poem draft.

In a recent interview in Fifth Wednesday Journal, *you said that for a long time you were more interested in studying poetry than in writing it and that you think "reading about literature is as intense as writing it, maybe even more so." How do you introduce this intensity into the classroom?*

I don't know if this is the answer to the question, but I feel as though being honest about reading, and being patient with students and their fear of and/or resistance to literature, I can create a place that allows them to discover that they don't hate it. I get the feeling more and more that any literature they've come in contact with via education has been given to them only for a test or something: take this story and boil it down to a moral or an aspect to be memorized that the teacher can ask you about on an exam. They come into class feeling like they have to know: what is the message this book is trying to convey? Can I distill it down to two sentences to remember for the exam? And so literature, which isn't trying to convey any message, but is only being, and opening the world, and inviting them into a landscape … many of the students haven't been exposed to just reading for pleasure, which leads to thinking, which leads to the kind of depth and increased feel for reality that we read for. Students initially feel compelled to reduce to a nutshell-type summary, resisting any part of the literature that might allow them to imagine, to wonder, to *not know*, because they read to accumulate data for the test. But literature, poetry, fiction are there to do exactly the opposite of that. Eudora Welty said,

"There is absolutely everything in great fiction but a clear answer" [(Welty 1978, 149)]. So how would a test work with that? Literature is not for testing.

I ask for the students' patience as we scratch through something difficult, like Faulkner. I certainly avoid lecture, and instead create opportunities for what we used to call group work: getting students into small groups to discuss the literature among themselves. It's an insider secret that students learn more in class when they are listening to their peers as well as the teacher. If the teacher is up at the front of the classroom dispensing data, the students become passive, as if they were watching a television program. If their peers are speaking, it's much more of an active discussing, a learning situation for them.

And then, there's the plain fact that I can't not get choked up sometimes—which is embarrassing, but whatever—when I read something as beautifully written as the ending of James Baldwin's "Sonny's Blues" or Kate Chopin's *The Awakening*, say. Or Stevens or Larkin. I am frank with my students about literature. I teach things I love, and I also teach things that I don't love. I don't hide my frustrations with it, and I don't hide my love. I don't know if this frankness helps, but I think it does. My students are surprised when I tell them I have times when I love T. S. Eliot's work and times when I really dislike it and him. In a recent discussion about the character Edna Pontellier in Chopin's *The Awakening*, I said, "I tell you what; I just don't get Edna a lot of the time. I can see how some see her as a woman out of place, but she can be irritating." There was visible relief on the faces of some students. It's okay to have a visceral response to a character that goes against the standard reading. My mind changes every time I read a book, and letting students feel the way they want to feel—informed at the very least—fosters a place where they can express themselves, and think, and change.

Do you have a favorite assignment that helps students connect research with the creative writing process? Any memorable classroom moments or writing break-throughs that have resulted from this assignment?

Research and poetry go hand in hand, in my opinion. Once you start looking into something that has been compelling to you, you discover intimate relationships, little correspondences. Books wherein the poet has explored this relationship become models for student research. I've used Natasha Trethewey's *Native Guard*, her book exploring a number of things—among them: the Louisiana Native Guard, one of the first black regiments, her mother's history; and her own complicated relationship to Mississippi—as a model for students. We study this technique of rescuing historical narrative (not many of us are aware of the story of Ship Island which forms a central sonnet sequence in the book), and also of examining one's correspondence with a past. In conjunction with that book we read Daniel Cross Turner's interview with Trethewey. We consider what Turner [(2013)] calls "the metaphor of 'crosshatching'" in Trethewey's sonnet sequence "Native Guard": a confederate soldier (formerly a slave) is writing in the lines of a journal he finds in the abandoned home of a White Southerner (the term also refers to this soldier's back crosshatched with marks from a whip). Turner asks Trethewey whether "crosshatching" may be read as metaphor for her technique of exploring history as a part of her writing search. She responds:

> It's the integration of my personal story, my history, crosshatched, written over and within the public histories and more dominant narratives I have received. I like the idea of how these strands are interwoven, because our stories are never simply two trains running on separate tracks. They are much more like the basket weave of that crosshatching [Turner 2013, 160].

A number of poetry books rescue lost narratives, crosshatch this way: Martha Collins' *Blue Front*, Eavan Boland's *Outside History*, and recently Tarfia Faizullah's *Seam;* these books use a personal voice to explore, study, and rescue from the dustbin of history some event. The poets begin by exploring a historical event or time period, and find themselves immersed and obsessed and a part of the material. Writing into this subject, researching it, they rescue it from an obscurity. My students' responses to these books often begin "I had no idea that…"

Having long stressed that poetry isn't a relaying of what you know, but a kind of submission to what the world wants you to learn, I assign crosshatching to my poetry students: what event or issue, what history or interest, has tapped you on the shoulder, but you never explored it and its correspondence with you? That has yielded some beautiful work. One will note a compelling fascination with the mistreatment of whales at Sea World; one cites an interest in Egypt. Someone mentions hearing about the Spanish American war; another starts talking about the first women in prison. These sometimes become semester-long chapbook projects.

The publishing industry is undergoing tremendous change driven by the web and social media. How have these changes had an impact on your approach to publishing your work? What advice do you give to your students?

The web has generated many venues for publication. So in one way having these alternatives to place work means more publishing opportunities. But reading online doesn't feel to me the same as reading in print. I always have the feeling, when I read online, that the material is going to a different part of my brain than when I read hard copy.

A bit of the advice I give my students about publishing online or in print: look at the work you love, see where those poets you admire have published, look at the acknowledgments pages in book and the contributor's notes in journals to see where work that you think is similar in aesthetic to yours might find a home, and send there. This suggestion doesn't distinguish between print and online venues.

But in terms of reading, studying, and researching, I have found that students don't read as deeply when the sources are delivered electronically, unless they print them out. Our university is going through a budget crisis, as are so many universities. In an effort to reduce expenditures for my department, I no longer photocopy materials for students to study in classes, but instead scan and send them out electronically. My small and unscientifically verified study, which is only comprised of me comparing student response this year to years previous, shows that students just don't retrain, absorb, or even consult electronic materials. Maybe it's because the screen, which has the potential to offer so much, flattens whatever it offers.

We are still in the middle of knowing how we will feel about print in the years to come. Many university presses have been in danger of getting sliced and even closed. In the case of The University of Akron Press, public response restored the press when the university tried to shut it down [(Farkas 2015)]. So many readers are still clamoring for print and the kind of experience and quality selective print publishing conveys.

Works Cited

American Heritage Dictionary of the English Language. 1976. New York: Houghton-Mifflin.

Blackmur, R.P. 1987. "Statements and Idylls." In *The Legacy of R.P. Blackmur: Essays, Memoirs, Texts.* Ed. by Edward T. Cone, Joseph Frank and Edmund Kelly, 247–249. New York: Ecco.

DeFrees, Madeline. 1996. Resolution and Independence: John Berryman's Ghost and the Meaning of Life. *The Gettysburg Review* 9.7: 9–29.
Eliot, T.S. 1974. "Tradition and the Individual Talent." In *The Sacred Wood: Essays on Poetry and Criticism,* 47–59. London: Methuen.
Farkas, Karen. 2015. University of Akron Press Staff Rehired Two Weeks After Positions Eliminated. Cleveland.com, August 17. http://www.cleveland.com/metro/indexssf/2015/08/university_of_akron_press_staf.html. Accessed April 29, 2016.
Kirby, David. 2016. Review of *On This Day in Poetry History* by Amy Newman. *The New York Times Book Review,* February 26. http://www.nytimes.com/2016/02/28/books/review/on-this-day-in-poetry-history-by-amy-newman.html?_r=0.
Mariani, Paul. 1994. *Lost Puritan: A Life of Robert Lowell.* New York: W.W. Norton.
Miller, Brett C. 1993. *Elizabeth Bishop: Life and the Memory of It.* Berkeley: University of California Press.
Newman, Amy. 2011. *Dear Editor.* New York: *Persea.*
_____. 2004. *Fall.* Middletown, CT: Wesleyan University Press.
_____. 2016. *On This Day in Poetry History.* New York: Persea.
Stafford, Jean. 1986. The Interior Castle. In *The Collected Stories of Jean Stafford,* 179–193. London: Hogarth.
Stevens, Wallace. 1997. From the Notebooks. In *Collected Poetry and Prose,* 899–922. The Library of America, 96. New York: Literary Classics of the United States.
Turner, Daniel Cross. 2013. Southern Crossings: An Interview with Natasha Trethewey. In *Conversations with Natasha Trethewey,* ed. Joan Wylie Hall, 156–167. Jackson: University Press of Mississippi.
Welty, Eudora. 1978. Must the Novelist Crusade? In *The Eye of the Story: Selected Essays and Reviews.* 146–158. New York: Random House.

How One Library and One Poet Reached 1,200 Readers for National Poetry Month

DIANE KENDIG *and* LAURIE KINCER

This is the story of how a library that supports poetry, a librarian who loves poetry, and a poet who loves libraries came together to create a daily blog, *Read + Write: 30 Days of Poetry*, for National Poetry Month. The blog exceeded all expectations, attracting 1,283 subscribers over the course of two years, 2014 and 2015. Approaching its third year, it is still going strong.

A Library That Supports Poetry

Located near Cleveland, Ohio, Cuyahoga County Public Library—the nationally ranked number one large library system in the U.S. for the last six years—has long supported and promoted poetry. Its support has been due largely to director and 2015–2016 American Library Association President Sari Feldman, an avid reader and poetry lover.

In 2004, Feldman sold out a 1000-seat theater by bringing Irish poet and Nobel Laureate Seamus Heaney to Cleveland to raise funds for the library foundation. A year later, in 2005, she established the William N. Skirball Writers Center Stage, a ticketed author series, to raise ongoing funds for the library foundation. Now in its twelfth year, Writers Center Stage has hosted a who's who of famous writers, including an impressive list of poets: Robert Pinsky, Mary Oliver, Billy Collins and Rita Dove.

Feldman also created a Poem of the Month project in 2009. Each month, CCPL posted on its website a video of a visiting author reading his or her favorite poem. Among many memorable performances, Colson Whitehead read "In a Station of the Metro" by Ezra Pound, Nancy Pearl read "Wild Geese" by Mary Oliver, and Jonathan Lethem read "Thank You" by Kenneth Koch. Poem of the Month continued for over a year, ending only when obtaining copyright permissions for the poems became too difficult. Nevertheless, Feldman had positioned CCPL squarely in support of poets and poetry for years.

In addition, this twenty-seven-branch library system had a librarian on staff, Laurie Kincer, who had read widely, attended author events, and followed national and local writers since the late 1980s when she moved to Cleveland and studied for her master's degree in literature from Case Western Reserve University. She had had poems published in two local collections under her former name of von Mehren. Joining CCPL in 2003, she had led the library's programming efforts around National Poetry Month, National Novel Writing Month, and visiting author events. Since 2011, her work at the library had focused on programs around books, author visits, and writing workshops.

So when Kincer proposed in 2013 that the library celebrate National Poetry Month with an online poetry blog in April 2014, administrators approved the idea.

A Tailor-Made Library Blog for National Poetry Month

There was no shortage of quality poetry available online through reputable national organizations. Every day of the year, poetry readers could turn to Poem-A-Day from the Academy of American Poets, Poem of the Day from the Poetry Foundation, and The Writer's Almanac with Garrison Keillor. During the month of April, they could also try writing thirty poems in thirty days with inspiration from NaPoWriMo.net.

What could CCPL add to the crowded field of online poetry?

The library believed that it could make a niche for itself in the online poetry world by creating a special blog for the month of April that promoted local poetry, featured the library's poetry books, and inspired readers to try their hands at writing poetry through writing prompts. They named this blog *Read + Write: 30 Days of Poetry.*

Its prominent features, as they took shape over two National Poetry Months in 2014 and 2015, became:

1. A poem each day by a poet who had lived or worked for some period of time in the Cleveland or northeast Ohio area.
2. A poetry writing prompt each day.
3. A poetry book each day available from the library.

The library would find that featuring local poets was a key advantage. First, permissions were easier to obtain. Second, it expanded local poets' reach to a wider audience. Finally, it provided content that frequently delighted readers through familiar northeast Ohio settings, incidents, history or people.

The Collaboration Between a Library and a Poet

How did CCPL connect with the right poet for this project? It happened at former Poet Laureate Rita Dove's event at Writers Center Stage in the spring of 2013. Cuyahoga County Public Library's Kincer and local poet Diane Kendig met through a series of accidents. While Kincer's husband, Tom Kincer, and Kendig waited next to each other in the lobby, they discovered that they lived a block apart (in different decades) in a small community near Lake Erie.

Tom Kincer introduced the librarian and the poet, and an immediate connection formed over the many things they had in common. As they talked, Kincer sensed that Kendig had the right mixture of knowledge, background, temperament and connections for a future poetry project.

Kendig had grown up in the northeast Ohio area and been part of the vibrant Cleveland poetry scene in the 1970s and 1980s, studying poetry at Cleveland State University.

She became a writing professor at The University of Findlay (Ohio), where she ran a writers' series and taught on campus and in a nearby prison for eighteen years. Kendig had recently returned to Ohio after a decade teaching near Boston, happy to be home and reconnecting with the writing community.

Kincer and Kendig exchanged e-mail addresses and planned to meet again to brainstorm about partnering on a poetry project. When they finally met in the summer of 2013, Kendig proposed a number of traditional poetry workshops. From past programming experience, Kincer believed these workshops would not draw a very large audience.

Kendig paused, sat back, and said, "Then let's see what we get when we bring poetry *to* people."

She told Kincer about her online course at The University of Findlay, E-Poetics, which examined the influence that poetry and the Internet had on one another. Students who took it tended to be upper-level, non-traditional, adult students, most of whom majored in hazardous waste engineering and business. These were not the typical poetry audience. Most admitted that they took the course out of necessity, not desire, and with much trepidation. But as the class studied contemporary poetry online, considering online videos and websites such as the Electronic Poetry Center at the State University of New York at Buffalo, they surprised themselves by how engaged they were with online poetry. Kendig had been looking for a way to bring poetry to such non-traditional readers ever since, and the CCPL audience seemed the perfect opportunity to try.

Over the course of the fall of 2013, Kendig and Kincer came up with a general outline for *Read + Write: 30 Days of Poetry*. While neither of them knew exactly what would be involved in turning this blog into a reality, they settled on a stipend for Kendig of $1500, which broke down to $50 per day of content which she would curate and provide to the library.

Choosing the Poets and the Poems to Feature

Kendig, with her extensive poetry background and knowledge, was responsible for coming up with thirty poems by poets who currently or formerly lived in the Cleveland or northeast Ohio area. From a lifetime of living and writing in Ohio, Kendig had known and read many of the area poets. Kincer, too, compiled a list of poets she believed should be included. When they put their lists together, they had far more poets than days in April.

Kendig attributes this to northeast Ohio's rich tradition in modern poetry, including Hart Crane, Vachel Lindsay, Langston Hughes, Mary Oliver, and Rita Dove. The area continues to be a center of activity for poetry, with the academic resources of the Northeast Ohio Master of Fine Arts in Creative Writing program, a consortium of four state universities—Cleveland State University, Kent State University, The University of Akron, and Youngstown State University.

Outside of academia, a monthly public poetry workshop has existed in the Cleveland area for forty-two years, supported by various sponsors. In 2011, CCPL adopted the workshop and kept it meeting when its former nonprofit sponsor of thirty-seven years disbanded. With these poetry resources, Kendig had many talented, published poets from whom to choose.

Kendig wanted to include as wide a range of poets as possible since the northeast Ohio poetry scene has prided itself on its open tent. Academic poets, slam poets and street poets all mingled, workshopping and reading their work. She strove for a diverse group of poets.

Kendig also had one requirement: that a poet had at least one non-self-published book. Having this one prerequisite helped Kendig narrow the field considerably while still allowing for plenty of fine poetry from which to choose.

When it came to selecting the poems, Kendig favored ones that would reach a general audience or what Virginia Woolf called "the common reader." She also favored poems that were not available on the Internet, often existing only in out-of-print books, giving these poems a new, online life through the project. On occasion, she also chose recent poems that were not yet in books.

For the first year of the project, Kendig was able to obtain copies of most of the poems from her own poetry library. Often she remembered and chose poems that fit the season or the day, such as a poem about cold, wet April days or one about a full moon. While Kendig preferred clear lyrics that tended toward narrative, she also chose a few poems that were more challenging to read. As with the poets, she wanted a wide variety of types of poems.

Choosing the poets and finding their poems proved in many cases to be easier than finding the poets themselves to obtain permissions. Academic poets had listings on their university websites, but not all of them answered their university mail in December when Kendig first reached out to them. Poets with their own websites were ideal, but some of Kendig's requests via email forms went unanswered there, too.

One particularly helpful source for finding writers was the "Directory of Poets &Writers" on the *Poets & Writers* website. Another useful list was the Ohio Arts Council's "Ohio Creative Writers Directory," with listings for over 450 writers. In the final stages of sleuthing for contact information, Diane used social media and word of mouth.

In each case, Kendig contacted the poet, explained the project, and asked for permission to include his or her poem. She also collected short biographies from each poet and, in the first year only, a photograph. As the library learned in that first year, many fine poets did not have appropriately formatted or sized digital photographs, so they did not ask for photographs in the second year.

Creating the Poetry Writing Prompts

Drawing on years of writing and teaching poetry, Kendig was well suited to creating thirty poetry writing prompts. In addition to her twenty-eight years of university teaching, she has taught creative writing in grades K–12 for Ohio's Artist in Residence program and other Writers in the Schools programs. She has also led workshops in prisons, libraries, senior residences, and writers' organizations in the United States and abroad.

She turned to what had worked best for her in those settings. She also took into consideration specific days, such as Earth Day and the first day of spring, or tried to play off the topic or form of the day's featured poem to create the prompt.

Kendig tested each prompt herself, having used it with a group of writers in the past. She wanted these prompts to be inspirations to write but also ways of sharing other knowledge, such as knowledge about Cleveland, about Ohio, and about poetry forms.

For the most part, Kendig chose the date on which each poem and writing prompt appeared, ordering the poets and topics as she saw fit.

Choosing the Poetry Books and Websites

Meanwhile, Kincer handled the selection of thirty books of poetry from the library's collection. The library's purpose in showcasing these works was to encourage discovery of poetry resources that were available for free with a library card. If it boosted circulation of these titles, that was an added benefit.

In the first year, Kincer also selected thirty poetry websites to feature. In subsequent years, the library discontinued this daily feature out of a desire not to repeat content from past years.

Building the Blog

The library's Information Technology Department handled the creation of the blog. In the first year, they built a site from scratch with different elements that came together each day: a poem to read, a poem to write, a library book to check out, and (in the first year only) a poetry website to visit.

In the second year, they simplified the process, using a blog template from the library's content management system and customizing just a few elements.

CCPL's Graphics Department also designed an eye-catching logo and styled headlines that matched our library's branding, plus a colorful graphic for each daily poem.

Once all of the poems, prompts, library books and poetry websites had been collated, staff in our Communications and External Relations Division uploaded the content in March to be ready for the April 1 debut.

The Unknowns

Even as they were planning the content and imagining the structure of the blog, Kincer and Kendig had two important questions. First, would local poets freely give the library permission to use one of their poems in this new blog? The answer was that most responded quickly and positively and, within days, had granted permission and sent in biographical copy.

A second question loomed: would the blog find an audience? Again, the response far exceeded expectations. When *Read + Write: 30 Days of Poetry* went live in mid–March of 2014 and through the month of April, nearly 600 readers subscribed to it. Another nearly 600 would sign up again in the same time frame in 2015. Additionally, year-round online browsers found it and became subscribers in months outside of March and April, bringing the total as of this writing to 1,283.

Getting the Word Out and Attracting Subscribers

So, how exactly does one library attract over 1200 readers to its National Poetry Month blog?

In the first year of the project, Robert Pinsky happened to be appearing at the library's

For the first year of Read + Write: 30 Days of Poetry, Cuyahoga County Public Library's website included four elements which combined each day in April to create a unique page. The elements were Read a Poem, which included a poem by a local poet, along with a photograph of the poet and a short biography; Write a Poem, a poetry writing prompt; Visit a Poetry Site, highlighting outstanding poetry websites; and Check Out this Book, featuring a poetry book available through the library.

Writers Center Stage in April. Those who subscribed to the blog before April 1 had their names entered into a drawing for two free tickets (a $60 value) to attend Pinsky's event.

Three other factors also helped boost subscriptions to the blog.

1. The library sent an e-mail to its complete mailing list of thousands in early March, inviting them to subscribe to *Read + Write: 30 Days of Poetry*. It also used all of its social media outlets to promote the blog and encourage readers to subscribe.

2. The featured poets themselves became ambassadors for the blog. Most posted a link to the website on their website or social media the first day and again on the day their poem appeared. A few of the featured poets were college professors who shared the blog with their classes, in some cases offering extra credit to write poems using the daily prompts. Two poets mentioned it during their weekly poetry radio show, on a local college radio station. Two other poets posted it on a local poetry blog which serves as a popular clearinghouse of local literary information.

3. Kendig herself promoted it online far beyond Cleveland to her contacts across Ohio and the United States. One high school teacher, a former football player and college student of Diane's, read about the project on her Facebook page and wrote to say that he was using it as a class project. Kendig also shared it with WOM-PO, a well-regarded listserv created in 1997 for the purpose of discussing women's poetry.

Community Response

In its first year, in addition to having nearly 600 initial subscribers, the blog had an extremely high e-mail open rate ranging from 30 percent to 60 percent. Over both years, the library received positive feedback from many in the community. They expressed gratitude and appreciation, spoke of what it meant to the local poetry scene, and lauded the library for its support of poets and poetry.

Helpful Hints: What to Do

Here are a few recommendations for anyone considering a similar project.

1. Obtain written permissions from poets. A simple email works fine. Put it in a file and forget about it. You just need to have it to protect yourself from any misunderstandings.

2. Work from a scanned image of the published poem for accuracy's sake. This is particularly crucial with concrete poetry, but it is important for any poem since a scanned image avoids human transcription errors and settles all questions.

3. Begin early. In November, brainstorm a list of poets to contact, in order of preference. Spend December and January contacting poets, collecting poems, gathering permissions, writing poetry prompts and creating a list of poetry books. Use February to edit content. In March, upload content and graphics, so you're ready to begin publishing posts on April 1.

4. Create opportunities for interaction. In the blog's second year, the library added three elements that created opportunities for online and in person interaction. First, they inserted a comment section in the blog. Readers could comment, compliment and even post their own work there. The library also added a Twitter feed on the page and created the hashtag #readwritepoetry. Using this hashtag, readers often commented about their own writing progress during the month and tagged other sites, too, so that the library became part of a wider conversation. Finally, the library added a live open mic at one of our branches on the last day of April, inviting everyone, particularly those who had been writing in response to the daily prompts. The open mic attracted over twenty participants, including a wide range of ages, experiences and styles.

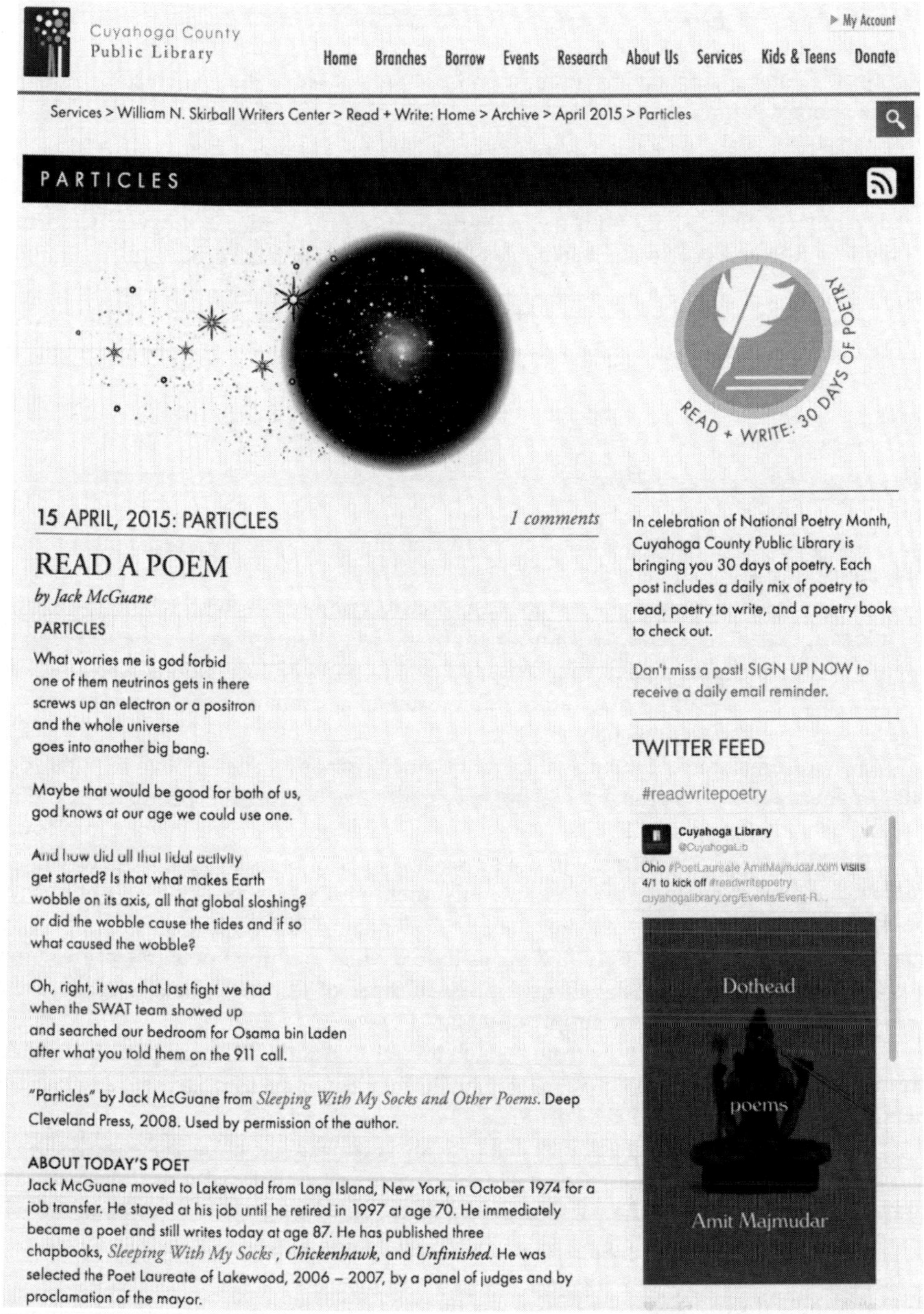

In the second year of Read + Write: 30 Days of Poetry, Cuyahoga County Public Library streamlined the site by creating daily pages that could be archived in their entirety. The library retained the elements of Read a Poem (a poem by a local poet and a short biography) and Write a Poem (a poetry writing prompt). It added a comments section and moved the library poetry book recommendations into a Twitter feed. Each day, the Library posted a different book in its collection to Twitter with the hashtag #readwritepoetry.

What Not to Do

In the interests of having the best end product possible, here are a few pieces of advice about what not to do.

1. Do not attempt to pair representational art with the poems. Representational art assigns too restrictive a meaning to poems, which are purposely subtle and multilayered. Graphics should not try to do the work of the reader in any way. Colorful, subtle and abstract patterns can complement the poems without reducing them simplistically.
2. Do not conduct an open call for submissions, which would necessarily lead to the unpleasant business of rejecting poets. Instead, choose poets and poems and invite their participation.

Trying It at Your Library

This project is something that any motivated library can do with the right community connections.

Where can librarians find the right community connections with whom to partner on a local poetry blog? They will find them by paying attention to the poetry scene in their area, attending local poetry readings, being familiar with local poetry websites, and reading local poets' work. When librarians are aware of and attentive to their community's poetry scene, collaborations happen organically.

If your library cannot identify thirty local poets, expand your scope to include your state or your region. You probably will not have to do that, but the Internet makes reaching out to poets in other parts of your state as easy as reaching out to one in your own town.

More likely, your challenge will not be too few worthy poets to feature but too many. In that case, making sure that you feature only poets with at least one non-self-published book is a useful filter to apply to your search. Kendig and Kincer knew in the first year that they wanted to continue to the blog as long as they had fine poets to feature. They are working on year three now, bringing the number of featured poets to ninety, and they haven't yet exhausted the supply of talented poets.

While CCPL created a blog from scratch in year one and used a template from their content management system in year two, any library could customize the free blogging platforms available online, like WordPress, Blogger or Tumblr.

The support that a larger library can provide is convenient but even a small library can bring local poetry to your patrons' inbox. Chances are that many of them will take time to write and express their appreciation, as they did with CCPL. Your library will make a name for itself as a supporter of local writers and writing.

Beyond that, there is the appreciation of the poets themselves. Not a single poet has turned Kendig down. As she contacts poets in preparation for year three of the blog, she has received enthusiastic responses expressing delight and honor to be included in 2016's *Read + Write: 30 Days of Poetry*.

So, in answer to the question, "What could the library add to the crowded field of online poetry?" the library says, "We have brought it home."

Rich Soil for Poetry in Rural Cajun Louisiana

PATRICIA BROWN, MAURA GAGE CAVELL *and*
AVA LEAVELL HAYMON

"You want to write? There's the library. You've got to go in and read."—
U.S. Poet Laureate Charles Wright, quoting poet Theodore Roethke.

Introduction to Rurality

In this turbulent time of privatization, commercialization, and electrification, poets William Carlos Williams (1988) and Adrienne Rich (1993) remind us that

men die miserably every day
for lack
of what is found there [in poems].
Hear me out
for I too am concerned

about poetry and the human nurture it provides. The rich culture of rural rice-and-crawfish south Louisiana is home to many poets and performers, though getting larger audiences together with them can be difficult. The Eunice campus of Louisiana State University (LSU) is thus fortunate to have a literary journal on campus and two state poets laureate within easy driving distance. With several published poets on its faculty, LSU Eunice is fertile ground for the creation, appreciation, and study of poetry. The Arnold LeDoux Library's collection of contemporary poetry includes regional authors such as Miller Williams, Ava Leavell Haymon, Robert Penn Warren, Darrell Bourque, Dave Smith, Pinkie Gordon Lane, and George Garrett. Since 2013, the LeDoux Library has increased its support of local live poetry by inviting Louisiana poets laureate to speak and by establishing an annual public reading event.

However, like any agricultural endeavor, cultivating poetry is a communal process. At LSU Eunice, it is also an interdepartmental, boundary-crossing endeavor. LeDoux's reference and instruction librarian, Patricia Brown, worked with professor Maura Gage Cavell and other colleagues and students in a collaboration which has become increasingly significant on campus. Although libraries have come to rely on computerization, their primary mission is still to bring people together with knowledge. James K. Elmborg

(2011) described how libraries might guide them across the border between their private selves and the larger world. In Eunice, the boundary is partly a physical one: the campus of LSUE sits between the town to the northeast and the fields from east to southwest. New students and employees cross from present to future to explore new ideas and new lives in the classroom and at the library. Teacher-librarian Amy Price Azano (2014) suggests that "libraries offer students and teachers a unique opportunity to consider place and rurality" (63).

Narrative Background: The Librarian's Perspective

Patricia Brown, Librarian and Professor

After a career of teaching English in college, I moved to south Louisiana to work and teach at the academic library of LSUE. The job combined my interests in literature, books, and students, and an outdoor poetry event seemed like a good venue for all three. I sat in on a poetry-writing class to find out what poetry was like from a student-writer's view. Dr. Cavell and I had worked together on library instruction for freshman English classes, so the poetry event was a natural expansion of library-classroom collaboration. While arranging for National Poetry Month to be officially recognized by the mayors of Eunice and Crowley, we planned an open reading called "Refreshments: Spring Poetry." Held on the quadrangle in front of the library building, the noontime event has continued every April, providing a microphone for readers, chairs for an audience, food and drink for both, and balmy spring beauty for all.

There had, of course, been poetry readings on campus before my arrival. In addition to regular events arranged by library directors, for some years *The Louisiana Review* held a reading series downtown at the locally owned Cafe Mosaic. Poet laureate Darrell Bourque had pitched a literary double-header in October 2013, reading at Cafe Mosaic and the LeDoux Library. When I learned that Ava Haymon had been also named poet laureate, I arranged for her to visit Eunice for a triple bill of readings and class sessions. Under her tutelage, each class wrote a line-poem, comprised of one line from each student which began with the same phrase, "the student who." None of those responses were specifically rural, nothing like "the student who does chores before class."

For the 2016 "Refreshments: Spring Poetry," we were inspired by Azano's "Rural: the Other Neglected 'R'" to use rurality as a theme. As a guest lecturer in Dr. Cavell's poetry class, I explained the evolution of this poetry project; then I taught the quatrain form and we did a found-poetry exercise. First I arranged two sentences from the Elmborg article (p. 346) into four-line stanzas, without changing any words or punctuation.

> The extreme orderliness of the library provides
> a thin veneer over an otherwise seemingly
> endless and sometimes chaotic context
> for discovery of the unknown....
>
> Every user of the library can be understood
> as a borderland person, intellectually crossing
> boundaries and moving between what she or he is and
> what she or he hopes to become.

Then the students "found" or assembled quatrains from a previous assignment. They had written prose about horses and cows and fields, about positive attitudes and character traits, about hunting and fishing and riding horses in Courir de Mardi Gras. Most of the responses valued their rural life, whereas only one (an urban transplant) called it negative.

Here are three representative quatrains from the found-poetry exercise:

When I was young, I lived in Buras, Louisiana
My family consisted of crawfish farmers and shrimp men
I wore a string of pearls while my sister wore muddy feet
I believe in individuality despite the crowd who raised you
—Keonna Clark

growing up in a close knit community
one becomes involved with rural life
whether it is helping a family harvest rice
or riding a horse for Mardi Gras
—Wesley Blanchard and Dylan Reed

As a child, I lived in a rural area
There were no near neighbors
And animals ran free
It provided me with a way of life
—Holly LeJeune

Even in these short stanzas, one can see the variety of rural experience. Rather than separating themselves from their upbringing, the poets kept the sense of life they had learned, as they grew up and moved on.

Interviews: Poets Speak About Rural Influences

First in this section are several responses by LSUE faculty to a question about how the rural setting influences their work. Then follows a written interview with visiting poet Ava Haymon.

Maura Gage Cavell, Poet and Professor

I find crawfish ponds, fields, reeds, water, egrets' flight—the details and images around me as I'm driving to and from work and other rural areas—pervade many of my poems. Horses, farmers, babies on porches, tea, barns, burning fields, and sugar cane have become some of the details in the fabric of my poems.

From "Her Farmhouse Porch" (2016):

she grabs the baby and heads inside
perhaps to make a meal for the men

who are tending to crops
and burning what was not wanted.

The people with whom I work and teach influence my vision of the world as there is a closeness they share with the land, a sense of family life and ties to the area that are a part of who they are. I write of their fishing details shared with me, their love of the water and boats, their love of music and dance. One cannot live here and not be touched by what is the Cajun culture.

Mardi Gras may be colorful and lively, but it the Cajun people who fill the air, the sky, and the land with its richest hues.

Kenneth Elliott, Poet and Administrator

... the short answer is that I am not influenced in my work—at least not in any way that I can abstract and articulate from experience—by my small-town life and job at a rural college....

What influences my poetry is not settings so much as events, real or imagined. I have written about farmlands when living in suburbia. I've written about industrial zones dense with factories and grit when living next to an open field, deafened by the chirruping of tree frogs. About beaches I conjure from the beaches I've visited. About forests and mountains and chaparrals that I've never visited or that I have made up whole cloth.

I suppose I'm much more influenced by books and nature documentaries than I am about the rurality of my current life. I tend to write about things that have ended for me long ago as I try to understand them, put them in some context for my life as I live it now. Most of what I've ever written about "rural life" I wrote before I ever moved to a small town, to an agricultural area. I made it up. It was a setting for events, the unfolding and unraveling of relationships; it was a well of images to concretize the decay and loss of love, of connection. It was sensual desolation distilled into words, as in these lines from my "Pouring Libation" (2015):

> There's not much to do but drink and watch the rain.
> Midget trees on the horizon move closer, become dusky travelers
> overburdened with distance, their feet padded in blisters.
> The grass catches flame in the wind, burns smokeless, holds fire
> deep in every twisting blade.

Diane Langlois, Poet, Professor, and Painter

I am a city person, born and raised in Hartford, Connecticut. I have since lived in Washington, D.C., and smaller cities. I neither live on a farm nor way out in the country although as a child one summer, I stayed with my grandparents on their farm in remote northern Maine. I loved it. The place smelled of natural stuff, like hay and pigs and sweet rain, and all I had previously experienced at that time were man-built constructs, like museums and movies and libraries available on foot. I loved this, too. In my child's experience, that farm meant peace and quiet. The city meant frenzy and life. Both were fine with me.

Now, many, many years later, there is no doubt I prefer living in cities, but there is also little doubt that I could ever write or paint—or engage in thoughtful ventures—without periodically embracing a quiet, introspective escapism. I drive forty-five miles one way to my job (teaching English at a branch of LSU), and I find myself deliberately seeking the back roads. I never turn on the radio. I see white egrets and orange traps in crawfish ponds; I see pretty horses beside simple homes; I hear the wind; I listen to nothing (but my own thoughts). Sometimes, I am even fortunate enough to remember a few thoughts that bubble to the surface—as seeds of poems, stories, and even paintings. "Rurality," or whatever it is called, affords that peace that contrasts with energy. Both mean life, and both are necessary. I can't construct a complete picture unless I have first looked at a complete picture.

Billy Fontenot, Professor and Short Story Writer

I grew up in the Acadiana area of Louisiana, and now I teach college English in the same rural area. In the classroom, this has affected my teaching in a beneficial way. I have a good idea of my students' backgrounds and the breadth of their knowledge of the world at age seventeen or eighteen. One of a teacher's jobs is to help students make connections, and since I came from the same place as my students, I often can relate aspects of literature to things/events found in Acadiana life (such as Mardi Gras, Cajun food, Cajun customs). For example, the carnival season in Edgar Allan Poe's "The Cask of Amontillado" is readily understandable to my students when I compare it to Mardi Gras. During their visits to the library to research their essay topics, perhaps this connection reinforces their understanding.

I also write short stories (my Ph.D. is in English—Creative Writing). Most of my stories are set in rural South Louisiana, and I often consult texts from the library that describe pre-twentieth century Acadiana. For example, one of my stories concerns Cajun *traiteurs*, or healers, who practiced homeopathic medicine in rural areas until the mid–twentieth century, and several library texts offer invaluable descriptions of this practice.

Ava Leavell Haymon, Poet Laureate and Teacher

How was your laureate visit to Eunice? Did it affect your work afterwards?

Being in Eunice and at LSUE was a high point in my term as poet laureate. The faculty was welcoming and fun to hang around with. The librarian had arranged for me to stay in a beautiful historic place, a restored 1910 house with access to old cypress outbuildings—including a 19th-century country store moved from Turkey Creek, Louisiana, where it was a location of one of the last attempted robberies by the infamous couple, Bonnie and Clyde. The house and buildings now are surrounded by natural landscape, plant life, insect life of course, and birds.

The students appealed to me in their unspoiled curiosity and openness. Most had never seen "a poet" before, many had perhaps never thought about there being any still alive. They were willing to try any activity I proposed, even risking vulnerability, and to share their ideas for a poem readily even in a large class.

I suspect that they have kept this openness and genuine curiosity because they are mainly from rural families. They have not moved to town and become jaded.

How do you see the connections among your art and your teaching?

Making art and teaching both come very naturally to me. And teaching poetry writing seems to arise from the same ineluctable place that poems do. I'm as happy when a student pulls off a good line, as I am when I do it myself. I do try not to teach students to write like I do. I want them to learn to write like THEY do, which is much more difficult than copying someone else. I work hard to get students to find their own best material—those things that they are most driven to say. That drive will fuel the astonishing amount of work that it takes to get a poem down on paper and to get it revised. Once the student learns that those explosive and honest words can find body, clarity, and communication if they are used as the driver of poems, then, I know that student is in for life. I do teach craft, I teach craft intensely, but if that connection to personal expression is missing, not only is there no energy to learn craft, but the poems that might get made are boring.

The connection with my work? The right material is found and expressed in the act of writing; craft is learned in the work to express it and to express it clearly. This is what I learned during my long apprenticeship in poetry writing (which is not over, I hope), and this is the strategy for writing that I seek to teach. When I see it happen, I am thrilled, and that usually powers me into a new poem of my own.

How has being Louisiana's Poet Laureate been important to you?

I have found the formal position of Poet Laureate affirming and valuable, and it's made possible for me to produce some very satisfying work. I have traveled all over our endlessly interesting Louisiana, met many people fascinated with the great art form and working at writing their own poems. I gave forty-two readings by informal count, taught poetry writing to thousands of school children, presented poetry writing workshops in colleges and universities, to groups in libraries, coffee shops, book clubs, and high school poetry clubs. I spoke to elementary and secondary teachers about good ways to teach poetry in their classes. I gave a reading and a workshop at Angola to incarcerated men who were reading and writing poetry of their own.

I have sought to encourage Spoken Word poetry which is a groundswell everywhere I've been and to introduce the poets all over the state to each other in the hopes that we can make common cause and support each other. I've done whatever I could to bring poetry into the public discourse. It was a strenuous and full two years. I wouldn't have missed it for the world.

Interlude: "Groundhog's Prayer of Petition," from *Eldest Daughter*.

Weather
Before our eyes
Close

Two lines from "Reentry: Agricultural Horizon" in *The Strict Economy of Fire*:

that portion of food measured out
on a common scale I acknowledge

You were not raised in rural areas, but from reading your poems, I can see that you must have spent a lot of time there. What are some of the less obvious ways rurality has affected your poems?

A: I grew up living in cities during the school year but traveling for some part of every summer, and most holidays, to my grandmother's house in the country in the Mississippi Delta. I have written a good deal about being there, and just writing these words has brought back the smell to me of alluvium and DDT. A tomboy at all times, in the city I climbed trees, played with lizards, and slept in the back yard, but in the country not only did I do all these things but I rode horses bareback, picked some cotton, watched crops come and go, jigged for "crawdads" by the creek, jumped in hay in the barn, chased pigs and churned butter. I could see both sun and moon through the entirety of their arcs because the ground is so flat there.

The country is so much quieter than the city. When your ears can calm down, your other senses can grow more acute. Land and water, sky and mud, are experienced in smell, taste, sight, touch, and sound equally. This touches memory in a different way.

In the country, you do not learn to be squeamish. You see people shoot deer, you see piglets suckle, grow, and know they'll be butchered (always after I was back in the city, of course). You see blood and death, and you face different dangers than you face in the city. I know I am marked by this, and in a valuable way.

I do not, however, sentimentalize life there. Education is poor in many cases, good medical care is hours away, you have few choices in friends and in entertainment. It appeals to me because I love to be outdoors, and I'm an introvert and a reader, but I'd be one of the ones sometimes lamented as they move into the city as soon as they possibly can. My mother had grown up in that very place. She could "put down" her own beloved dogs when they got too old, but she never could get over her fear of life in the city. She raised me in the city, but from her I always knew that I was being raised away from home.

Conclusion

In April, the LeDoux librarians print event flyers for bulletin boards and local media, submit work orders for arranging chairs outside and serving light food and drink, procure a podium and a microphone, urge people to attend, and hope for good turnout and nice weather. The poets who live, work, visit, or write at LSU Eunice engage in a reciprocal encounter with students, faculty, the library, and our lush rural setting. Because "Refreshments: Spring Poetry" is held outside, the poems of place and particularity come alive environmentally as well as poetically.

Poetry will persevere—
printed in books,
penciled in spiral notebooks,
penned on paper coffee napkins,
tapped out in 140 characters or txt-msgs,
performed during spring noontides to new audiences.

And libraries? Insofar as they free those minds to create, guide them across borders, and nourish them with the work of other writers, libraries shall not pass away.

Works Cited

Azano, Amy Price. 2014. "Rural. The Other Neglected 'R': Making Space for Place in School Libraries." *Knowledge Quest* 43, no. 1: 60–65. ERIC (EJ1041889).
Cavell, Maura Gage. 2016. "Her Farmhouse Porch." *Louisiana Literature* 33, no. 1: 12.
Elliott, Kenneth. 2015. "Pouring Libation." *Illya's Honey* (Fall): 13.
Elmborg, James K. 2011. "Libraries as the Spaces Between Us: Recognizing and Valuing the Third Space." *Reference & User Services Quarterly* 50, no. 4: 338–350. JSTOR (edsjsr.20865425).
Haymon, Ava Leavell. 2013. *Eldest Daughter*. Baton Rouge: LSU Press.
_____. 2004. *The Strict Economy of Fire*. Baton Rouge: LSU Press.
Rich, Adrienne. 1993. *What Is Found There: Notebooks on Poetry and Politics*. New York: W.W. Norton.
Williams, William Carlos. 1988. "Asphodel, That Greeny Flower." In *The Collected Poems of William Carlos Williams*, vol. 2, edited by Christopher MacGowan, 310–337. New York: New Directions.
Wright, Charles. 2015. "Charles Wright, the 2014–2015 Poet Laureate Consultant in Poetry, Discusses His Love of Poetry." *Library of Congress Magazine* (March/April 2015): 28. http://www.loc.gov/lcm/pdf/LCM_2015_0304.pdf.

Outreach Through Play, Creation and Inquiry

Classes and Workshops at the University of Arizona Poetry Center

Wendy Burk, Sarah Kortemeier *and* Cybele Knowles

The University of Arizona Poetry Center is a special collections library located on the campus of The University of Arizona in Tucson. The Poetry Center is home to one of the nation's most extensive and accessible collections of contemporary poetry. The institution offers a wide array of public literary programming, including a Reading and Lecture Series, children's programs, and discussion groups. In this article, we discuss one of the Poetry Center's most popular offerings, the Classes and Workshops program, a fee-supported program that employs professional writers as teachers and connects these authors with the local writing community.

Goals of the Classes and Workshops Program

The primary goal of the Poetry Center's Classes and Workshops Program is to provide high-quality education that helps students improve their writing, develop a better understanding of the literary landscape, and create publishable work. Related goals are to engage Classes and Workshops students with other aspects of the Poetry Center and to provide employment opportunities for local writers to teach creative writing.

The Classes and Workshops program strives to function as a close-knit community of writers who return for multiple classes, growing their writing through the program. This provides a sustained experience of community that is accessible to writers at all stages of development, from beginning writers to those with graduate degrees. In 2012, the program began hosting an end-of-semester public reading, in which students and teachers read from their writing in the Poetry Center's auditorium. This reading helps students prepare and experience their writing in a new way, by reading it in front of a public audience. The event also reveals the Classes and Workshops community to itself and to others, reinforcing connections in the community.

Students and Teachers

A wide range of students enroll in the Poetry Center's non-credit community classes, including many students who have had lifelong aspirations to write and are pursuing this goal later in life. A majority of Classes and Workshops students are between the ages of forty and sixty-five. Other students are alumni of the University of Arizona's Master of Fine Arts program in Creative Writing who are seeking additional opportunities to develop as writers. Occasionally, university and high school students enroll in classes. A special Parent/Child Writing Summit is offered for families with children over the age of eight.

Teachers for the program include two groups. First, emerging and established writers from the local Tucson community teach most of the long-format classes, which typically range from six to eight weeks in duration. Locally based teachers have typically earned an M.F.A. degree, often from the University of Arizona, and have published professionally in literary journals or single-author books.

Second, shorter-format classes taught over the course of a single day or weekend expand the Poetry Center's teaching opportunities to writers based outside of Tucson. Visiting writers who teach in the program typically do so as part of a previously arranged visit to Tucson to present their writing in the Poetry Center's Reading and Lecture Series. Tucson boasts a vibrant writing community that appreciates opportunities to study with well-known authors based outside of Southern Arizona. In spring 2016, classes taught by visiting writers Mark Wunderlich, Kimiko Hahn, Khadijah Queen, and David Baker have quickly filled.

Structure and Administration

While most of the Poetry Center's programming is free and open to the public, the Classes and Workshops program is supported by registration fees. In the 2014–15 year, the Poetry Center offered 17 courses, employed 14 writers as instructors, and sold 179 registrations. This represents $23,258 in registration fees, or an average of $130 per person, per class.

After financial transaction charges, scholarships, and course material reimbursements are deducted, the registration fees for each course are split sixty percent to forty percent. The course instructor receives sixty percent of the fees as an honorarium, and the Poetry Center retains forty percent. In the 2014–2015 academic year, the Poetry Center's income from the Classes and Workshops program was $7000. This income is invested in the Poetry Center's free community programming, including the Reading and Lecture Series and literary programs for children and families. While the income represents a small percentage of the Poetry Center's annual programs budget, it does make an impact.

Although registration fees are modest by design, some community members cannot afford to take a class at full price. The Poetry Center works to make classes and workshops accessible to writers with financial need in various ways. The Mary Ann Campau and Will Inman Scholarships Program provides $75 scholarships to three students each during the fall, spring, and summer class sessions. In addition, Poetry Center docents, staff, and weekly volunteers receive a discount when they enroll in classes and workshops.

Administration of the program is primarily carried out by one employee and represents approximately fifteen hours of work per week, with an increased workload at the beginning and end of each class session. The program coordinator plans the course schedule up to two years in advance, scheduling courses based on demand, instructor availability, diversity, and variety. In selecting teachers and classes, the coordinator aims to bring in new instructors, bring back well-received teachers, be diverse in hiring, and offer a wide variety of course topics.

Sometimes, instructors request the coordinator's assistance to develop new courses or fine-tune a course proposal. The primary key to success in a course proposal or description is representing the goals and format of the course as specifically as possible. This ensures that the Poetry Center can promote the class or workshop effectively and that the students begin the course with accurate expectations. When students are accomplishing what they expect to accomplish, they view a class as successful. Students can understandably be disappointed by a course that does not match their expectations, even if the quality of the instruction is high.

The coordinator begins publicizing the courses about a month prior to the start of each fall, spring, and summer class session. Most students learn about classes and workshops through the Poetry Center's web site. Classes frequently sell out, or come close to doing so. For this reason, returning students often call the Poetry Center to find out on what day the course schedule will be first available. The Poetry Center's e-news bulletin and Facebook, Twitter, and Instagram accounts are other avenues by which students learn about upcoming course offerings.

Registrations and payments are primarily processed online, while the scholarship program is directly administered by the coordinator. At the start of each session, the coordinator attends the first meeting of every class to ensure that the students and the instructor know how to use the library and its resources. Throughout the session, the coordinator offers individual support to instructors and students. At the end of each course, the coordinator administers online course evaluations, which are compiled and shared with the course instructor.

Writing Classes Offered Through the Program

The Poetry Center's Classes and Workshops program specializes in poetry writing workshops. Workshop topics offered in recent years include introductory poetry writing, lyric poetry, poetic forms, poetry of witness, prose poems, and haiku. Other workshops have focused on writing poems that address specific subject matter, such as healing, disability, or ecology.

The Poetry Center also offers an increasing number of courses that reach beyond poetry. Highly successful workshops have been taught in literary translation, fiction, nonfiction, playwriting, letterpress printing, and improvisation. Lastly, the Center offers literature courses focusing on topics such as sound poetry, women poets, the New York School, and postmodern poetry.

Of all of the classes and workshops, foundational and introductory courses enjoy enduring popularity. Introductory workshops also work best as courses that can be repeated multiple times to attract new students to the Poetry Center. For example, the course with the highest enrollment in the spring 2016 is simply titled Writing Poems. On the other hand, many of the Poetry Center's experienced instructors have followings of students who are eager to take any classes that they offer, on any topic.

A number of the Poetry Center's classes and workshops help to connect students and teachers with the Center's library collections. For example, in Fall 2015, poet Joni Wallace taught a class on "The Art of the Chapbook." In this course, students wrote and revised ten to twelve pages of poems, then assembled their poems into chapbooks ("little books") of their own design and construction. The first class meeting of The Art of the Chapbook included a field trip to the Poetry Center's L. R. Benes Rare Book Room, where students experienced an exhibit of chapbooks prepared for the course by the Center's library staff in consultation with Wallace. At the end of the course, Wallace arranged for an exhibit of her student's handmade chapbooks, which remained on display for a month in the Center's Jeremy Ingalls Gallery.

Other courses have been designed specifically for students to interact with the Poetry Center's digital collections. For example, the curriculum of a course titled Women's Voices in Poetry was built around Voca (http://voca.arizona.edu), the Poetry Center's online audiovisual library of author recordings. To date, Voca includes more than 800 recordings, representing more than fifty years of writers reading their work as part of the Poetry Center's Reading and Lecture Series. In the Women's Voices in Poetry course, students used Voca each week to listen to the actual voices of twentieth and twenty-first century women poets reading their own work.

Because many writers come to the library seeking information on how to publish their work, the Poetry Center has offered, and plans to repeat, a free one-day class on literary publishing for authors. The class is designed to introduce writers at all levels of experience to the process of researching the writing market and submitting work for publication. Most writers of literary poetry, fiction, and nonfiction begin publishing their work in print and online literary journals. The Poetry Center subscribes to more than 250 print literary journals, which often serve as a good starting point for literary market research.

While anyone can come to the Poetry Center and browse the Periodicals section, many writers are not aware of how to start the process. In addition, many writers have questions about how the Internet has changed the publishing landscape. A free literary publishing class helps writers navigate these questions. It also helps them understand how using library collections is an important part of furthering and promoting their own writing.

Teacher and Student Professional Development

The Poetry Center's Classes and Workshops program provides meaningful professional development for both teacher and student participants. Professional development benefits to the working writers who serve as instructors center around the joys of teaching in a generative, playful, non-evaluative environment geared toward creation, self-paced progress, and discovery. At the same time, the Classes and Workshops program also offers teachers tangible benefits with regard to current and future employment as writers. For many teachers, Classes and Workshops are the first opportunity to teach creative writing after receiving a graduate M.F.A. degree. A number of teachers have gone on to full-time creative writing faculty positions after teaching classes and workshops at the Poetry Center.

Whether they are new to creative writing or already have an undergraduate or graduate degree in the subject, students benefit equally from the playful, generative, creation- and inquiry-driven focus of the Classes and Workshops program. Students have described the Classes and Workshops experience as the most fun they have ever had while writing. Free of outside expectations and formal evaluations, students can focus on developing writing projects that matter to them.

In addition, having working writers as teachers provides students with role models that encourage their professional development as writers. A number of student projects started in the Classes and Workshops program have gone on to be published. Likewise, students who plan to apply for graduate study in Creative Writing find the classes to be a good venue for them to strengthen their writing samples and pursue letters of recommendation, which are the most important components of the graduate M.F.A. application.

Teaching as Librarians

Many staff members at the Poetry Center have earned graduate degrees in Creative Writing. Not surprisingly, the Poetry Center provides opportunities for library employees with an M.F.A. degree to participate in the Classes and Workshops program as instructors. At the Poetry Center, all instructors, including staff members, are hired as independent contractors. They receive the same stipend as other instructors within the program, and their responsibilities as teachers fall outside of their regular work responsibilities.

Depending on the employee's responsibilities within the Poetry Center's library and individual teaching style, the roles of librarian and teacher may intersect a great deal. For example, the daily responsibilities of the Poetry Center's Library Specialist include coordinating field trips and building curricula for university students. Thus, her daily work in the library is closely tied to the introductory and foundational poetry courses she teaches through the Classes and Workshops program.

The concept of teaching as librarians opens a door for libraries that are interested in starting a classes and workshops program, but that do not have a mechanism to accept registration fees or that do not wish to launch a fee-supported program. Librarians who work in public programming and instruction are accustomed to providing programs that promote a deep engagement with literary works. The Classes and Workshops model promotes a longer-term, more sustained version of this engagement with literature and writing. It also promotes deep student engagement with the library as a community resource. Librarians teaching in a classes and workshops program may find, as the Poetry Center's library staff have found, that occasional library users deepen their engagement with the library first by becoming students, and then by becoming volunteers, docents, and donors.

Advice on Adapting the Classes and Workshops Model

The Poetry Center's Classes and Workshops model draws some of its strength from its unique organizational aspects, such as its world-class collection of contemporary poetry, and the proximity and support of The University of Arizona's thriving Creative Writing program. Indeed, Tucson is particularly notable for the richness of its literary community. Yet the concept of a classes and workshops program for community writers is highly adaptable to other settings and other types of libraries.

A library that is interested in offering creative writing classes should take time and care recruiting teachers who can be effective with their potential student group. Significant time spent thinking about the needs of the communities of students to be served is time well spent. This planning process will enable the library to recruit teachers who can effectively meet students' needs. In assessing student needs as well as recruiting teachers, libraries should consider who are the trusted writers, storytellers, and teachers already practicing in the community.

Equally important, we advise the creation of courses that are broadly defined and can be offered on a repeat basis, such as introductory and foundational courses. Courses with inclusive titles, such as Writing Poems, have appeal for advanced as well as beginning writers. This can promote a multi-level classroom environment in which students learn from each other's experiences and proficiencies.

At the same time, setting accurate expectations of what will happen in the classroom is key. To be satisfied with the outcomes of a course, students must feel that they accomplished what they expected to accomplish and feel that the pace of the course was appropriate to them. At the Poetry Center, this is facilitated by the non-credit, non-graded format of the community classes and workshops. Students come to the classes expecting a generative, playful, and safe environment for them to explore their writing. This permits students with varying goals to experience positive outcomes.

While the Poetry Center's courses are instructor-designed, or designed in collaboration between instructor and Classes and Workshops coordinator, this model is not necessary for a successful program. We strongly encourage libraries to consider creating an in-house template for an introductory creative writing course that can be taught by many teachers. The Poetry Center's web site includes a free library of creative writing lesson plans for students of all ages, from young children to university students and adults. These lessons cover literary genres including poetry, fiction, and non-fiction/memoir.

Lastly, we advise libraries offering creative writing classes to think in terms of questions rather than rules. Particularly in the genre of poetry, a widespread public perception exists that writing must fit within a narrowly defined structure. For example, teaching or studying poetry may seem intimidating if one believes that poems must (or should not) rhyme, make sense, or address certain subjects, such as personal experience. We believe that poetry can raise questions and expand existing structures, rather than reinscribe those structures or prescribe rules.

Conclusion

The Poetry Center's Classes and Workshops program promotes meaningful, accessible personal and professional development for the writers who teach and learn within the program. It encourages occasional library users to return to the Poetry Center on a regular basis and deepen their engagement with the library's resources. It provides a source of income for writers who teach in the program, as well as for the Poetry Center, which uses income from course registration fees to support its wide array of free public literary programming.

We believe that the affective aspects of the Poetry Center's Classes and Workshops program contribute strongly to its success. As creative writers ourselves, we know that it can be difficult to keep writing alive as a practice in one's daily life. It is meaningful to see Classes and Workshops students continuing to grow as writers, and to hear about their successes in completing creative projects and achieving publication. In many cases, we are given the opportunity to observe the path taken by their creative work over a period of years. We appreciate the fact that our library provides an open, flexible, safe space where writers can develop new works of literature within a supportive community. When we look up from our desks and see a class taking place, or when we engage in conversation with students or instructors, we are given a new way to think about the value of our workplace, and the value of libraries in general.

Publication Talks and Book Review Workshops

Spotlighting Faculty Publication, Emerging Authors and Book Reviews as an Effective Personal Branding Strategy

NINA Q. ROSE,
RAÚL FERNÁNDEZ-CALIENES *and*
HAGAI GRINGARTEN

Universities are home to authors of all kinds, from scholarly authors publishing journal articles and monographs to authors of creative works teaching in departments such as humanities. While publishing once was thought to be the domain of faculty and graduate student authors of theses and dissertations, undergraduate students are increasingly securing first publications with the burgeoning emphasis on undergraduate research, the rise in student-edited journals, and the ease of self-publishing on blogging applications and widely disseminating one's work on the Web. Libraries not only provide access to the knowledge that faculty publish, they provide the platforms for faculty and students to produce journals and blogs, openly disseminate student and faculty work in digital repositories, and teach about maximizing scholarly impact by making one's work freely available on the Web, including via social media. Academic libraries are now playing integral roles in the production and dissemination of scholarship and other works through various library publishing activities (Lippincott 2016).

Within this environment, libraries can provide additional services to support student and faculty publishing such as hosting publication event series, where selected authors are invited to the library to give talks about their recent publications. Alongside these talks, libraries also can host workshops on how to break into scholarly publishing by writing a book review. This is particularly important when most faculty members in the United States self-report never having published in a peer-reviewed journal (Gringarten, Fernández-Calienes, and Mitchell 2015). Why book reviews? Book reviews are an easier start for students and staff looking to publish their first article. While they are low-hanging fruit for faculty, book reviews provide opportunities for reviewers to consciously develop their personal brand.

Not an academic librarian? Many of the ideas presented here can be morphed into event series featuring local authors, and working professionals in your community may be equally interested in publishing book reviews to shape their personal brand.

Faculty and Student Publication Talks

Faculty publication talks are an easy event series for libraries to host, particularly for those libraries that already track and feature recent faculty publications on the library website or on a physical display. At St. Thomas University Library in Miami Gardens, Florida, we have a "Hot Off the Press" shelf featuring faculty books and articles published in the past year, and we include faculty biographies alongside the publications. The Provost also hosts an annual faculty publication reception where faculty members are celebrated. Maintaining the physical display and using subject liaisons to solicit new citations is one way of developing your potential list of speakers.

From here, the outreach librarian invites newly published faculty to give talks about their publications in the library and promotes the various talks as a Faculty Publication Series, developing digital flyers that the library can disseminate on social media and that faculty can add to their portfolios and email to their students and colleagues. Talks are scheduled at a time when the faculty member's students are more likely to be on campus to maximize attendance or at a time when class is held should extra credit opportunities be offered. Of course, celebrity faculty may draw a wider audience. You should factor this in when scheduling the talk, reserving the space, and marketing the event. Another type of event to consider is a panel discussion: Faculty publications on related themes or publications offering divergent or complementary perspectives on an issue could be combined in this format, and another faculty member or librarian could be invited to moderate. These events typically draw a larger audience and can serve as a showcase event for the library.

Students and alumni also may have publications that can be featured through a publication talk. University, department, and alumni affairs newsletters or social media posts may feature recent student or alumni publications, so ask your subject liaisons to be on the lookout for these as well. Featuring student and alumni authors also can encourage budding writers and scholars to consider turning some of their course papers and projects into publications and to begin developing a personal brand.

Book Review Workshops

A complementary event to promote alongside a Faculty Publication Series is a workshop on some aspect of academic publishing. If your library has a scholarly communication librarian or digital scholarship librarian, approach this person for possible workshop ideas. Another resource is the Faculty Center for Teaching and Learning or other university unit charged with supporting faculty research and publishing.

With its Faculty Publication Series, St. Thomas University Library hosted a workshop "How to Write a Book Review That Will Get You Published." It so happened that the two faculty members who gave the talk had recently published an article on how to write a book review, but there are likely prolific book reviewers on your library staff or faculty within other departments who could host this workshop.

Promote the event in a way that pointedly invites students and staff to the workshop. Highlight the fact that the book review can be an easy first publication and a way for staff and students to get more mileage out of reading those books already on a professional reading list or books otherwise listed as recommended on a syllabus. Alumni now working in their chosen fields and other area professionals also could be invited to attend, since some scholarly journals, newspapers, and trade publications publish book reviews written by both professionals and practitioners.

If you also manage your library's social media accounts and have a user population in mind that might be interested in writing book reviews, consider creating a book list or Pinterest board, "New Books Worth Reviewing in the [Fill in the Blank] Field," and promote it on social media. A physical book display also can be created with the same theme. Related resources may include a library guide on identifying new books to review, finding new calls for book reviewers, and publishing a book review, along with suggested database and Internet searches for finding journals, magazines, newspapers, and other periodicals that publish book reviews in a specified field. The alumni services office also could be made aware of the LibGuide as a useful resource for alumni professionals and practitioners. Search the Web for *libguide write OR find "book review"* and *libguide submit "book review" publisher* to get started on developing one for your library users.

Reviews of Other Media

Consider expanding the scope of any workshop or resources you create to include reviews of other products and tools that are covered by reviewers, including databases, software, apps, educational curriculum materials, websites, video games, movies, documentaries, short films, services, and, with the evolution of electronic commerce, practically anything sold on the Web. Signing on to be a beta user of a new app or website that would be useful in one's target profession and finding a trade publication that reviews these types of tools (or reviewing it on one's own blog) is a way to learn about the tool and to add "mass appeal" and cutting-edge to the personal brand.

Early Publication: Being Brand New

Early publication is a good strategy for personal branding for several reasons including the following:

- Highlights the author's skills in written communications (e.g., analysis of text or subject matter)
- Increases the author's scope of knowledge
- Increases the author's experience with editors and publishers:
    - Scholarly
    - Commercial
    - International
- Raises the author's visibility:
    - Among peers
    - In his or her field(s)
    - Among colleagues in other fields

    - Among other authors and editors (who may be planning future publications)
    - Among publishers (who may be seeking authors with specific characteristics)
    - Among administrators (who may not have known about the scope of an author's competencies or skills)
- Increases possibilities for networking
    - Internally (own organization)
    - Externally (other organizations)
- May enhance opportunities for collaborative work (e.g., to join ongoing research projects)
    - Internally (own discipline or organization)
    - Externally (other disciplines or organizations)
- May increase the number of leads or options for employment opportunities
    - Short-term (volunteer placement, internship, job)
    - Long-term (career)
- May improve opportunities for advancement or promotion
- Adds the author's voice to the scholarly communication on the related fields

Personal Branding and the Selected Book

The world is evolving at lightning speed toward more efficiency, productivity, and effectiveness—leading to greater interaction between consumers, retailers, and corporations than ever before. As a result, employees, recruiters, and students face tough challenges and competition while enhancing personal branding importance. Pioneered by Tom Peters (1999), personal branding evolved into a necessary platform and strategy for students, recruiters, and employers alike. According to Peters (1999), every person is a brand and can be managed as one. For our purpose, we would define personal branding as marketing oneself through establishing a personal brand identity, differentiating through positioning strategy, and enhancing self-brand image while achieving personal goals through mutually satisfying relations (Gringarten 2016).

Book reviewers can help create, maintain, and enhance their personal brand and professional image (Gringarten, Fernández-Calienes, and Mitchell 2015). Developing and positioning a certain personal brand can start with the decision of what books to review. Positioning is about placing your product or service in the mind of consumers in reference to competing products and services (Keller 1998; Ries, Trout, and Kotler 1986). By choosing well-targeted books to review, reviewers can position themselves as experts in their fields or subjects. The types of books an individual reviews can create certain secondary brand association, which is based on consumers' prior knowledge and experience with existing brands and is critical to brands' successes, while helping create brand image and reputation. Secondary brand association is a positive image or experience one brand delivers to another brand simply by association. Choosing titles that fit the reviewer's positioning strategies will generate a good secondary brand association. Reviewing *Good to Great: Why Some Companies Make the Leap...And Others Don't* by Collins (2001) creates a very different brand association and image than reviewing a novel.

Reviewers should always consider categories of books they plan to review, since some book categories are more popular for reviews than others (*New York Times* 2014). They also should review books that can add to their knowledge, expertise, or preferred research areas, which can enhance personal brand and professional image. For instance, if they continuously review books on finance, they can create an image of a finance professional or expert in the field.

Branding and Where to Publish the Review

Positioning is also impacted by the type of journal reviewers target for publication of a review. Faculty seeking to develop their portfolio for promotion and tenure are well aware of the impact publishing their work in the leading peer-reviewed journals of their field can have on their prospects (Liebowitz 2015). This singular focus of promotion and tenure committees can make it difficult for scholars to choose new journals or other venues more aligned with a developing research interest. Consequently, some reviewers with less latitude may opt for journals bearing the "stamp of quality" associated with rankings by such organizations as the Chartered Association of Business Schools. Emerging authors should look at journals with low acceptance rates, wide enough circulation and visibility, and preferably a high impact factor. The good news for emerging authors is that although it is becoming more and more difficult to get published in a highly ranked journal, journals have a continuous need to receive submissions due to the evolution of electronic media and the proliferation of academic journals and other publishing venues. Prospective reviewers should research their target publications and identify those that have a need for book reviews in general and those that publish reviews on their book subject in particular. Previous research by Gringarten, Fernández-Calienes, and Mitchell (2015) showed that only about half of ranked journals accepted book reviews. Reviewers also can look at popular media such as magazines and newspapers. Those venues can increase mass appeal or brand awareness, but authors should balance the reviews carefully, not to dilute their personal brand equity.

Not all reviewers can handpick their publishers. Students may find more welcoming venues for publishing reviews if they look in specific places, for example, by type of degree or by academic discipline.

Reviews by Type of Degree

Undergraduate students may find venues on the list of journals maintained by the Council on Undergraduate Research (http://www.cur.org/resources/students/undergraduate_journals/) or in any number of student-edited journals typically published by universities.

Graduate students may find outlets by researching the publications of the professional societies in their own fields for example, the very brief, partial list below:

- Humanities and arts students: the Website at Humanities Net, specifically its dedicated Reviews section "H-Net Reviews" (Humanities & Social Sciences Online 2016), lists thousands of reviews on a wide range of subjects.
    - American Historical Association (2016).
    - American Philosophical Association (2016).
- Mathematics and computer science students:
    - American Mathematical Society (2016).
    - Institute of Electrical and Electronics Engineers Computer Society (2016).

- Natural science students: see, for example, "Journals" on the website of the American Association for the Advancement of Science (2016).
- Social science students:
    - American Anthropological Association (2016).
    - American Psychological Association (2016).
- Professional and applied science students:
    - Chartered Association of Business Schools (2015) publishes a Directory.
    - National Education Association (2016).
    - American Society of Civil Engineers (2016).
    - American Medical Association (2016).
    - American Nurses Association (2016).
    - National Association of Social Workers (2016).
- Law students may find venues in law reviews that focus, specifically, on including book reviews—see, for instance, the law reviews at Alabama, California, Michigan, and Texas (Rostron and Levit 2016). In fact, one of the major resources for assessing law reviews lets the researcher distinguish his or her search, specifically, by student-edited versus faculty-edited publication (Washington and Lee University, School of Law, Law Library 2016).

Publishing success with any of the entities above also may have a positive impact on students' personal brand because they raise their profile among present and future peers.

Open Access as Brand

If open access is part of your personal brand then submit the review to an open access journal, many of which are listed in the *Directory of Open Access Journals* (https://doaj.org/). Publishing your work in an open access journal enables you to disseminate the book review more widely, since the articles are not subscription-bound and are freely available on the Web. Professionals without access to subscriptions journals may consciously target open access journals for their reviews so their review can be more widely read by those in the profession.

Conclusion

Faculty publication talks are an excellent way to showcase recent university publications, and engage faculty and students, while bringing greater visibility and traffic to the library. Book review workshops also can introduce new writers to publishing and personal branding concepts. Encouraging early publication among students and getting book reviewers to consider what types of books to review and what publishing venues they might target are all aspects of personal branding—which is critical for young professionals. Hosting publication events and workshops has the added benefit of enhancing the library's brand as a center for library publishing services and activities.

Works Cited

American Anthropological Association. 2016. "Publications of AAA." http://www.americananthro.org/StayInformed/Content.aspx?ItemNumber=1980&navItemNumber=685.

American Association for the Advancement of Science. 2016. "*Science* Journals." http://www.aaas.org/science-journals.

American Historical Association. 2016. "Publications & Directories." https://www.historians.org/publications-and-directories.

American Mathematical Society. 2016. "Journals." http://www.ams.org/publications/journals/journals.

American Medical Association. 2016. "JAMA Publications." http://www.ama-assn.org/ama/pub/jama-publications.page?.

American Nurses Association. 2016. "ANA Publications." http://www.nursingworld.org/MainMenuCategories/ANAMarketplace/ANAPeriodicals.

American Philosophical Association. 2016. "Publications." http://www.apaonline.org/?page=publications.

American Psychological Association. 2016. "APA and Affiliated Journals." http://www.apa.org/pubs/journals/index.aspx.

American Society of Civil Engineers. 2016. "Welcome to the ASCE Library." http://ascelibrary.org/.

Belcher, Wendy Laura. 2016. "How to Write an Academic Book Review." http://www.wendybelcher.com/writing-advice/how-to-write-book-review/.

California Law Review. 2016. "Articles and Essays." http://www.californialawreview.org/submissions-articles-essays.

Chartered Association of Business Schools. 2015. *Academic Journal Guide*. London: Author.

Collins, Jim C. 2001. *Good to Great: Why Some Companies Make the Leap…and Others Don't*. New York: Harper Business.

Directory of Open Access Journals. 2016. https://doaj.org.

Gringarten, Hagai. 2016. "Personal Branding." Lecture in Personal Branding Class at St. Thomas University, Miami Gardens, FL, April 14.

Gringarten, Hagai, Raul Fernández-Calienes, and Lloyd Mitchell. "Publishing Book Reviews in Accounting Journals: A Lost Art?" 2015. *Journal of International & Interdisciplinary Business Research* 2, no. 3: 18–29. http://scholars.fhsu.edu/jiibr/vol2/iss1/3.

Humanities & Social Sciences Online. 2016. "H-Net Reviews." https://www.h-net.org/reviews/home.php.

Institute of Electrical and Electronics Engineers Computer Society. 2016. "Publications." https://www.computer.org/web/publications/.

Keller, Kevin Lane. 2013. *Strategic Brand Management: Building, Measuring, and Managing Brand Equity*, 4th ed. Boston: Pearson.

Liebowitz, Jay, ed. 2015. *A Guide to Publishing for Academics: Inside the Publish or Perish Phenomenon*. Boca Raton, FL: CRC.

Lippincott, Sarah K., ed. 2016. *Library Publishing Directory 2016*, 3rd ed. Atlanta: Library Publishing Coalition. http://www.librarypublishing.org/resources/directory/lpd2016.

Michigan Law Review. 2016. "Book Reviews." http://www.michiganlawreview.org/book-reviews/.

National Association of Social Workers. 2016. "Journals." http://www.naswpress.org/publications/journals/index.html.

National Education Association. 2016. "Our Publications." http://www.nea.org/home/606.htm.

New York Times. 2014. "Inside the List." *Sunday Book Review*, p. BR 22, February 23.

Peters, Thomas J. 1999. *The Brand You 50: Fifty Ways to Transform Yourself from an "Employee" into a Brand That Shouts Distinction, Commitment, and Passion!* New York: Knopf.

Ries, Al, Jack Trout, and Philip Kotler. 2001. *Positioning: The Battle for Your Mind*. New York: McGraw-Hill.

Rostron, Allen, and Nancy Levit. 2016. "Information for Submitting Articles to Law Reviews & Journals." *SSRN*, February 1. http://papers.ssrn.com/sol3/papers.cfm?abstract_id=1019029.

Texas Law Review. 2016. "Book Reviews." http://www.texaslrev.com/book-reviews/.

Washington and Lee University, School of Law, Law Library. 2016. "Law Journals: Submissions and Ranking, 2007–2014." http://lawlib.wlu.edu/LJ/.

How Would You Use It?

Designing a Library Workshop to Engage Young Writers with Resources in Their Field

KARLA FRIBLEY

While students generally understand how a library can help with research papers, it can be harder to help them see how a library can help in their creative pursuits like writing or film-making. To make things more challenging, librarians can't possibly be subject experts in every topic, so may lack the disciplinary knowledge to completely understand if and how a particular resource may be of use. Addressing both challenges, this chapter will outline a one-hour workshop that I designed with a creative writing professor to engage undergraduate fiction writing students with resources that can help them get their work published. At the same time, the design of the workshop helped the library capitalize on students' input regarding a library research guide on writing.

Background

In the fall of 2015, I was approached by a faculty member teaching a short story writing course at the undergraduate level at Emerson College. She wanted to integrate a library research workshop into her course to introduce students to resources for writers. This was an exciting moment for me, as our library had been eager to work more frequently with creative writing courses. Although we have an active library instruction program, and over 800 Writing, Literature, and Publishing students, librarians rarely work with any of the fiction or poetry writing courses. In the past when I'd brainstormed with colleagues about how we might work more with these courses, many of our ideas had centered around supporting them as they do background research for setting a story or creating realistic characters. However the faculty member teaching the short story writing class saw a different need—that of supporting students in getting their stories published.

In the past, the faculty member would use part of a class period towards the end of the semester to talk about resources that could help students understand the publishing process. For example, she would highlight potential literary journals that publish short fiction (both print and online). She would talk about books such as *Literary Market Place* (a directory of book publishing industry) and *Writer's Market* (a book and magazine publishing directory and manual) that could help students decide where and how to submit work. She'd highlight magazines and websites that can help students keep current with publishing industry news or help them track their submissions. However, she sensed students would benefit from actually getting a chance to use and test out the resources. She approached me to see if we could bring the students into the library to explore some of the resources.

From my perspective, I was excited about the opportunity to work with the class, but I was nervous about several things. For one, I didn't want the class to feel like a lecture, where I rattled off lots of resources, and slowly marched students through them one by one. I wanted it to be a more active learning experience that would have them engaging with the resources in a deeper way. If I were to try to lead the students through all the resources, students would most likely leave with only surface-level understanding of them, and very likely wouldn't retain much of the workshop content after our session had ended. I wanted it to be an active learning experience where students would need to engage in higher-order thinking (e.g.: analyzing, evaluating, synthesizing) as a part of their experience.

In addition, while the professor was able to provide me with a list of possible resources for students to look at, for many of them I felt I lacked the disciplinary knowledge to fully understand how they might be useful to a writer. For several of the items she mentioned, I had little to no experience with them. While I could attempt to review them all in time for our workshop, in the end I would probably only be able to offer a generic summary of the suggested resources. I would likely miss key things that a writer would find most valuable.

Given this, I proposed that we design a workshop that would ask the students to become the experts on a particular resource, and to share their insights with their peers. In this model, their learning would be enriched by having to synthesize all the information about a particular resource, and then teach that to their classmates. At the same time, this workshop would help librarians as we finalized a new online research guide for Writers.

Structure of the Workshop

Rather than try to guess which resources would be helpful to the students, I largely relied on the faculty member for recommendations of the resources (or types of resources) she wanted her students to explore. These were the items she recommended:

- *Writer's Market* (a book and magazine publishing directory and manual) (Information Today, 2015)
- *Literary Market Place* (a directory of the book publishing industry) (Brewer 2015)
- sample literary journals like *Ploughshares* (https://www.pshares.org), *Tin House* (http://www.tinhouse.com)/, *McSweeney's* (http://www.mcsweeneys.net/books), etc.
- sample books from our collection on authors' legal rights and issues
- *Poets & Writers* (non-profit magazine and website on writing) (http://www.pw.org)
- *Writer's Chronicle* (magazine and website on writing from the Association of Writers and Writing Programs) (https://www.awpwriter.org/magazine_media/writers_chronicle_overview)

- *Publishers Weekly* (magazine and website on publishing industry) (http://www.publishersweekly.com/)
- *Duotrope* (subscription-based website for tracking submissions) (https://duotrope.com/)
- *Publishers Lunch* (subscription-based newsletter on the publishing industry) (http://lunch.publishersmarketplace.com/)

In some cases (example: *Publishers Lunch*; *Duotrope*) the resources were not "library" materials, in that we did not own or subscribe to them. For these non-library sites that required some sort of subscription-based content, students were asked to explore the site, without subscribing, to see what they could learn about the potential usefulness of a subscription. For the sample literary journals and sample author's rights books, I explored generally what the library offered in these areas and picked a handful of items for students to review.

For the workshop, the faculty member and her students came to the library's computer classroom for a one hour session. In advance of their visit, I created a publicly editable Google Doc listing the resources, instructions for the activity, and a sample entry. At the outset of the workshop, I explained to the students that they would be exploring a resource and sharing their findings with their classmates. By the end of the workshop they would leave with a better understanding of resources available to writers seeking to be published. This would also be their chance to help future writing students, as I hoped their insights would help the library improve our library research guide on Writing. I showed them the draft library research guide on Writing, and noted that it included many of the resources that they'd be exploring during the workshop.

During the workshop, each of the 13 students chose one of the resources. I then asked each of them to take five minutes to explore their resource, and asked them to consider "How would you use it?" To help them as they examined the resources, I provided them with a list of questions to consider:

- What is it? A book or a website or a magazine or a database or some combination?
- Why would a writer use this?
- Key features?
- Limitations?
- Call # and/or link?

After exploring their resource for five minutes, they were to take five minutes to write a summary of their item in the Google Doc. For their descriptions, I asked for the following:

1. a brief one-sentence summary of the item (15 words or fewer)
2. a longer summary of the item (100 words or fewer)

By asking for the two summaries of different lengths, I hoped to give them the space to describe the resource, but then also to give them the challenge of having to distill their findings into a much shorter version. After writing their descriptions, they would be presenting their resource to their classmates, so this would force them to decide what was most important about the resource. The shorter description would also be more similar to the kinds of descriptions librarians would use in the in-progress research guide on Writing resources. To help them understand what they'd be doing, I provided them with the following sample description I had written for the *Literary Market Place* book:

Short summary: Directory of the book publishing industry in US and internationally

Longer Summary: Literary Market Place (LMP) is the directory of book publishing covering publishing houses and personnel in America and Canada, as well as 180 other countries. Includes category indexes. Use it to find names, addresses, submission guidelines, and representation (agents), along with distribution, writing conferences and retreats, competitions and fellowships, and library associations. Access is limited to 4 users at one time. Available in print [X ReadyRef] PN 161 .L5 at library's reference desk or online [link to online access].

After the students had spent ten minutes exploring and summarizing their resources, I asked them each to present their resources briefly to their classmates. For each presentation, I encouraged the rest of the class to think of one or two questions we could ask each presenter. At this point, the professor and I were able to chime in with additions or clarifications.

Results

Overall this format worked well. The students wrote thoughtful, useful descriptions of the resources they examined. Perhaps because they regularly workshop and discuss each other's writing in class, they seemed to function well using this format. They listened to each other's presentations, and asked good questions. As I had hoped, they were able to pinpoint strong features for some of the resources that were not as obvious to me. For example, several students noted that their resource contained guidance on finding grants and scholarships for writers. This was not something that had jumped out at me when I perused the resources, in part because it was often one feature out of many others. However, finding funding was something of interest to them as they considered pursuing their writing careers or pursuing graduate school, so it would make sense to highlight this as a useful feature for young writers.

Having the students record their definitions in a shared Google Doc was also a good choice. I was able to share that link with the professor after the class, so she and her students could refer to it later if they wished. It was also helpful to have something to refer to beyond just my general notes of their presentations. As an instructor I often find it challenging to take meaningful notes while still engaging with the class. While I still took some notes as students presented their resources, I found their written descriptions from the Google Doc more helpful after the fact. They tended to be more concise and focused in their written descriptions. After the workshop, I worked with the librarian who curates our research guides to compare the students' insights about each resource with the current summaries on the Writing research guide. In several cases, we ended up modifying our descriptions based on something a student had noted as useful.

For assessment, I checked in with the professor after our workshop to share the link to the Google Doc and to follow up on some questions, and asked her to share any feedback she received from her students. After our session she surveyed her students for their thoughts about the experience. She asked them if they thought a workshop like ours would be useful for future students in her classes, and 100 percent of them said yes. She made sure to note that I could feel fairly confident about their honesty—given the amount of workshopping of each other's work they do each semester, they were not afraid to share when something did not work. In other words, they weren't afraid to be critical! Using the Google Doc and having the students do verbal reports were other useful assessment tools. They allowed me to see what the students were taking away from each resource, and to check for any misunderstandings.

Modifications for Future Versions

Perhaps the most surprising moment for me occurred at the outset of the workshop, although in hindsight it made perfect sense. After I went over what we'd be doing, I shared how excited I was to hear their insights. I explained that they would be of great help to the library and future students, as the library was in the process of revising our research guide on resources for Writing. I hoped this would help them feel that their work had even greater purpose than that of helping themselves and their classmates. However, shortly after I finished explaining this, the professor interrupted to ask if it was really necessary that students write their definitions in the shared Google Doc. She explained that not everyone may wish for their work to be used by future students or the library. At the time, I was admittedly somewhat taken aback. Using the Google Doc had been a last-minute idea of mine, so it wasn't one I'd discussed with the professor in advance. We had discussed having the students summarize the resources, so I had just assumed it wouldn't matter if it were also to be captured online. To respond to her concern, I thanked her for raising the issue, and modified the instructions. While the students would all use the Google Doc to locate their item and to read the activity directions, I left it open to them whether they wanted to write their summaries online for others to see. In the end, all students did use the Google Doc to write their entries, although to be fair I don't know if any of them had lingering concerns.

In retrospect I can see the flaw in my assumption that everyone would be open to "bettering humanity" by sharing his or her summaries, potentially for future use by the library. People working in creative fields are frequently asked to share their work for free, with the assumption that they'll be content with getting the experience or exposure. Actor and writer Wil Wheaton recently called attention to this issue in a widely discussed series of tweets and blog post after *The Huffington Post* (http://www.huffingtonpost.com) approached him about using some of his writing on their site, without compensation, presuming he would be glad for the exposure (Wheaton 2015). For someone hoping to earn money in a creative field, it can feel frustrating or even insulting to be asked to share your skills without appropriate compensation. I appreciated that the professor was sensitive to this issue, and raised it during the workshop. For future versions, she's going to discuss the activity with them beforehand to gauge their feelings, and I'll make sure to emphasize the optional nature of the online entries. I may also add a question as part of each entry that asks each student if they would feel comfortable with the library using their summaries to help with future research guides.

For future versions of this workshop, I plan to identify ways to help students engage more with each other's resources. For the first half of the short presentations, students were engaged and asked good questions. However, after the fifth or sixth presentation, I could sense that some of the energy had been lost from the experience. Students still listened to their classmates, but asked fewer questions. One way to fix this could be to incorporate an activity in the middle that would break things up and provide a change of pace. Perhaps they could all explore a resource together, or have a reflection question to discuss in pairs. Similarly, I'd like students do some kind of cumulative reflective activity that has them consider which resource(s) overall seemed most useful to them, or something else that has them considering the resources as a whole. I'd also appreciate knowing if they think there are useful resources that we left out, or other types of help that would be useful to young writers. Both these activities would help them evaluate the resources as a whole. If time allows, I'd also like give them time to look at the library's existing Writing research guide, and hear their suggestions on how we can make it more useful.

In future versions of this workshop, I anticipate incorporating some new resources for the students to review. Generally speaking, the resources the professor recommended fit into the following categories:

- Guides and handbooks regarding getting published
- Examples of where one could be published
- Directories or tools for figuring out where one should submit work
- Tools for tracking submissions
- Sources for industry news
- Listings of conferences and workshops
- Listings of grants, scholarships, and contests
- Legal information for authors (copyright, rights, contracts, etc.)

Librarians or faculty members wishing to offer a similar workshop experience could choose their own favorite resources that fit these categories, and add new categories or resources as they see fit. Beyond consulting the resources previously mentioned, the following sites may be helpful as one considers other resources for writers:

- *Poets & Writers* website—"Tools for Writers" (http://www.pw.org/toolsforwriters)
- *NewPages* website (http://www.newpages.com)
- *Writing Career* website (http://writingcareer.com)
- *Review Review* website (http://www.thereviewreview.net)
- *The Writer* magazine and website (http://www.writermag.com)
- *Winning Writers* website (https://winningwriters.com)

Conclusions

Overall, I look forward to using this workshop format again for this particular class, but also to adapting this workshop format for other classes I teach. This format could easily be used with other disciplines. Beyond it being a helpful way for students to engage in-depth with a resource and learn from each other, it was beneficial for me to hear their insights. I believe the students appreciated the opportunity to become experts on their resources, and listened more intently to their fellow classmates more than they would have if I had been the one talking about all the resources. I'm especially interested in using this format going forward to learn from students about how we can improve our library research guides. I would recommend others consider this workshop concept and workshop format as they look for ways to support writers seeking to be published.

Works Cited

Brewer, Robert Lee, ed. 2015. *The Writer's Market.* 95th ed. Cincinnati: F&W.

Information Today. 2015. *LMP 2016: Literary Market Place: The Directory of the American Book Publishing Industry with Industry Indexes*, 76th ed. Medford, NJ: Information Today.

Wheaton, Wil. 2015. "You Can't Pay Your Rent with 'The Unique Platform and Reach Our Site Provides.'" October 27. http://wilwheaton.net.

A Workshop Is Learning by Doing

RITA KEELEY BROWN

When I think about what the word means, my mind goes to my dad's workshop. It was his haven to build, repair, try new tools, find out why something wasn't working right and fix it. He had frustrations, recognizable by the swearing under his breath, as he'd start over and try another approach. When he came into the kitchen smiling for a fresh cup of coffee and a piece of Mom's cherry pie, we knew he had conquered it. That also applies to a workshop on writing. It's through the hands-on "doing" that we learn best. We need room to write what is significant to us. A writing workshop should give inspiration, make participants feel confident that they do have unique stories to tell, and that they possess the ability to write them.

Libraries are the ideal venue for a writing workshop as librarians understand the importance of writing from many perspectives and the atmosphere of a library is extremely receptive to such an event. One such experience I had was with the Lied Scottsbluff Public Library in my hometown of Scottsbluff, Nebraska. I live in California but was going back there for a family reunion in September. When I contacted the library on another matter, the librarian asked if I would give a talk on my books. Communicating by phone and e-mail over the following months, we scheduled a talk and book-signing for a Friday evening and added an all-day workshop to encourage people to write their own stories on Saturday.

The library handled publicity (including newspaper articles, flyers), made copies of material for handouts, and assisted with audio-visual equipment. They also packaged six-copy sets of two of my books that people could check out for a month to use for discussion groups. Over forty people attended and were very responsive. In a newspaper article following the event the librarian, Jana Kehn, stated, "From the attendance at the writer's workshop, it is clear we need to do more of this type of programming. I was very impressed with the talent of our budding authors and Rita's comments were quite helpful.... I look forward to the day when this column will be reviewing titles from these local talents" (*Scottsbluff Star Herald*, October 14, 2012, book review).

Another example of working with a library here in Los Angeles brought the same type of comments from the librarian as a result of a four-week session of two-hour workshops, one per week, which I presented at one of the regional libraries. This was offered free of charge as part of community outreach sponsored by the California Writers Club–San

Fernando Valley Branch (CWC-SFV). The CWC-SFV President and I met with the librarian to set up a program that answered the needs of the library and the perceived interests of participants. About thirty people signed up and most were there throughout the program.

Programs of this kind are valuable to all. They are opportunities that offer guidance and encouragement for people to write their life stories, to explore and express their thoughts and ideas, and to enjoy the experience and learning that takes place through writing. Most will say they would like to write but don't know if they are "good enough" or just don't know where or how to start. With a little inspiration and confidence most will give it a try and find they are able to express themselves and their stories in ways they had not thought possible.

It's Never Too Late!

I came late to writing and even then, not willingly. In college, I majored in music and minored in English. After my children were grown I wanted to continue my education. I knew what good sentences looked like, but never gave any serious thought to writing my own stories, let alone, books. So, what was it that changed all of this? Odd as it may seem, it was a course in psychology.

I needed another class to fill the required credits for that semester. I had heard there was an instructor in the psychology department who was an especially good teacher, so I thought his course might be interesting. In the early weeks of the class, he projected the first line of a story on the overhead screen and told us to complete the story with whatever thoughts popped into our mind. We had fifteen minutes to write and then we would share what we had written.

I did not want to do this! I sat there conjuring up a list in my mind of all possible excuses to get out of doing this. I then saw that the other students were all busy writing and five minutes were lost in my attempt to find a way out of doing it. With great reluctance, I wrote that line at the top of the page, thought about it, and did come up with a few lines. I only hoped to survive the embarrassment of reading my fumbling effort to the class.

To my complete surprise, everyone liked what I'd written and encouraged me to develop it further. This small exercise opened the door to a confidence I needed to pursue. I still felt insecure about writing, but knowing that I could write what others enjoyed reading gave me the impetus to learn to write well. I read books about writing, took writing courses and workshops, absorbed feedback from others to help move me along this new path.

One of the most valuable resources was my library. It is an endless resource for reference materials not only in books, periodicals, but recorded books on tape and CDs which I could listen to while driving to and from work. Librarians are usually very interested in your project and eager to suggest resources you may not be aware of and provide them or at least, offer information on how to acquire or contact other resources on your subject.

When I was asked to write a biography about a Chinese man who was "sold" as a young child, *A Pawn of Fate,* I was not well informed on Chinese history. I needed to understand what conditions were in China that led to this family's decision to "sell" their four-year-old child in order that he and they might survive. My librarian gave me excellent resources that provided the clarity I needed to construct the scenes and background surrounding this family's life particularly in the 1930s and 1940s. I did not want, nor did I have the time, to go through a complete history of China. I wanted to understand what led to this alarming situation and why it was so devastating and insoluble during that time period. What did daily life look like for people living in those conditions? Her suggestions were extremely helpful.

Learning is the underlying theme in all my workshops. A well-prepared lesson plan is essential, but it must be flexible. The most important considerations are: What is the best way I can help participants learn to do this? How can I help them shut down that "inner critic" that keeps telling them their writing isn't good enough, or what they write is amateurish, and no one will be interested in it? These and so many other negative thoughts hold us back. As instructors, we must have our "antennae" alert to what the group needs to know and the areas in which participants show interest.

Before my workshops begin, I place an Information Sheet on each desk or chair and as students settle in I ask them to respond to the questions. I prefer having them write their answers rather than respond verbally, because I want them to focus on why they came, what they need help with, what worries them about writing, and what they would like to be able to write. If we do this aloud, people usually listen to what everybody else says and give those "Me, too" answers. Those give little information about where they are with writing or where they would like to be. The Information Sheet asks the following questions:

- What kind of books or stories do you enjoy reading most?
- What writing have you done (thank-you notes, memos, stories)?
- What type of writing would you like to do?
- What are some questions/concerns you have about writing in general?

I ask for their name and e-mail address and assure them it is only for my use should I need to contact them and this information will neither be used or seen by anyone but me. I collect the sheets and quickly look them over. This gives me an idea of their expectations and needs, where they are coming from. This helps me understand and address their concerns, so they can feel that "they got what they came for" in some measure.

At the end of the workshop, I ask them to answer a few questions anonymously on an Evaluation Form for my use only. It asks:

- What was most helpful in the workshop?
- What was least helpful?
- What are your overall comments about the workshop/s?

These comments have been extremely valuable to me in planning future workshops and help me become a better teacher.

Writing is a very personal activity. The participants need to feel at ease about sharing what they write. They also need to know that their privacy is protected: this is a critical factor in most of us. To begin, I strive to build a level of trust with the group. I introduce myself by sharing what my writing life is like to give a sense of who I am and where I am coming from as a writer.

I also ask them to agree that the readings and whatever personal feelings are expressed here stay in this room and not repeated outside of class. The first time I announced this, I was amazed to hear sighs of relief and to see many nods of agreement. Now I always make a point of establishing this rule.

In these first steps, we have taken the time to know each other (the group and me) and have an idea of where we are coming from. The next step is to get students to know each other. One way is to have them interview the person to their right or another participant they don't know. That person will, in turn, interview them. They then introduce that person to the rest of the group. I suggest two questions to ask that help keep them on target:

- What kind of reading and/or writing interests you most–fiction, nonfiction, poetry, etc.?
- What are your hobbies or things you enjoy doing and do well?

This entire exercise takes a total of fifteen minutes. I allow five minutes for each of the two interviews (total of ten minutes) and the last five minutes is for them to briefly introduce each other to the group. For example: "This is Laura. She likes reading nonfiction and she makes jewelry like the lovely ones she is wearing today."

Timing is dependent, of course, on how many people are in the group and the overall time restrictions. It is well worth the time if it makes everyone feel more at ease about sharing. When you can accomplish that, everything else you have planned will go much smoother and closer to schedule. If the class is large, this can be done by introducing each other only to their neighboring pairs (six people maximum) instead of to the whole class. All later sharing should be done to the whole group, if possible.

I speak from experience when I say establishing this comfort-zone is critical to presenting a productive workshop. Not only does each person have a unique personality, but the group takes on a personality of its own. This can either move the workshop along, or inhibit progress. These beginning activities are designed to establish trust and acceptance, and are major contributors to the personality and success of the group.

It is also important to give suggestions regarding comments during the sharing. It is vital to clarify the tone of comments made. These should be helpful comments regarding what was liked about that person's writing, such as:

- what was most interesting to you in the story?
- what would you like to know more about?
- what words in the story caught your ear?

These comments are meant to encourage the writer, not criticize or condemn. We are all there to support one another. Spontaneous writings are not a finished product and negativity is not helpful. The participants should be encouraged to "write what is in your heart." No one is expected to be a William Shakespeare or Maya Angelou. Every person is unique and so is their story. Many of us are surprised to learn that others are interested in what we have to say and they often bring to light interesting elements in our writing of which we were not aware.

What Happens Next?

The content of what ensues depends on the specific purpose and the time allowed for the workshop. If asked to present a workshop on specific topics such as character development, editing, plot, or a specific genre, that is where your focus must continue. You may be working with people who are already writing and have different needs. They may already enjoy reading aloud to others and may even be acquainted with each other. It is important to know this. Using a tool like the Information Sheet mentioned earlier, or having them introduce themselves, will give a good sense of this and help you adjust the emphasis of your workshop plan when needed.

Whatever the focus of your topic, give your students examples of "good, better, and best." Use PowerPoint and handouts to clarify basic points they will need for reference. It is important to have the students work with these points, give them an example that needs improvement and have each person improve it. This could be an exercise deleting unnecessary words, correcting confusing voice, inconsistencies in verb tense, singular/plural errors, spelling mistakes and homonyms that sound the same but give the wrong meaning. By doing these exercises and discussing each one they will better understand the difference between incorrect, so-so, and what makes the words come alive and move the story forward. We humans learn by hearing, but if we both hear it and see it, we will retain it. And if we hear it, see it, and do it, we can master it. The more senses involved, the deeper the learning.

Let the Editing Begin

That first draft is for you alone. It is where you get your ideas down. From there you develop the story. What's next? You reshape and smooth out your sentences, consider your choice of words, review facts, check the grammar, and make sure the story flows. You might find it better to move the last paragraph to the beginning, the beginning to the middle, change the order of sentences, add more description of characters and scenes, delete superfluous words, etc. Welcome to editing! It's a major part of writing. John Updike said, "Writing and re-writing are a constant search for what it is one is saying."

The workshops I most often present are described below. They are suitable for any age and adaptable to any particular group. I prefer to present a series of three or four two-hour sessions which allow time for input about writing, as well as individual writing and sharing; or, an all-day workshop which allows time for a reasonable grounding in the writing process.

Each workshop has a different emphasis. Basic skills are covered in each session as appropriate. All apply to both fiction and nonfiction. Poetry is included in reading and writing but is not covered in depth. I encourage workshop participants to write poetry as well as prose, but poetry is best presented in a full-blown workshop of its own, in order to understand its unique qualities and processes.

I accumulate an ongoing personal library of hand-outs, visuals, PowerPoint slides, and resource materials to illustrate whatever is important in each workshop. During the presentation, I'm guided by a timed outline. Without it, I run the risk of losing track of time. If we're flexible enough to go with whatever interests the group, we must be aware of time. This outline guide keeps me on schedule.

Each of the following workshops has a different aim and structure.

- *Creative Writing—An Unopened Gift* gives a broad approach and exploration of writing in general. It develops confidence in the participants' ability to write through timed writing/sharing exercises and focuses on development of a story, editing and improving it, and includes resources for publishing.

- *You Have a Story Waiting to Be Told* focuses on more specific genres, formats, subjects, development and editing skills. Whether we choose to write to publish or simply to share with family and friends, it should be the best we can do. Resources and procedures for publishing are included for memoir, biography, autobiography, essay, short story, poetry, and/or anthologies.
- *Just Write* was inspired by participants who wished for a longer experience to "just write" from the ten- or fifteen-minute exercises based on unfinished sentences, first lines of a story, and other prompts. I expand these prompts to include works of art, music, photographs, objects, colors, animals, nature, and other topics.

If time and circumstances permit, I offer to compile an anthology of writings done in class. I set a deadline that allows time to edit and polish their work. They e-mail their work to me. I use a local printer for copies and we split the costs that come to around a maximum of $5.00 a copy dependent on the number of pages and the number of copies. They can share their writing with friends and family in a published form. This gives quite a boost to their belief that, yes, they are writers.

One of the classes from a Just Write workshop has continued to meet independently for several years. They have researched their own resources and prompts from which to write. They e-mail their writings to each other and meet weekly to read and discuss their work. It is exciting to recognize the interesting thoughts, feelings, and wants we have within us that come out when we relax and write, without inhibition, whatever pops into our mind. One woman from that group is now publishing a gorgeous illustrated children's book from a story she wrote in the class. She loved her story. All of us did, too, and urged her to publish it as a children's book. Getting past all those "what if" worries to focus on writing ideas as they emerge, is a thrilling experience. When your writing excites you, it will excite your readers.

Librarian Writer Supports Courageous Conversations, Critical Multiculturalism and Communal Networks

ROLAND BARKSDALE-HALL

As mentioned in my chapter, "Building Dialogic Bridges to Diversity: Are We There Yet?," "acquisition of a research skillset" was the primary reason I became an academic librarian.[1] During my freshman year and later as graduate library science student I worked as a page and senior page in the Langley Biological Sciences and Psychology Library in Pittsburgh, Pennsylvania. I viewed the head librarian, Drynda J., as a mentor, who was professional, knowledgeable and possessed a mastery of courageous conversations. I silently cheered for her one day when she told a co-worker that she would never have visited apartheid South Africa on the university-sponsored Semester at Sea and certainly not got a stylish haircut there of all places. Harriet B., another library aide, invited me to her home for dinner with her husband and young son. I felt part of a communal network and found the academic library to be a pleasurable environment.

I was coming out of a personal tragedy when I received a bachelor of science degree in biological sciences from the University of Pittsburgh in 1983. As a result, I had financial concerns and decided to change my career interest. I realized that my scientific background coupled with my love of reading and research might be good qualities to possess for a biomedical librarian. Fortunately, I received a scholarship to attend library school. I earned a master in library science degree from the University of Pittsburgh School of Library and Information Science in 1984.

Shortly thereafter I relocated from my native Pennsylvania to the metropolitan Washington, D.C. area. I served as a part-time academic librarian at Capitol Institute of Technology, Laurel, Maryland; then as a reference librarian at NASA Science and Technology Information Center Headquarters, Washington, D.C., from 1985 to 1986; Johns Hopkins University Milton S. Eisenhower Library, Baltimore, Maryland, from 1986 to 1988; and a biomedical librarian and Coordinator of Black Health History at the Howard University Health Science Library, Washington, D.C., from 1988 to 1990.

During a stint in Washington, D.C., I launched a writing career. I participated in various cultural and educational enrichment activities. At the 1985 Afro-American Historical and Genealogical Society Conference held at the Library of Congress, I presented my first scholarly paper, "Stayin' a Little Ahead," which was subsequently published in the fall 1987 *Journal of the Afro-American Historical and Genealogical Society.*[2] I became book review editor for the *Journal of the Afro-American Historical and Genealogical Society.* I participated in the Federal Poets, the D.C. Chapter of the National Federation of State Poetry Societies and of the Academy of American Poets which met at a local branch of the Washington, D.C., public library. My first published poem, "Rent Parties (A Tribute to Langston Hughes)" appeared in the fall 1987 *The Federal Poet.*[3] I pursued additional graduate studies in the Publication Specialist Certificate Program, George Washington University, Washington, D.C., from 1987 to 1989. Following a disability from an accident in the library workplace I returned back home to Sharon, Pennsylvania.

In 2002, I was recruited by the president of the Black Caucus of the American Library Association Gladys Smiley Bell to serve as the managing editor of the organization's official publication, *The BCALA News.* I then was the Peabody Special Collections Librarian at Hampton University, Hampton, Virginia. From 1997 to 2001, I served as a *BCALA News* columnist.

Visit to My Alma Mater

"Would you come and give a presentation on leadership to the PAWS class?" Ms. Christal J., Penn State talent search coordinator at Sharon High School, greeted me. With the school mascot being the tiger, the acronym PAWS stood for Pause for Academic Work Session. I was thrilled by this invitation. This indeed was no ordinary presentation. I was a Sharon High School alumnus.

Before I had a chance to do the presentation, something dreadful happened to change the context of my visit. Lee Lee, an outgoing youth in my son's sophomore class and a popular basketball player, was killed by gunfire at a house party a couple blocks from the school during the weekend. There was shock, hurt, anguish and grief.

I now faced a challenge. I felt I could no longer do an idyllic presentation I envisioned before. The tragic chain of events took its toll. I needed to scrap the presentation I planned earlier and regroup. I needed to make my visit more relevant to the life of students. Reevaluating the significance of an author's visit at this particular time, I asked myself: "What need exists for teens in an urban culture?"

Two weeks after Lee Lee had been laid to rest I visited my alma mater. These were familiar haunts. The dormant flower garden at the entrance took me a few decades back. It seemed like just yesterday I along with the members of the Greenhouse Gang planted geraniums as a service project. An article describing the project was published on the front page of the June 3, 1977, *Sharon (Pennsylvania) Herald.* At the time, I was so thrilled with this article, I cut it out and pasted it on the front page of my scrapbook. The movement in the hallway brought me back to the present. The lunch time was over and the Commons area was quiet. I went around the corner and paused. A faculty office was now where the *Gazette* office had been before. It was nice to walk up the steps without being jostled by other students.

The second floor housed the language arts department, social studies department and the media center. When I was a student, I often played chess after school. Mr. Q, the soft-spoken librarian and the chess club advisor made the library an inviting space, Even now I can picture him twirling his thick coal-growth beard when faced with a challenging move. Chess in the library meeting room was at the heart of my school day.

Everything around me looked pretty much the same. The lockers were orange rather than the drab beige but still looked like the ones during my school days. The science and mathematics departments still were on the third floor. I peeked into Miss Julie G.'s classroom. We both enjoyed science and graduated from Sharon High School together. She now was the science teacher. I then walked into the science classroom where my presentation was supposed to take place.

I now stood before the crowded classroom of sophomores. My daughter Vonita, then a senior at the same school, was the muse on this particular occasion. "Pops, do a PowerPoint presentation. Include slides about the time when you were there in high school—and then about where you are now in your life." And that was exactly what I did. In addition to the opening title slide, I had seven frames each with a "before" and "after" image. "Help me Lord to bring something of meaning to our hurting children," I whispered a prayer. I then took a deep breath and began.

Who, Me?

I started by talking to students about the reasons we choose or get chosen for certain paths in life. "Who, Me?" was the headline for the first frame. A particular experience from my childhood was an inspiration for it. In the winter of 1977, I remember my Pops waking me before morning. "Window," he said, adding something about wind blowing out the attic window. Pops needed me to hold the window while he nailed it back in. It was brutally cold, what we called "a Russian winter." "Who, me?" I thought, but back then you knew to keep your thoughts to yourself. Otherwise you would be in for some trouble.

It was around the same time that the school newspaper, the *Gazette*, resumed its publication after a lapse of several years. Ms. Agnes O., the newspaper advisor, chose me as the editor. She did not really know me since I never took any of her English classes. I guessed since I earlier had submitted a writing sample, she decided that I was the most qualified. Still I was surprised. "Who, me?" I wondered.

How Do You Create a Positive Climate?

I continued my conversation with students by stressing that everyone has responsibilities and opportunities to bring about positive changes. At the time when I became the student newspaper editor, the school experienced racial unrest. The school felt the necessity to improve interpersonal relationships and suggested to form a Human Relations Council. Initially, I was skeptical. "You want us kids to solve problems the adults themselves can't fix? Ummmh…" I thought.

The charge of the Human Relations Council was to "create a positive climate for people-to-people relationships, to investigate reports of discrimination, and to make recommendations to the school principal, Mr. Donald B." I was chosen as president of the Human Relations Council and later received a Sharon High School Alumni Scholarship for my student involvement thanks to Mr. Donald B. "Who, me?" I asked.

How Do You Get Your Message Through?

As I continued my talk, students sat motionless and stared at the typed front cover of the *Gazette*. The black and white issue with tiger paws running up one side had to appear to them like something retrieved from a time capsule. An article entitled "Human Relations Council Formed," on the front page of the November 1977 issue of the *Gazette* carried the following story: "This year Sharon High has initiated a new organization, the Human Relations Council. The Council was formed to discuss prejudices and problems at the school and to find solutions. The council is made up of five students and four adults. In forming the group, students were chosen to represent different facets of the school. Seniors on the Council are Mark I., Leslie M., and Roland B-H; the representative of the junior class is Patty C., and the member of the sophomore class is Wanda H. Adult members of the Council are Miss Peggy M., social worker for Mercer County, Mr. Charles H., assistant principal at Sharon High, Miss Nadine H., educational liaison [sic] person for the Urban League, Mr. Carl E., social studies teacher at Sharon High.... Mr. H serves as group facilitator and reports directly to the principal. The Council meets at least once a month, with sub-committee members meeting as often as needed."[4]

Youth compared and contrasted the typewritten newspaper to a modern digitally published one. It was the glitzy New York City-based bold red, black and gray *QBR The Black Book Review* I now edited. *QBR The Black Book Review* front cover with a larger than life techno image of James Brown's face, formed by his various nicknames, including "Godfather of Soul," with a background of word-picture rays took front and center stage.

I pointed out "Life Before Trayvon," an interview I had done with Sharon Flake, teen author of the *Skin I'm In*,[5] which topped the list of headline stories on the side of the page.[6]

I explained that formats changed and will continue to do so, but your message has to have a strong impact regardless of its packaging. As I mentioned earlier, I served as managing editor of the *BCALA Newsletter* from 2002 to 2007. I laid the groundwork for a design change of the *BCALA Newsletter* and transition from print to an electronic publication. I added several new feature sections to promote current awareness. In the December 2002 the section with reviews of print and electronic resources appeared. In August 2003, I began interviews with notable librarians, authors and publishers. The first installment was an interview W. Paul Coates, librarian and founder of Black Classic Press. In February 2004 the Issues and Actions feature first appeared. The March 2005 issue introduced a design change followed by the first electronic version in January 2007. In May 2007 H.W. Wilson agreed to index the publication. Regardless of all the exterior changes, the main thing remained—the newsletter and I as a managing editor were committed to supporting the goals, objectives, and mission of the Black Caucus of the American Library Association.

With all these examples, I tried to drive one point home: you have got to have something to say, the rest is just bells and whistles. So here I asked the students: "What is your message?"

What Are the Right Questions to Ask?

"Ask???????" was the headline for the second slide. In 1977, Alex Haley's *Roots* aired on television. The same year Momma pressed a yellow weathered clipping in my hand

and told me, "Keep and preserve this." "Who, me?" I asked. I projected the image of the clipping onto the screen. Students looked into the face of an older, kinder, gentleman with a plat tie. He appeared to greet them from over a half a century ago. It was the face of someone who had lived a long life. Perhaps, he attained the status of a grandfather, maybe great-grandfather. It was a full life, in any case. "Dad Stevenson Celebrates His 109th Birthday Today," was the headline above his receding hairline.

Momma gave me a gift from the heart. Scrawled above the headline in pencil was the year 1947. "The gentleman, Dad Stevenson, was my slave ancestor. A journalism background gained at the school newspaper helped me to know what to ask, Who? When? Where? How? Why?" I said. "Asking the right questions led me to a story." I pointed to a historical document. It was a page-length list in two columns: first names only and dollar amounts. "You're looking at an 1849 Inventory and Appraisement for the Estate of Moore Stephenson, listing my enslaved ancestor, along with his brothers, sisters and parents." Students zoomed right in in on Wilson's list price of $300.00. They were unable to reconcile his stately appearance with a list price.

"You got to ask the right questions in life." I indicated.

In *American Libraries'* article an image of Wilson, his wife Rillis and family appeared as an example of the "cultural nuances … that permeated"[7] my earliest book, *People in Search of Opportunity: The African American Experience in Mercer County*.[8] Beverly Goldberg, the author of the article, discussed that I became interested in research during "student days at Sharon High School, but keenly felt the absence of resources that could answer his questions about local African-American history. To fill in the blank for today's schoolchildren he conducted nine years of painstaking research that included gathering oral histories…." An appreciation for diversity coupled with my interest in local history led to writing the book when I was the head librarian at Pennsylvania State University Shenango Campus Library, Sharon, Pennsylvania, in 1995. This example Illustrated my point about the importance of asking the right questions when you want to become a writer.

How Can You Discover Your Voice?

Teens were captivated by the photograph on the third slide, "Discover Your Voice." Their thirsty eyes seemed to be longing for an adventure. The slide captured their imagination. A party of twenty youth, both male and female, on a rocky summit, seemed to be beckoning them to join in the fun times.

I told students the story of the photograph. I always had an interest in traveling and back then there was an opportunity to join a summer study program in Mexico. I shared this with Poppa who did not ask any more questions. To earn money for the trip, I cut grass and washed cars.

That summer I visited my dream land. It was the Plaza of Three Cultures and Temple of the Sun in Mexico. I climbed high on top of the rocky mound. I asked the students if they could identify me in the photograph. I was the one in blue jeans and tee-shirt, lying on my side in front of the others seated. I believe that was the summer when I discovered my voice.

I later traveled to many new destinations. I stood tall at the base of the Kwame Nkrumah Memorial in Accra, Ghana, when I attended Association for the Study of Ancient

African Civilization Conference. I now gained a footing, traveled solo with confidence. I have served on the inaugural editorial board for *The Journal of Pan African Studies*, founded by librarian Itibari Zulu, and *Information Equality Africa, Newsletter of the Progressive African Library and Information Activist's Group* (PALIAct). I advocated for oppressed poor communities in Africa. As I told students about these experiences, I encouraged them to discover their voices, to foster friendships with people from diverse cultures. I repeated that the need for better human relations has remained constant in our society.

Who, Me, a Storyteller?

"Me, an Author?" was the caption of the next slide. I told students about the time I wrote and performed a one-man skit about the three wise men for a Christmas pageant. "You're a storyteller," my Sunday school teacher exclaimed. "Who, me, a storyteller?" I asked.

Today, I have written several storybooks, *Under African Skies*[9] and *Lion Pride*,[10] based on African folklore. I have done storytelling at the Harlem Book Fair and other urban venues. I showed students a group shot of me with children's authors Sharon Flake, Elizabeth Howard, and Kelly Starling Lyon at an Ujamma Collective Children's Literary Festival in Pittsburgh's Hill District. I was dressed in a white cotton kufi and traditional Ghanaian dress with a blue and white ceremonial cloak from the Ewe culture in the Upper Volta.

How did I become an author? I read, read, read. In middle school I loved reading science fiction, historical fiction about slavery and Greek and Roman mythology. I later learned about the Aztecs, Mayans and Incas. I now know about ancient classical civilizations, namely Ghana, Mali and Songhai. I have incorporated African folklore, animals and vegetation into character development stories.

Teen Power

"Teen Power" was the headline of the fifth slide. "What could the possibilities have been, if only I did this or that?" you sometimes might ask. "Well, you're not alone."

Teens have power. I showed students a goofy picture of me and my high school friends on wacky dress day. Through the Human Relations Council I was responsible for program planning and held assemblies where international students from India, South Korea and Germany presented. I also set up exhibits on different cultures. My newly found friends from India and Germany helped me organize the dress-up party. At that time, we took home the realization that it was not our dress that defined us but the content of our character and the way we fostered a climate for better people-to-people relationships. I then encouraged cross-cultural exchanges with students from South Korea, who wanted to improve their English.

Now, many years later, I still have an appreciation for diversity. I emphasized that this experience influenced me later to write two books in the Arcadia books series, *Farrell*[11] and *African Americans in Mercer County*.[12] I told the students the story of writing these books. Miss Margaret, the public librarian at the Stey Nevant Farrell Public Library, asked me if I would be interested in writing a book about Farrell. This request was in response to a query from a publisher that was sent to the Farrell City Building and then passed on to the public librarian. I submitted a book proposal and it was accepted. This book celebrated multiculturalism and showcased families in traditional costume dress from countries of origins in our community.

Celebrate Life

"Celebrate!!!!!!" This slide brought awwwes, hoots and howls. Youth were ecstatic to see my book, *The African American Family Guide: Healing, Understanding and Restoring Our Families*, on a postcard with books about Jay Z, Beyoncé and Destiny's Child. I had a high energy storytelling image to show to a packed audience.[13] Two underlying legends read: "You have got to know and like yourself" and "join clubs and networks." I shared how my role as managing editor of *QBR The Black Book Review*, took me on gigs to New York City. Being back in Harlem evoked childhood memories of hot dog stands on Lennox Avenue, lunch at the post office box style Automat and roller coast rides and prizes at Coney Island.

I told teens about the time at the Schomburg's specious Langston Hughes Auditorium when I co-hosted the kick-off event, "My Favorite Book Story: Bring your Book" with Max Rodriguez, famed founder of the Harlem Book Fair, I expressed my deep gratitude for seeing the mahogany faces of nurses, tailors and other professionals I saw during my summer in the Big Apple that carried me through the bluster of each new school year.

I encouraged youth to explore their interests, join clubs and networks. You can begin building the skill set you need to reach your dream land today. Youth follow what we say as well as what we do. I recalled the euphoria I felt autographing books at Book Expo America.

Becoming a Leader

"Build Leadership Skillset" was the wrap-up slide of my school presentation. I showed an image of me seated in the *Gazette* editor's chair with school newspaper staff. Seems like just yesterday, when I was editor of the high school newspaper, I began building my leadership skills. Today, I make presentations at national conferences and guest appearances on television shows. I presented a paper, "Spirit of Sankofa: Retrieval, Historical Interpretation and Publishing," as a panelist for a plenary session, "Getting Our Voices Heard; Black Librarians and Publishing," at Clark Atlanta University in Georgia for ALA Annual Conference in Atlanta, June 13–17, 2002. I showed a picture of me making a guest appearance on the set of the WPXI television show *Black Impact* with hostess Brittiny M. in Pittsburgh.

Is There Life After This?

Following the Q&A after the presentation, there was some downtime. The kids were talking and I was chatting with a teacher. "After I graduated from high school my father died on I-80 in a car accident. I was in college. My mother died a few years later. She had breast cancer."

Students stopped talking. You could have heard a pin drop. Youth strained to hear what happened next. I had no prior intention of talking about this, maybe this was an "aha" moment.

"Was I prepared to revisit this emotional landmine?" I thought.

I cautiously pressed on. "My mother knew she had a floating tumor. She did not return to the doctor soon enough after she experienced discomfort, because she felt the need to stay home and raise her children. That's me."

"I did not want this to happen to anybody else's mother," I said. I told students that I later researched and wrote a story "Breast Cancer: Lightning Does Strike Twice" published in *Sisters Magazine*, the official publication of the National Council of Negro Women when I served as a biomedical librarian and Coordinator of Black Health History at the Howard University Health Science Library, Washington, D.C.[14] It was a piece about my mother's struggle with breast cancer. The story was so successful that it was circulated at an international women's conference in Cairo, Egypt. Youth broke out into spontaneous applause time and again at the conclusion of this inspirational message.

Final Thoughts

My visit and presentation at my former high school was a valuable experience for me as well as for the teens. Not only I delivered profound messages to the students, but the preparation for the visit and the conversation itself allowed me to take a second look and re-evaluate some of my experiences. In retrospective, I was fortunate to have met many remarkable people and have life experiences that inspired some difficult conversations and revelations, helped me understand and appreciate the complexity of multicultural human relations, and become an integral part of my community. As a librarian and a writer, I feel it is my responsibility to continue inspire youth by encouraging them to find their place and role in life.[15]As a writer and a storyteller, I have a wealth of life experiences that I will continue sharing with young people encouraging them to continue promote multiculturalism, develop the sense of community and interpersonal relationships.[16]

Notes

1. Roland Barksdale-Hall, "Building Dialogic Bridges To Diversity: Are We There Yet?," in *Where Are All The Librarians of Color? The Experiences of People of Color in Academia*, eds. Rebecca Hankins and Miguel Juarez (Sacramento: Library Juice, 2015), 265–298.
2. Roland Barksdale-Hall, "Stayin' a Little Ahead," *Journal of the Afro-American Historical and Genealogical Society* 8, no. 3 (1987), 114–121.
3. Roland Barksdale-Hall, "Rent Parties (A Tribute to Langston Hughes)," in *The Federal Poet* 44, no, 3 (1987), 23.
4. "Human Relations Council Formed," *Gazette* 44, no. 1(1977): 1.
5. Sharon Flake, *The Skin I'm In* (New York: Jump at the Sun, 1998).
6. Roland Barksdale-Hall, "Life After Trayvon: Q&A with Author Sharon Flake," *QBR The Black Book Review* 1, no. 3 (2012): 11–14.
7. Beverly Goldberg, "When Opportunity Knocks," *American Libraries* 26, no. 10 (1995): 997.
8. Roland Barksdale-Hall. *People in Search of Opportunity: The African American Experience in Mercer County, Pennsylvania, A History and Guide* (Sharon: Penn State Shenango, 1995).
9. Roland Barksdale-Hall, *Under African Skies* (Cherry Hill: Nefu, 2010).
10. Roland Barksdale-Hall, *Lion Pride* (Cherry Hill: Nefu, 2011).

11. Roland Barksdale-Hall, *Farrell* (Charleston: Arcadia, 2012).
12. Roland Barksdale-Hall, *African Americans in Mercer County* (Charleston: Arcadia, 2009).
13. Roland Barksdale-Hall, *The African-American Family's Guide to Tracing Our Roots: Healing, Understanding & Restoring Our Families* (Phoenix: Amber, 2005).
14. Roland Barksdale-Hall. "Breast Cancer Lightning Does Strike Twice," *Sisters Magazine* 2, no. 3 (1989): 9–10.
15. Roland Barksdale-Hall, "Cultural Issues in Health," in *Practicing Prevention: How to Be Healthy and Whole*, eds. Pamela Payne Foster and Roland Barksdale-Hall (Cherry Hill: AHLP Communications, 2013), 77–96.
16. Roland Barksdale-Hall, "I Indeed am a Griot," *BCALA News* 42, no. 2 (2015), 61–62.

Authors on the Inside

A Decade of Connecting Correctional Inmates with Writers

DANIEL MARCOU *and* PATRICK JONES

Although it is called the County Home School, it is doubtful that any of the incarcerated teenage girls who live in a cottage set in a wooded campus in suburban Hennepin County (Minnesota) think of it as home. However, when author Coe Booth (*Tyrell* [Booth 2006]) visited, she was welcomed like an anticipated houseguest. Booth sat in the same room where the girls held group meetings, answering their questions. They inquired about her writing, her life growing up in the Bronx; one even asked, "What is it like to be famous?" As the too short one-hour session ended, Booth signed copies of *Kendra* and listened intently as the "tough girls" approached her in awe.

The next morning Booth's visit to the Hennepin County Juvenile Detention Center began by listening to a rap recording by two residents about her books. As often happens in a pre-adjudication facility, both residents had left: one for home, another for placement. Many of the residents, new to the facility, had not read her books. Others, however, had read them and were prepared, thanks to their teacher, with a list of questions. Even the drab setting didn't dampen the mood of the curious residents, as Booth answered their questions.

After leaving the facility, Booth stopped at the Hennepin County Library—Minneapolis Central—to meet with girls from a teen parenting program, an issue she tackles in her book *Kendra*. At this session, Booth spoke about her background working in child protection. For these girls, the visit wasn't only about meeting an author, but also someone who (they noted in evaluations) understood their lives.

Booth's long day ended at the women's section of the Hennepin County Adult Corrections Facility where residents had their first chance to meet an author of a book t hey had read. For the adults, she made an even shorter presentation, letting the women drive the discussion and answering their questions about her life and writing. Also in the audience asking questions were stakeholders, including a Hennepin County Commissioner.

And that's just one experience of the twenty-plus authors brought into Hennepin County correctional facilities by Hennepin County Library (HCL) Outreach over the past decade.

A Hennepin County Adult Corrections Facility resident at the Coe Booth author visit.

Outreach to Correctional Facilities in Hennepin County

HCL Outreach provides library service to county residents who face barriers to using the library, including the incarcerated. For over thirty years, HCL has provided outreach service and programs at the Hennepin County Adult Corrections Facility (ACF), Hennepin County Public Safety Facility (PSF), Hennepin County Juvenile Detention Center (JDC) and Hennepin County Home School (CHS). This longstanding partnership between HCL and the Hennepin County Department of Community Corrections and Rehabilitation has been built through time, trust and national recognition. It has brought onsite libraries and library service in the facilities as well as ongoing programs like Read to Me (family literacy), employment workshops and job training opportunities. The level of library service varies by facility based on agreements with HCL.

The ACF provides short-term (up to one year) custody and programming for adult offenders convicted of a felony, gross misdemeanor, or misdemeanor offenses. The facility has a capacity of 399 to 477 residents in the men's section and 78 in the women's section—with an average length of stay of forty days. The PSF is not operated by the Department of Community Corrections, but instead by the Hennepin County Sheriff's Office. It is a pre-sentencing adult detention center with limited programming.

The JDC is a detention facility for juvenile offenders up to age 18 who have been arrested and are waiting for court disposition or placement. The facility has a capacity of 87 residents with an average length of stay of seven days. Residents 18 years old and younger who have not graduated from high school or have not earned a GED are enrolled in the Stadium View School in the JDC.

The CHS is a residential treatment center for juveniles found delinquent and committed by the court. The facility provides a safe, secure, and healthy environment in a

Authors inside:

Author	Titles	Visit location
Bao Phi	*Sông I Sing*	ACF (men's)
Coe Booth	*Kendra*	ACF (women's), CHS, JDC
David Mirambeaux	*Count-Time*	ACF (men's)
Deborah Jiang Stein	*Prison Baby*	ACF (women's)
Jacqueline Woodson	*Miracle's Boys*	ACF (women's), CHS
John Coy	*Box Out*	CHS
Jon Scieszka	*The Stinky Cheese Man and Other Fairly Stupid Tales*	ACF (men's)
Matt de la Peña	*Mexican White Boy*	ACF (women's), CHS, JDC,
Michele Norris	*The Grace of Silence*	ACF (women's), MC
Ryan Holiday	*The Obstacle Is the Way*	ACF (men's)
Sarah Fox	*Because Why*	ACF (women's)
Sharon Draper	*Hazelwood High Trilogy*	CHS, JDC
Steve Healey	*Earthling*	ACF (men's)
Tommy Watson	*A Face of Courage*	ACF (men's)
Will Weaver	*Claws*	CHS

167-acre rural setting. Intermediate School District 287 provides education and vocational opportunities to all residents.

During a year, more than 60,000 county residents will cycle through one of these four correctional facilities and during their time there, have access to library materials. At PSF, residents may only read books, while at the ACF, residents have access to onsite libraries and weekly library service and may take part in programs. Youth at the JDC receive twice-monthly library visits, while the collaboration between HCL and the CHS has resulted in literary magazines, creative writing workshops, and other programs.

Benefits of Bringing Authors into Correctional Facilities

In many ways, an author visit to a correctional facility is no different than one to a school or a library except that the author is literally speaking to a captive audience. What also might be different are the impactful outcomes for the audience.

An author visit to a correctional facility produces positive results for everyone involved. Residents (or inmates, the term varies), most of whom spend their time reading, learn that the books they read emerge from real people who look, talk and think like they do. For some residents, the author is a role model: often a person from a troubled background who made good. For almost all residents, however, an author visit provides the rare internal feeling of freedom: to ask questions, meet a new person, and interact with others in a positive way around a shared loved of reading.

For HCL, an author visit turns the library's mission statement—to nourish minds, transform lives and build community together—into reality. While the mission of a correctional facility is different than that of a library, there is a shared goal of helping people improve their lives. Author visits, especially when accompanied by book discussion groups or activities to extend the visit, present such opportunities. When institutions work together on author visits, the project itself is a "win" for collaboration as the library and facility demonstrate the strength of working together. This can serve as a springboard for future partnership or funding opportunities.

Planning for an Author Visit to a Correctional Facility

Planning for an author visit starts by gathering a team of library and facility staff to talk about the visit. Facility contacts will not only help the library plan the visit, but also will work with other staff at their location to resolve any potential issues.

Before a conversation about choosing authors and arranging other program details, everyone on the team needs to be clear about what they want to achieve. While goals may vary, most often they center on outputs such as the number of people reading the book and outcomes related to behavior, knowledge and attitudes. After the "why" is answered, the next step is to review the funding. Some funding sources may not pay for author visits that are not open to the general public, while others may not pay for books. Once everyone agrees on the goals and understands the resources available, focus can shift to the most important question of an author visit: "who?"

Choosing an Author

There are many factors to consider when choosing an author. One of the most important is finding an author whose books will be relevant to the residents' lives as well as their interests and needs. It's pointless to have an author that no one will want to read. Decisions are based on who has an engaging book about topics such as mental health, parenting or reentry that would also appeal to readers from different backgrounds and literacy levels.

For HCL, it has been important to have authors who can speak to both adults and youth. Some like Matt de la Peña and Jacqueline Woodson write for young adults, but also pen picture books of interest to the many adult parents at the ACF. Coe Booth's book *Kendra,* about teen motherhood and pregnancy, worked at adult and juvenile facilities.

Another important factor for HCL in choosing an author has been role modeling. Due to as disproportionate minority contact (DMC)—the over-representation of minorities in the criminal justice system compared to the general population—choosing an author of color was a consideration in our selection process. Many of our program evaluations mention the fact that the author "looked like me" as a plus.

As in most library decisions, the cost has been another factor. Hennepin County was fortunate to book Jacqueline Woodson before her National Book Award and Matt de la Peña before his Newbery Award, but both authors would probably no longer be in the target price range for programs at our county facilities. With few exceptions, an author's popularity and notoriety come with an expected author visit fee.

Since funding can be limited, it's good to look for partnership opportunities. For example, Michele Norris and Matt de la Peña visited facilities after they agreed to be part of different community programs. Jon Scieszka visited when he was in town for a library conference. Other author visits, like those by Steve Healey, Bao Phi and Sarah Fox were through a partnership with Minneapolis book publisher Coffee House Press. Local authors not only bring local connections, but also usually cost less since their travel expenses are minimal.

Some of the authors have visited multiple county facilities, plus the Minneapolis Central Library and a community school. But many of them visited only the ACF as part of the One Read or Big Idea book discussions. One Read programs are offered at the ACF women's section because its smaller population allows for all of its residents to participate. While normally libraries prioritize "bang for the buck," that is the wrong approach to authors on the inside. The work is about making connections, thus smaller groups that allow for more interaction work best. The positive outcomes related to changes in behavior, knowledge and attitudes are far more valuable than the numbers entered as program attendance statistics.

Making Arrangements

Once an author is selected and the correctional facilities are aware, a series of possible dates are determined that will work for the schedules of the author, library and facilities. Most "big name" authors book at least six months in advance. Some authors will book directly, while others have agents. Most authors' websites spell out the process of booking them to visit a library. A daily schedule that outlines which facility the author will visit is compiled including information on how many residents, what type of room, and any other details that might help the author plan effectively. Simply put, it needs to be clear what the author agrees to do during their visit so there are no last-minute surprises. A correctional facility runs on routine and anything that disrupts it will not be appreciated.

To prepare for any author visit, books should be ordered early. These come unprocessed, and if possible, in paperback to reduce costs. A set is given to facility staff, while other copies retained for the author to sign during their visit. Once the books arrive they need to be distributed to those residents who will still be in the facility at the time of the program. Residents get a copy of the author's book two weeks before the program.

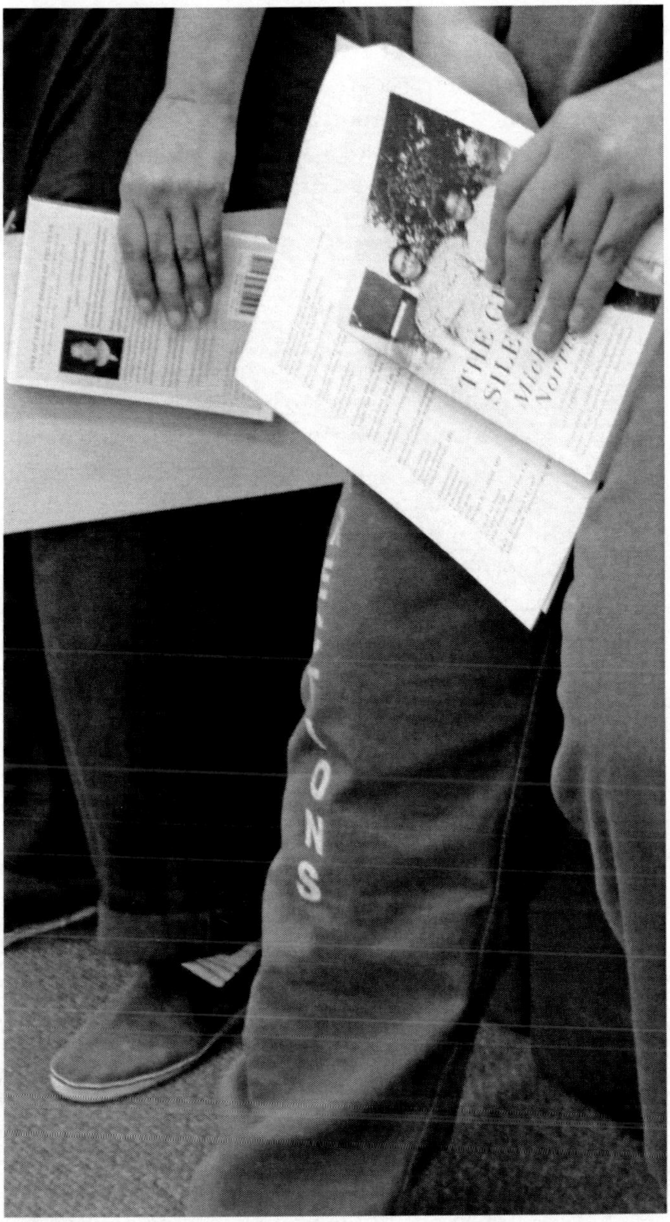
At the Hennepin County Adult Corrections Facility during the Michele Norris author visit.

Every correctional facility requires some sort of security clearance. With increased security due to the recently enacted Prison Rape Elimination Act (PREA), facility requirements might include asking the author to undergo a criminal background check or something similar. It needs to be made clear to the author that they must agree to complete background check paperwork and meet any other security clearance requirements of the facility. Since this takes time, it needs to be done early in the planning process.

At the same time in the process, invitations should be sent to stakeholders. HCL has typically invited a small number of community stakeholders, including library and facility administration as well as area elected officials. It is important that key supporters have the opportunity to attend the program, meet the author, and observe the program's impact on the residents, yet not so many as to overshadow the event.

It is also a good idea to get contracts signed early so the author can be paid promptly and to handle travel details as soon as possible including booking flights and a hotel, and arranging local transportation. Everything from making sure someone is available to pick up the author at the airport to ensuring the facility allows bottled water needs to be handled. Are there rooms booked? Is someone willing to arrange the chairs? Is there a sound system? Most libraries have a programming checklist going over such details, but corrections staff may not have experience in this area. Last minute doesn't cut it within corrections.

Building Excitement

A month before the program, HCL prepares flyers, bookmarks, and other promotional materials. The key is to build buzz around the program with facility residents and staff. The best advertising inside a facility is word of mouth—when you get people talking, good or bad, things can go viral very quickly. To enhance the buzz, make sure residents hear about the upcoming program when they pick up their library materials or attend other library programs. Promote authors on the inside as you would a public program. Involve corrections staff in promotion, especially those who have been part of your planning team from the beginning. While residents read, librarians can prepare additional materials, such as evaluations, book discussion questions, and "if you like" or similar readers' advisory lists. All of these materials allow the excitement and impact of the author visit to last beyond the day of the event.

The Day of the Author Visit

While every visit to a correctional varies based on the author, audience, and circumstances, the typical format for HCL is a one-hour program starting with 30 minutes of the author reading from their books and talking about their life as a writer. The author's talk is followed by an opportunity for residents to ask questions for 15 minutes. Some authors, like Coe Booth, interweave the time for questions throughout their talk, and in that case, it facilitated more questions and a deeper discussion. John Coy planned to talk about his young adult novels, but ended up instead discussing his picture book *Night Driving* (Coy 1996), including showing drafts from the book's illustrator. Most programs end with an opportunity for the residents to get their books signed by the author.

Authors like Jacqueline Woodson and Jon Scieszka also visited with ACF residents during the HCL's Read to Me program where incarcerated parents learn about early literacy and then record themselves reading books for their children. After meeting with fathers at the ACF men's section, Scieszka shared a very short story based on a question a dad had asked during Read to Me. At the ACF women's section, Woodson shared readings from several of her books with residents at Read to Me and answered questions. She also inspired several residents to request more of her books and books about writing from the library. At the end of the program, each resident received a book written by Woodson, then had the opportunity to have her to sign it so it could be sent home to their child.

At the end of every HCL author visit, participating residents are asked to fill out an evaluation. During the program, photos are taken. It is important to note that no identifying photos are taken of residents to respect their right to privacy. A photo release form is used if needed, and the facility also reviews all images from each program. The images are used, along with evaluation results, to create a PowerPoint summary of the program's success that is shared with all of the program's funders and stakeholders.

One consistent theme in program evaluations has revolved around how the author's writing and experience "connected" with the audience. It has become apparent that themes in the discussions are just as important as the book and author being well received. At the ACF, this has led HCL to focus more on local non-fiction writers who have "walked in the shoes" of the residents.

The Big Idea

HCL's Big Idea program is similar to a One Read program; however, the Big Idea focuses on a topic that is very relevant to the residents' life and explores it with the hope that it will help the residents after their release. HCL has hosted authors for three Big Idea programs at the ACF men's section.

The first program featured Tommy Watson's talk about motivation. He shared his experience growing up with incarcerated parents and how he overcame many challenges, including homelessness, to eventually become an elementary school principal. Facility residents who participated received a copy of Watson's book *A Face of Courage*. (Watson 2008). Eighty-three percent of the residents said that the program made them think about the changes they wanted to make in their lives while seventy-two percent were inspired by Watson's life story.

David Mirambeaux discussed strategies for success at the second program. Mirambeaux honestly revealed past mistakes he had made in life, including the events that led to his incarceration, and how he was able to make significant changes that eventually led to his current work as a case manager for the Goodwill-Easter Seals FATHER Project. Residents who participated received a copy of his book *Count-Time: An Offenders Guide to Successful Reentry* (Mirambeaux 2010) Ninety-three percent of the residents said that the program made them think about their lives. Eighty eight percent were inspired by Mirambeaux's life story.

Because many of the residents who attended these two programs could relate to the authors' life experiences of poverty, ongoing family issues, street life, and incarceration, they appeared to be more open to the suggestions each presenter gave about making positive changes. Each program served as an opportunity for the residents to meet someone who had walked in their shoes, but then did the hard work of change and found a way out to a better life.

Ryan Holiday visited for the third program to talk about his book, *The Obstacle is the Way* (Holiday 2014) and how the residents could use philosophy to better face challenges in their lives. Only thirty percent of the participants had ever read about philosophy or overcoming obstacles before reading Holiday's book; however, after the program, ninety-five percent of the participants felt that philosophy, and the public library, could help people with the obstacles they face when leaving a correctional facility.

Outcomes from an Author Visit

Evaluations allow HCL to know what worked and what could be improved. They are also helpful to get ideas for other possible authors the residents would like to hear from at their facility. HCL's evaluation model has evolved over time, from capturing outputs (how many residents attended) to low level outcomes (did you like the program) to impact indicators based on the library's mission.

Sometimes, the thoughts of program participants are captured using a digital recorder. While it can be difficult to get in-depth written qualitative data, these recordings allow people to freely talk, which they are apt to do after an exciting program. Any use within a facility of a camera or other recording equipment needs prior approval. There also must be enough staff to distribute and collect evaluations. After an HCL program, participants are given a paper evaluation to complete. The evaluations remain consistent with the same questions asked in similar programs to document improvement, but new questions are also added for each author. Multiple-choice questions seek to determine if the goals of the programs were met, while open-ended questions allow ample opportunity for residents to offer authentic feedback.

While evaluation questions and responses vary, across them all, HCL has seen clear evidence that before a program, most residents have never met an author or participated in a book discussion. But more important, the evaluations document that in the short term, the visit changed attitudes, increased knowledge, and inspired positive behaviors.

Obstacles to a Successful Author Visit

Despite these positive results, there are obstacles facing other libraries attempting to replicate HCL's efforts. Many issues emerge from the differing core philosophies of libraries and corrections. Libraries are about access and choices, but for many reasons, correctional facilities limit access and choices. Libraries break down walls, correctional facilities are made of them. The aforementioned PREA legislation puts up additional barriers to library staff, volunteers, and authors looking to get into a correctional facility. One author even refused to visit a facility because of the background check requirement.

Once inside, there are additional challenges; therefore, adaptability is an essential skill for offering any programs inside a correctional facility. On the day of the visit, a hundred things could go wrong. The facility could, due to fights or other issues, go on "lockdown" where no one is allowed to enter. In a short-term detention facility, like the JDC, many of the residents who read the author's books may have departed, leaving new students unfamiliar with the author as the audience. In long-term facilities, residents anticipating the visit might not be able to attend. They might be "in the hole" (solitary) for discipline problems, on a home visit, at court, at work, or absent due to another scheduling conflict.

Another hurdle leading up to an author visit stems from the competing priorities of staff in each institution. For the librarians and some corrections staff, an author visit is a big deal. It is something they've planned for months; for many corrections officers, it might be seen as another demand on their schedule. Their job remains the same: keeping order and maintaining safety. An author visit might be seen as contrary to those goals, so it is good to talk with all facility staff and offer copies of the book so they can share in the excitement about the visit.

The attitude of frontline corrections staff might be shared by members of the public, stakeholders, and even other library staff. As the warden in the movie *Shawshank Redemption* (Robbins 1994) tells Andy about the request for money to buy library books, "there's only three ways to spend the taxpayer's hard-earned money when it comes to prisons. More walls. More bars. More guards." While an author visit to a public library or school involves press releases, social media posts, and photo opportunities, programs inside a facility are rarely promoted in advance and outcomes, no matter how outstanding, aren't typically shared outside of the library after the program, except in reports to stakeholders who already understand why author visits matter.

Conclusion

Creativity expert Sir Ken Robinson spoke about the role of the arts in society noting "The arts especially address the idea of aesthetic experience. An aesthetic experience is one in which your senses are operating at their peak. When you are present in the current moment. When you are resonating with the excitement of this thing that you are experiencing, when you are fully alive" (Robinson 2010).

Author visits offer the opportunity for residents of correctional facilities to experience that they are alive and part of the world again, or as one resident noted, "Thank you for making me feel normal." This comment about normalcy has appeared in many HCL evaluations after an author visits a facility.

When an author becomes a real person, instead of just words on a page, correctional facility residents—and all of us—make a connection to the world bigger than the one we were in before. When the world we know is small and wrapped tight by steel bars, concrete, and barbed wire it is easy to stop feeling normal. You begin to feel alone. You start to shut down. Writers bring ideas, hope, laughter and tears. Most important they share their stories, and for an hour, we are one community, listening to one another.

Works Cited

Booth, Coe. 2006. *Tyrell.* New York: Scholastic.

Coy, John. 1996. *Night Driving.* New York: Henry Holt.

Holiday, Ryan. 2014. *The Obstacle Is the Way.* New York: Penguin.

Mirambeaux, David. 2010. *Count-Time: An Offender's Guide to Success.* Scandia, MN: Greystone Educational Materials.

Shawshank Redemption. 1994. Directed by Frank Darabont. Performed by Tim Robbins.

Robinson, Sir Ken. 2010. *Changing Paradigms.* February 4. https://www.youtube.com/watch?v=mCbdS4hSa0s (accessed May 28, 2016).

Watson, Tommy. 2008. *A Face of Courage.* Bloomington, IN: iUniverse.

A Campus or Library Lecture Series

The Perfect Outreach to Writers and Poets

John C. Burns

Not too long ago, as an eager undergraduate student studying art and graphic design, I had the good fortune of attending several extracurricular workshops, lectures, and other similar presentations on campus. The professional artists presenting at the workshops were exceptionally skilled and extremely creative, working in a range of different mediums. These men and women were the de facto professionals; the professionals vibrant in their craft and making a decent living doing what they love and excel at. I distinctly recall two individual guest lecturers that did much to cement my determination to continue on and pursue my degree.

The first artist I had the pleasure of interacting with was a ceramic artist who worked primarily in porcelain clay. She owned a business whose physical location housed a storefront for sales of her handcrafted work and a studio in back. The art department at the university had invited her for a week of lectures and demonstrations scattered throughout each day so as to cater to various student schedules. When I attended a demonstration, she showcased her skills as a magnificent craftsperson and made a signature piece similar to pieces she frequently sold at her shop. Each piece is a unique, one-of-a-kind creation and often is the result of client conversations or special commissions. The piece she was demonstrating was a white porcelain tea set composed of a beautiful serving dish, a delightful teapot, and two matching teacups. All of the pieces fit snugly onto the serving dish in an elegant ensemble. I was utterly entranced during the entire workshop and found the experience of watching her work, and watch her engage with the audience to instruct, as one of the most cherished learning experiences of my art education.

The other experience I had was similar, but involved a gentleman working as graphic designer and printmaker. He held demonstrations and lectures and I attended one of the last lectures he did while he was staying as a guest of the university. Here too I found myself entranced as his work was fresh and unique using traditional printmaking presses, recycled papers, and antique letter blocks. His lecture was a combination of wit, storytelling, and instruction combined with videos of him working in his studio. Like the experience with the ceramic artist, these two events ended up being two of the most memorable, enriching, and beneficial learning experiences I have ever had.

I would later come to refer back to both experiences in my current professional librarian position. I now have an undergraduate degree in graphic design with a minor in art history. I also hold a master's degree in library and information science and am a full time librarian at a public university. In my career as a librarian I have often been given the opportunity to extend outreach to many groups and individuals from all walks of life. Early on I started my career in public libraries and was in charge of programming and outreach to adults. I ran multiple book clubs and had many writers come to the library to speak. However, it was not until I became an academic librarian in the position I now hold that I was able to fine tune and expand my outreach efforts to encompass the literary arts including outreach to writers and poets. My outreach efforts would eventually take two forms. One form developed as outreach to established professional writers and poets inviting them to come to my university and speak. The other form was the outreach to students and amateur writers and poets seeking to better their craft by engaging with and learning from the pros. It all started when I decided that I wanted to create a lecture series for the community, students, and faculty on campus. Serving as the librarian liaison to the art department at my university, I wanted the lecture series to focus solely on the studio arts or traditional painting, digital art, ceramics, sculpture, photography, etc. I set myself to work and organized the lecture series in collaboration with the art department faculty. Quickly the lecture series grew and had great success; so much so that it caught the attention of the dean of the school of humanities. The dean approached me in my office and asked if I would chair a committee for another lecture series that had long existed on campus. Enthusiastically I said yes because this opportunity had three key ingredients that I currently did not have for my newly formed artist lecture series. First, it had a budget so I no longer had to rely on the pro bono goodwill of my invited guests. I also could extend my reach to additional topic areas like literature and poetry and have some funds to arrange travel for guests. The second item it had was a committee of faculty and students that I could utilize for some assistance. Lastly, it had some established marketing personnel and media connections that made getting the word out easier. When I began my work on this alternate lecture series in earnest, my mind drifted back to the aforementioned experiences I had as an undergraduate. I began to ask myself one question I was convinced held the key to success with the lecture series I was now in charge of: what made these lecture experiences so utterly engaging, memorable, and effective? I believe it was two components of the workshops that are worth exploring. In their own way each component caused the workshops to function well providing an enriching experience for all.

1. Each workshop or lecture was a glimpse of a potential future career for students in attendance. At the lectures students would listen to, observe, and learn from working professionals. Granted, the students were enrolled in courses with instructors who are working professionals too, but the guest artist was something uniquely different providing a magnificent supplement to the efforts of the faculty. Many of the students were able to learn what it is going to be like out in the "real world" after their time in school came to an end. They were exposed to everything from business practices to legal issues surrounding art, given to them by individuals who had already encountered and conquered such things. Students also heard the emphatic pleas from each lecturer encouraging them to never stop learning.

2. The lectures and the people giving them were profoundly inspirational. Every lecture or workshop I have been involved in, whether I participated as an undergrad or events I worked to put together later in my working career, has always come from

the heart and soul of the presenter. Passion and expertise gushed out of them in every event and you could tell they were doing what they loved. It made a huge difference and was at the core of why they were so inspirational.

I found myself able to do so much more with a lecture series that was far larger than the one I had originally created. I also came to realize how relatively easy it was to get a lecture series off the ground and how enjoyable it was to manage one. It has, and continues to be, an excellent outreach tool for the library and the campus and an excellent means of collaboration with faculty. Collaboration with faculty is really where outreach to writers and poets catalyzed. Shortly after I became the director of the lecture series and chair of the committee that put them together, I approached and was approached by several faculty seeking to collaborate with me. Before I share some stories of marvelous experiences I have had so far, let me first share some tips about how one might go about creating a similar lecture series. Without a doubt, if you can find one that is already established and offer to take it on, that may be easiest. If instead you have to start from scratch, here is what is needed.

1. A source of funding is ideal despite it being possible to do a lecture series with only your own blood, sweat, and tears. The first lecture series I created cost nothing more than my time and energy (and some blood, sweat, and tears … mostly sweat). I had no budget whatsoever and it was all a product of my time and labor. Fortunately, it was a labor of love and something I have always wanted to do. Another fortunate component that amazes me still was the generous souls who gave their time and talents to the lecture series. Every guest lecturer I hosted, before I had a budget, did it for free and I never felt like their presentations were less than what I would have received had I paid them. Funding sources can come from the school, an endowment, a grant, fundraising, etc.
2. Desire and hard work. These two components are a no-brainer, but it needs to be said anyway. There is a great deal of networking, planning, and preparation that goes into each well produced, well executed lecture.
3. Marketing, marketing, marketing! Without this you are sunk and will just be spinning your wheels. If you can grab an intern, a student worker, or a volunteer to help with this—great, but if not—make use of social media and do everything you can think of to get the word out. My advice is to partner closely with the public relations office at your institution and, at minimum, have them send out a press release for you. You could always do this on your own, but an office dedicated to public relations will make this easier for you. Some of the tricks of the trade that have been successful for me is finding a restaurant in town that would be willing to donate food for the event. I have done events in the past that offered free food and I put the restaurant's logo on any of my promotional material as a token of gratitude. A word of caution here is that you don't want to just have free food be the reason people come. Nothing will be as strong of an incentive to potential attendees as a great presenter with a great topic at a free event.
4. A great venue. If you can find a spot in the library to hold your lecture series that would be ideal. If you cannot hold it in the library, find another spot on campus that is easy to get to and has great parking nearby. If you are able to record them, do and make the recordings available on the web via a web site, YouTube, or other social media.

What follows are brief case studies of the experiences I have had with faculty, writers, and poets.

Poet Laureate

The first case study involves a wonderful opportunity I had working with one of the English faculty on my campus. She had been working to arrange several events for students to spend some time learning from a seasoned professional with abundant experience. She contacted me to see if I would be interested in co-sponsoring an event to host the first Poet Laureate in our state (an individual who was also runner-up for U.S. Poet Laureate). In addition to the event our guest held writing and critique workshops all week long for our English students. The actual culminating event was an evening of readings and conversation with the poet. Those in attendance not only enjoyed dramatic and heartfelt renditions and readings of his work by the author, they also heard him tell stories of his career, stories of his creative process, and stories of the inspiration he found for his work. The venue was off campus and the space was donated by a local resort. Refreshments were made available and the entire evening was absolutely outstanding. Good food, good company, and good entertainment. It was a pure joy to work on and a magnificent collaboration between me a librarian, faculty, and an incredibly talented poet.

Film Maker and Author

Another outstanding event I was able to put together centered on a very talented and extremely knowledgeable film maker and writer. My guest for the campus lecture series was a woman who had created a thought-provoking documentary on the Holocaust. Her film was held in our collection in the library and she was an acquaintance of another member of our English faculty. The faculty and I collaborated to bring her to campus from New York. She gave a fantastic and interesting lecture and we showed clips from her film. Many in attendance were in awe of the content of the film and were captivated by her story. She not only spoke about the research she had conducted to aid her writing, but also spoke of all the other facets that came together to make her piece.

Two Writers: One Doing Creative Fiction, the Other a Poet with a Knack for Humor

Once again I sought out and was presented with an opportunity to collaborate with our English faculty. On this particular occasion, I was able to work with our English Department and its faculty to bring two excellent writers to campus for one event. While the faculty utilized them for some workshops with students, I was able to host both at the campus lecture series. I made all the arrangements for travel and hospitality while they were guests of our university and hosted a lunch for them as well. One of the guests is a creative fiction writer who teaches at a university. She spoke about her successes and then gave two incredibly engaging readings of her work. The other guest split the time at the lecture and presented a brief overview of his career and teaching experience. He then presented several readings of his extremely humorous and entertaining published poetry.

A Poet for the Sciences

This case was one where I was given a name of a gentleman as a possible option for the campus forum I am in charge of. The referral was from one of our English faculty and it had a unique twist. I produced an invitation through email and he graciously accepted but he was not like anything I had previously hosted. In fact, he remains to this day as a completely unique guest as far as his writing was concerned. This particular guest is fascinated by the natural work and the study of the life and physical sciences. He is a professor of English at a state university and his poetry was a delightful commentary on some of his favorite subtopics in the sciences. Beautifully written and wholly unique, his words had all the elements of excellent poetry on topics that many in the audience likely never imagined could or would be woven into poetry. A satisfying side effect of his interesting fusion of science and poetry was the remarkable mix of individuals in the audience attending the lecture event. Some seats were filled with science faculty and science majors; others filled with English faculty and majors.

Professor of English and Expert of Middle Eastern Women Writers

Of all the cases presented so far this one had the most far reaching collaboration aspects to it. Many people came together with me to bring this guest to the campus lecture series and the results were most enriching. To understand the stakeholders in this joint venture, I need to write a brief sentence or two about a documentary film festival held on our campus. Every year my university holds a week-long international documentary film festival during the fall semester. Many events run in parallel to the festival including film screenings, academic seminars, and events to meet screenwriters. One such event centered on Muslim women and a film at the festival with the same theme. Several people on campus (the production director for the festival, the dean of the library, and the faculty in the English Department) including myself decided to come together and create events around the screening of this film. For the campus lecture series that I oversee we decided to invite a scholar and professor of English who specialized in topics surrounding Muslim women. Fortunately this person resided in the same state and was a close friend of our library dean. My invitation to her was accepted and we arranged for her to speak at noon at the campus lecture series and again at night following a screening of the film. She was outstanding and drew an impressive crowd at both events. Not only is she a talented writer but she was also a captivating speaker.

Award Winning Poet

I cannot emphasize enough how valuable the cultivation of a strong relationship with English faculty can result in a fruitful partnership. The case is yet another example of the wonderful outcomes from investing the time to liaise and collaborate with faculty on your campus (that is if you are an academic librarian). After consulting with one of our creative writing instruction faculty, I received the names of a few colleagues and other guest idea options. She felt that these people would be the most advantageous and beneficial to her students. I agreed and picked one from her list to invite to the campus lecture series as I felt they would be interesting to other potential attendees, as well. Our guest was an award winning poet who taught as well. Her writing was deep and passionate and centered on topics that struck a chord with many in attendance. Not only was her presentation and readings outstanding, she also donated her book to our library. Many of my guests have published and some of them are quite prolific. When they offer to donate their work, I am delighted to accept, and we now have a growing collection in our library of titles that were written by guests of the campus lecture series.

Tolkien Expert

I admit I am a fan of Tolkien and when the final Hobbit film was released, I went out on my own in search of a Tolkien expert to invite to campus for a lecture. I struck gold with this case and found a gentleman who was just that … an expert. He taught and is a director of an academic library. Having written about many unique aspects of Tolkien, he was a perfect match to what I was looking for. During his excellent presentation he delved into language, music, and obscure facets of Tolkien's writing and life. The audience and I were elated and I could tell just from the expressions on each attendee's face that this was pure delight for the audience.

Singer and Songwriter

The last case I want to highlight in brief is a good example of ways to add variety and diversity under the umbrella of outreach efforts I have engaged in at my library. I have been able to bring to campus several writers and it was important to showcase the wide variety of career paths writing can take. The guest for this case is a singer/songwriter. Her writing obviously relates to her composition of music but it was fun to see this different aspect of the writer and the writing process. Poetry is often found within her lyrics and the guest did more than just read her works and talk about her process. She also brought her acoustic guitar and performed for the audience unplugged. As a bonus my guest is also a teacher of writing and taught the audience many of the same techniques and methods she teaches her students in the classroom.

In conclusion, I cannot emphasize the importance of simply seeking out and making the attempt to reach out to the profusion of talented and professional writers and poets dotting the nation. I have had nothing but success and have found each guest to be warm, gracious, and generous. All were eager to take the opportunity to share their knowledge and experience to guide the next generation of artist along.

An Evolving Partnership
A Reading Series Finds a Home in the Library

ROBERT S. MEANS

Anyone who has been in one lately knows that libraries are not just secular temples devoted to learning and the preservation of the printed word. Public libraries have become "centers" of their communities, gathering places for groups, families and individuals, while still maintaining traditional library services. Academic libraries as well have evolved as online access has provided faculty and students with "the library" on their laptops. In this evolution, the Harold B. Lee Library (Lee Library), centrally located at Brigham Young University has worked to become more than just the physical center of the BYU campus, but indeed something like the heart of the university. To accomplish this, the library has reached out with programs like Art in the Library (that makes gallery space in the library available to B.F.A. and M.F.A. candidates, as well as faculty and community artists); an internship program for students interested in pursuing an M.L.S.; and the English Department Reading Series that hosts poets, fiction writers and creative nonfiction writers each week in the library auditorium.

Such outreach ideas are not new. Many libraries have been instrumental in providing a bridge between writers, artists and the public:

> [i]n the early 1920s, the 135th Street Branch Library of the New York Public Library [...] played a significant role in the Harlem Renaissance movement. By drawing on the resources of the community, the library staff facilitated connections between writers and their readers with literary gatherings; between artists and their viewers with art exhibitions; and between playwrights, performers, and their audiences with theatrical productions [Anderson, 383].

In fact, libraries need to reach out and get involved, because artists have a way of creating their own space to gather in to read, to exhibit, and to perform. During the 1960's, Yiddish poets in New York City created the Poetry Center at the 92nd Street Y (notice: not in a library, and not at a university, but a safe, neutral space of their own making), which became "the most venerable and sought-after venue for poetry readings in the United States" (Schwarz, 69).

Universities, encouraged by English Departments eager to make contact with the writers they study and teach, have been proactive in reaching out and bringing writers to campus to read and discuss their work. Today most universities have some kind of a reading series.

The English Department Reading Series

The English Department Reading Series (ERS) at BYU began around 1995, but the idea originated years before in a Mormon literature class at BYU. John Bennion, a student intern in that class was impressed that the professor had a writer visit the class each week. When Bennion became an English professor and began teaching Mormon literature, he continued the practice (Howe, 8). Bennion had also been impressed with the reading series at the University of Houston, where he completed his PhD, and proposed a similar reading series to department leaders and creative writing faculty at BYU (Howe 8).

Back in 1995, the ERS at BYU started as a very modest reading series in a small 50-some seat auditorium in the old humanities building. When the Harold B. Lee Library at BYU opened its 234,000-square-foot addition that included a 211-seat auditorium with all the audio-visual amenities, I invited John Bennion to bring the ERS over to the Lee Library.

With no experience, I asked myself (even as I extended the invitation in behalf of the Lee Library) "what is a poetry reading supposed to be like?" How do we "stage" a reading series? Poetry enjoys a certain mystique, and often the image of something like a smoky basement Beat café still comes to mind (and that's not a bad thing), as in this description of an Alan Dugan reading in Chicago more than twenty-five years ago:

> [f]ifty or so people are sitting in uncomfortable folding chairs facing a lectern. On the lectern are two "single-shot" bottles of *Southern Comfort.* On a chair nearby, facing the audience, sits a man with his head down, hunched into his shoulders. [...] The Audience is very quiet as Dugan moves to the microphone. He says something. The voice is hoarse, hardly audible, barely understandable, but heard—attention is focused, as in the quiet moments just before a string quartet's recital [Stern, 67].

We at the Lee Library felt we could provide the same cool, hip(ster) atmosphere in our auditorium (substituting *Dasani* for *Southern Comfort* because we're a Mormon school), but with better sound quality and comfy theater seating.

Professor John Bennion and the BYU English Department accepted my invitation (on behalf of the library), and gradually I (and other library personnel and resources) became more and more involved in the ERS. The basic schedule was (and still is) ten to twelve readers every fall and winter semesters at noon on Friday in the Lee Library auditorium. The mix of readers included BYU English Department creative writing faculty (poets, fiction writers, and a growing number of essayists/creative-nonfiction writers), and writers of all genres from outside the university. Mormon writers were still well represented, including writers of young adult fiction aimed at the Mormon market. Science Fiction writer Brandon Sanderson has read twice at the ERS: the first time before his career had taken off, at which time he read passages from works in progress that he was then shopping around, and that (no one knew at the time) would soon become best-sellers. And sometimes writers have even poked fun at themselves at the ERS, including in their serious readings examples of overwrought, pompous *PowerPoint* poetry, and bad haiku. As one writer observed,

> [f]or the regional writers, the ERS must be an important opportunity to share their work with a wider audience, and an occasion for public recognition—so important for writers, but so rare for all but the most famous. In my experience, the ERS is not only good for these regional writers, but also for BYU faculty members, who establish friendly and sometimes productive collegial relationships with them [Talbot].

Lee Library Involvement in the ERS

At first, the library began to create simple posters advertising the weekly readings (and to give to the readers as a memento). Then, in time, the Lee Library's Special Collections seminar room (conveniently next door to the library auditorium) was booked after each reading for an author reception where the audience enjoyed refreshments, and readers could mingle with the audience and sign copies of their books.

Consequently, the university bookstore was also involved to make sure that copies of each reader's books were brought over, and a temporary cash register set up and staffed. Poet and creative writing faculty, John Talbot recalls:

> I've read from my books of poetry several times, an in each case it's been a great benefit to me. [...] It's the ERS that puts me in touch with readers who actually live where I do. After the reading, I'm able to actually meet fellow locals who find themselves interested in my poetry, to sign books for them, and—in a number of cases—to become friends with them. Each time I've read there's been at least one BYU student who gets to know me and later comes to me for help and advice with his own poetry. All that's a good thing, both for me and for the students. To which I'd add that the people at the Lee Library who host the readings have always done a superb job. The audio-visual materials are always expertly in place, the venue is superb, and the posters they produce to advertise the events are works of art in themselves [Talbot].

The publicity posters have, indeed, evolved: from simple "flyers" with the author's photo, date and time, to symbolic statements representing each writers work.

Roger Layton, the Lee Library's Communications Manager, explains:

> [m]y student designers began creating posters with original art based on what they could learn about the authors. As it turns out the authors liked the new posters. Soon my designers began looking forward to the next season of readings so they could research the authors and design new work. Today the English Reading Series poster work is the top project in our workflow. Only the senior student designers get to work on it and they have established very high standards for themselves. It is interesting to watch them search the library catalog and the Internet to acquire books, poems, and stories that give them an understanding of the themes in each individual author's works. The research experience should serve them well when they are presented with new design challenges in their careers [Layton].

Author Douglas Thayer signs a copy of his latest novel after his reading at a weekly English Department Reading Series program in 2007 (courtesy Roger Layton).

During her reading at the ERS in October 2015, Terry Tempest Williams was so impressed with the poster created for her reading that she asked to meet the designer, Emma Zaugg, an undergraduate majoring in animation.

The meeting made quite an impression on Zaugg:

An example of the weekly English Department Reading Series posters produced by student designers (courtesy Lee Library Public Relations).

Student designer Emma Zaugg, left, and author Terry Tempest Williams in October 2015 (courtesy Lee Library Public Relations).

> Designing posters for the English Reading Series was a fun project for me, as I had the opportunity to become acquainted with a new writer's work each week. I would start each poster by first learning about the writer, and then would read his or her work so that I could understand their style and find any themes that might be common throughout their writing. After that I just tried my best to create a design that shared similar themes as their writing and hoped they liked it. The best day ever working on the project was when Terry Tempest Williams came to my office to thank me for the poster I'd made for her. She asked me to sign her poster, and even gave me her own personal copy of her book that she had just read from. I was honored to meet her and so glad that I was able to help make her experience at the HBLL a pleasant one [Zaugg].

In addition to involving the library's PR resources for making posters, I also brought in the library's multimedia crew and began to professionally record the weekly readings. These recordings have since become an important part of both the library's fiction/creative nonfiction collection, and the history of the Lee Library, itself. Also, the library makes DVD copies of the readings available to the readers for their portfolios. Chris Garcia, Lee Library Multimedia Production Manager, supervises the multimedia crew:

> The ERS has become the most frequently occurring event in the library's auditorium as well as the most frequent project we do. We've gone from just recording and editing the lecture and delivering them in DVD, to including preparing digital files for two streaming video serves, making the series available to students within days of the event happening. In recent semesters I've even had students

request to be the person assigned to record the event every week because they enjoy the experience of the readings [Garcia].

The Lee Library has tried to assume responsibility for all ERS facilities details so that the reader can concentrate on their reading, and the ERS faculty coordinator can concentrate on hosting the reader. It's an arrangement that's worked well:

> The ERS has become one of the most successful and long running collaborations I think the library has done with a campus department. When doing a recent interview with a former faculty in charge of the ERS, he commented on how easy a collaboration it is. He said that there are many times he doesn't even have to ask for something to be arranged or set up before it is already done [Garcia].

The ERS Expands and Partners

Where once it was a venue essentially for BYU English Department and Mormon writers, the ERS now hosts many more readers from outside the university than it does from within. Some of the readers who have participated in the ERS over the years include U.S. Poets Laureate Maxine Kumin, Billy Collins, Mark Strand, Charles Simic, Robert Hass, Robert Pinsky, W. S. Merwin, and Philip Levine, as well as two standing Utah State Poets Laureate Katherine Coles and Lance Larsen. Also, National Book Award winners Barry Lopez and Galway Kinnell, and Pulitzer Prize winners Marilynne Robinson and Yusef Komunyakaa have read in the ERS, as have international writers Eduardo Galeano (Uruguay), Tomaz Salaman (Slovenia), Adriana Lisboa (Portugal), Kevin Hart (Australia), Luisa Igloria (Philippines), and Ngũgĩ wa Thiong'o (Kenya).

After the ERS hosted Nobel Laureate in Literature, Derek Walcott, in 2004, two BYU faculty were able to organize a study abroad to St. Lucia where literature and painting students met with Walcott, enjoyed a poetry reading in his home, and discussed painting and literature with him. One faculty member involved recalled: "we managed to arrange the study abroad program because of the relationship we ended up developing while he was here" at BYU to read at the ERS (Handley).

The ERS has come to partner with other reading series,' local libraries, and foundations to host some of these nationally known writers, who then gave readings at a number of local venues. In these arrangements the ERS benefits by the added financial help from other series,' libraries, and foundations, while the ERS can offer in return the Lee Library's established PR operation, and experienced multimedia crew for filming a reading "on location" (away from its usual venue in the Lee Library auditorium).

Robert Pinsky's October 2014 visit to BYU and the ERS, was co-sponsored by the Ethel L. Handley Annual Reading, and held in a larger venue on BYU campus (outside the Lee Library) to accommodate the anticipated audience. Even so, the reading strove for the same intimate give-and-take between poet and hearers. "At the beginning of the reading Pinsky stated that he would not only share a selection of his works with the audience, but that his goal [...] was to make himself as useful to the students as possible" (Cutler).

Pinsky also read at the nearby Orem Public Library, where "Outreach Librarian Nathan Robinson said the reading was a great way to wrap up the library's seventh series of Orem Reads. 'When you get to see a poet of that caliber perform, you see poetry in the element that it's supposed to be in,' he said. 'Poetry is more than something on a page—it's partially music'" (Stevens).

The ERS: A Venue for Student Writers

The ERS has also become a venue where campus essay contest winners read their work, and the ERS devotes one reading per semester "to three advanced creative writing students—one poet, one essayist, and one fiction writer—who compete for the opportunity to read" (Howe 9).

Michael Lavers was one of the students chosen to read his poetry at the ERS, and the experience helped him develop as a poet: "[a]s far as the audience was concerned, my poems were only auditory. I was forced to become aware of [my poems] as sound objects, and I found myself making sound-based revisions that I otherwise would not have thought to make. That realization has stuck with me in my composition process" (Howe 9). Lavers returned to BYU years later to join the creative writing faculty in the English Department, and become a faculty coordinator of the ERS.

Another student reader, Claire Akebrand found that "[t]he Q&A made me realize that I needed more practice articulating my ideas on poetry … [b]eing chosen to read was a great confidence builder. I felt honored to get to read in the same place where famous visiting writers had read. It is a great way to encourage students" (Howe 9).

Robert Pinsky signing a copy of his book after his English Department Reading Series program in 2014 (courtesy College of Humanities, BYU).

The ERS Becomes a for-Credit Class

The ERS has also evolved into a for-credit class in the English Department, offered Fall and Winter semesters, with semester enrollment between 40 and 70 students. ENGL 321R, a one-credit class, is open to all majors and can be repeated three times. Students in the class read a selection of each author's work in preparation for the scheduled reading, and after the reading, write a response paper that is posted to the class blog for response from other class members. Students in ENGL 321R also learn some of the basics of running a reading series: for example, preparing introductions and introducing the readers. But it's the TA for the class (a graduate creative writing student) who becomes the expert in running a reading series, including coordinating publicity, transportation, hosting, refreshments, and even managing class assignments. The TA position for the ERS has become a plum job sought after by graduate creative writing students, many of whom have been former student readers in the series. Professor Michael Lavers who now coordinates the ERS, says:

> I can't emphasize strongly enough how influential the ERS was to me as an undergraduate and aspiring writer. It introduced me to so many great authors I wouldn't have otherwise discovered (or at least not until much later), but more importantly it was a weekly reminder that the writing life is possible, that people do it, and it's not just a dream—it can really be made into a reality. That was an important reminder to have week after week [Lavers].

BYU students still find the ERS to be life-changing, as undergraduate Calvin Olsen explains: "I will never forget when Billy Collins came to campus. I was brand new to contemporary poetry, and I wasn't sure what to expect. In less than an hour, he made me want to spend my life writing poetry. His reading was engaging, thought provoking, and instructive. I left the room thinking, 'If it's remotely possible to make a living doing that, tell me where to sign'" (Howe 9).

Added Benefits for Classes on Campus

Many writers also take time to meet with creative writing classes as part of their visit to BYU and the ERS. BYU creative writing faculty and poet, John Talbot, explains:

> We live in a remote part of the country. It's not New York or Boston, where in any given month you can hear any number of leading writers read their work. So it makes a huge impression on our students when they can sit in the same room with nationally acclaimed authors, hear them speak, and later actually meet them. What's more: the ERS may bring such writers to campus, but once they're here, they often stick around and participate in the life of the university in other ways. For instance: a few years ago I invited Willard Spiegleman to read at the ERS. [...] He gave a wonderful reading of his essays for the ERS, and afterwards met and chatted with all of the students who wanted to talk with him. But he stayed on campus for an extra day, teaching a class in the English department, and later giving a presentation—to an auditorium full of aspiring writers—on how to submit their work to literary magazines, with all kinds of inside tips derived from his experience as an editor. So one of the great benefits of the ERS is not only that it brings important writers to campus, but that, once here, they often contribute much more than their reading [Talbot].

The ERS (and its ENGL 321R class) is the largest weekly activity in the Lee Library, with an audience of around 150 at each of the ten to twelve readings (and following author receptions and book-signings), or about 3,000 attendees per year. And the ERS is a now a (library-faculty collaboration) highlight on the library's new-faculty orientation film, encouraging new faculty to explore ways of working together with the Lee Library and their subject librarians.

The English Department Reading Series, which began as a venue for creative writing students at BYU to meet Mormon writers (a function it still performs), has also become a window to the outside world for students and faculty. As Michael Lavers observes:

> I also think [the ERS] serves an important function here at BYU, one that similar reading series might not serve elsewhere. As exceptional and fantastic as BYU is, its demographic is rather monochromatic. Having weekly interactions with writers from all walks of life, and from all over the world, is something I definitely don't want our students to be without. It reminds us folks in the humanities that there are many wonderful and different ways of being human [Lavers].

The ERS at BYU gives students and faculty a fresh perspective, exposes them to new voices and ideas. Poet John Talbot sums it up this way:

> It's for all these reasons the ERS contributes tremendously to the culture of our university. It's all very well for us professors and students to spend our time reading, talking about, and writing about literature. But what a difference it makes when the writers themselves show up on campus, reading their works aloud, meeting the students, encouraging them, and talking about literature from the writer's perspective. The professionalism of the Lee Library staff impresses the participants and makes everything go smoothly. It's all done so well that it could easily be taken for granted, but without it, the literary culture of our university would be hugely impoverished [Talbot].

Of course libraries are still about books and reading, but they're also spaces uniquely suited for celebrations of culture, and for "makers" of literature. As our information sources go online, programs like the ERS help keep the Lee Library central to the university and the lives of students and faculty.

> The HBLL could not be a better venue. It's central to campus, making sure that the ERS is an event that is known outside of the English department and attended by people all over campus. Every week, our visitors are always surprised, sometimes even overwhelmed, by the preparedness and helpfulness of the HBLL staff, and the posters that not only promote the event but seem to show a familiarity with the author's work. The generous use of the auditorium is a big deal too, I think. We could host the ERS in any number of locations, but the auditorium is a gorgeous room in (arguably) campus' most important building. I think it makes visitors feel not just welcomed, but important, and that BYU values their contribution to our students' lives [Lavers].

The collaboration between the Lee Library, the English Literature Subject Librarian, and the BYU English Department on the ERS has enriched everyone involved, and has produced a weekly event (and a for-credit class) attracting writers, students and faculty, and community members to come to the library. The ERS has helped to keep the Lee Library the heart of the university.

Works Cited

Anderson, Sarah A. 2003. "'The Place to Go': The 135th Street Branch Library and the Harlem Renaissance." *The Library Quarterly: Information, Community, Policy* 73.4 (October): 383–421.

Cutler, Sylvia. 2014. "Robert Pinsky Speaks at the Ethel L. Handley Annual Reading." Brigham Young University Humanities (October 3). Last modified May 19, 2016. http://humanities.byu.edu/robert-pinsky-at-the-ethel-l-handley-annual-reading/.

Garcia, Chris. 2016. E-mail to author. May 13.

Handley, George. 2016. E-mail to author. May 24.

Howe, Susan. 2012. *Humanities at BYU: BYU College of Humanities Alumni Magazine* (Spring): 8–10.

Lavers, Michael. 2016. E-mail to author. May 13.

Layton, Roger. 2016. E-mail to author. May 17.

Schwarz, Jan. 2010. "Glatshteyn, Singer, Howe, and Ozick: Performing Yiddish Poetry at the 92 Street Y, 1963–1969." *Prooftexts* 30.1 (January 1): 61–96.

Stern, Frederick C. 1991. "The Formal Poetry Reading." *TDR* 35.3 (Autumn): 67–84.

Stevens, Keri Lund. 2014. "Orem Reads Finale Features Master Poet Pinsky." *Daily Herald*, October 2. http://www.heraldextra.com/news/community/orem-reads-finale-features-master-poet-pinsky/article_50f544ff-8c4d-506d-b1f1-92d6f0266b5b.html.
Talbot, John. 2016. E-mail message to author. May 23.
Zaugg, Emma. 2016. E-mail message to author. May 27.

The Nevada Writers Hall of Fame

A History of Collaboration

STEVEN R. HARRIS

The Nevada Writers Hall of Fame, sponsored by the Friends of the University Library at the University of Nevada, Reno, has a long history of collaboration with writers and the literary community in Nevada (NWHOF website, 2016). The Nevada Writers Hall of Fame is one of the few such statewide honor programs hosted primarily by a university library, a distinction it shares with the Georgia Writers Hall of Fame at the University of Georgia. Literary programming such as halls of fame provides a unique opportunity for libraries to promote literacy, highlight local culture, and form relationships with valuable partners. As observed, literary programming is not often associated with academic libraries, but it really is a natural arena for partnerships within the literary community (Harris, 2002).

Inaugurated in 1988 by the Friends of the University Library at the University of Nevada, Reno, Nevada Writers Hall of Fame had a fundraising and library development focus from the beginning. Throughout its history the program has been managed by the Friends in conjunction with the University development office (and particularly library development). The idea of the hall of fame was conceived by Marilyn Melton, then president of the Friends (Ray, 2012). The library Friends group at the university had been largely dormant throughout the 1970s. The annual report of 1981–82 for the group reports that it was revived in 1981 with the intent of "raising funds and raising friends" for the university library and providing interesting programming for the local community (Friends Records, 3, 1-citations to archival materials include collection name, box number, and folder number). Melton and other members of the Friends met in her living room to select the first two honorees (Ray 2012). Those recipients were Walter Van Tilburg Clark and Robert Laxalt. Clark, deceased at the time of the award, was best known for his western novel *The Ox-Bow Incident* (1940), which was made into a 1943 film starring Henry Fonda and Dana Andrews. His father, Walter Ernest Clark, was president of the University of Nevada during much of Clark's youth. Robert Laxalt was also a local product with university connections. The son of Basque immigrants, he was instrumental in the formation of both the University of Nevada Press and an academic program that would later be known as the Center for Basque Studies. His memoir *Sweet Promised Land* (1957) helped stimulate a growing interest in Basque heritage in the Mountain West. Its publication, as David Rio notes, "put an end to the invisibility of Basques in America" (Rio

2003, 61). The selection of Laxalt was fortuitous in other ways, as he was still rather prolific at that point in his career and was certainly the elder statesman of Nevada letters. The following year, his novel *The Basque Hotel* was nominated for a Pulitzer Prize. Such recognition served to start the NWHOF off on the right foot.

The Friends had great ambitions for their hall of fame from the start. An unsigned proposal in the Friends archives enumerates the benefits of such a ceremony. The first of these was that it would raise awareness of Nevada authors (NWHOF Records, 1, 11). The sense that Nevada's literary contributions and significance were not widely recognized is palpable in all the documents of the organization. Even 20 years after the launch of the Nevada Writers Hall of Fame, University of Nevada English professor Cheryl Glotfelty observes in the preface to her anthology *Literary Nevada*: "Today Nevada is well known—but not known well. Its literary heritage, for example, is virtually *incognita*. Who *are* Nevada's authors? How has Nevada been imaginatively explored and construed? What are its stories? Where are its poems?" (Glotfelty 2008, xxvii).

The minutes of the selection committee from October 21, 1988, assert that the "award will go annually to any writer who, in the judgment of the selection committee, has made significant and lasting contribution to the culture and literary tradition of the state of Nevada" (NWHOF Records, 1, 12). And later, in the 25th anniversary commemorative book, Kathlin Ray notes the importance of "a strong 'Nevada connection' through theme or residence" for all honorees (Ray 2012). In fact, all of the inductees have been Nevadans by birth or residence. Theme alone has not figured in the recognition granted to the writers; the geography of the writer has been much more important than the geography of the writing.

The selection committee developed other criteria for inclusion in the Hall of Fame besides the "Nevada Connection." The original award was intended to honor authors with an extensive and life-long record of publication, some critical recognition, and "good quality" publications. Two discretionary criteria were a national reputation and commercial success (NWHOF Records, 1, 12).

The initial Friends proposal also states that the Hall of Fame was intended to be an occasion for a ceremonial experience and especially to provide development opportunities with the sort of "good" donors they were attempting to attract who would enjoy "events of literary and cultural significance" (NWHOF Records, 1, 11). Thus, a public ceremony conferring recognition upon the authors was planned. It was to be the sort of event that would attract both a large audience and media attention. To lend some sense of gravitas, the Friends also wanted the Hall of Fame to award commemorative medallions and to create a physical hall, as it were, or an area in the library to permanently display placards naming the Hall of Fame inductees. The purpose of these elements was obviously to lend seriousness to the proceedings, but also, perhaps, to demonstrate to the world (and the rest of Nevada) that they were the proper authority, with requisite resources, to grant hall of fame status. Both of these ideas (medallions and exhibit hall) were approved through the Friends board and the library administration.

The medallions were designed by Soleil, a local design firm. The front side includes a depiction of the Getchell Library, the main university library until 2008. The lettering around the edges reads "Friends of the Library * University of Nevada–Reno." The reverse side reads "Nevada Writers * Hall of Fame" and includes a blank scroll image in the middle with an area to engrave the honoree's name. These have been engraved and awarded to each honoree from the beginning. The medallions posthumously awarded to Walter

Van Tilburg Clark (conferred 1988) and Sarah Winnemucca (conferred 1993) are held in the University Archives at the University of Nevada, Reno. Other posthumous honorees either had no medallion made or the award was presented to family members or other interested parties.

The Hall area in the Getchell Library was funded by Friends members Clarence K. and Martha H. Jones. They initially donated $15,000 for the project. As plans progressed, and costs increased, they donated an additional $10,500. The construction of this area was another opportunity for the Friends to collaborate. They worked with the donors, library administration, campus facilities, and design and construction firms to create the space. An interior design undergraduate student even helped with selecting wall and floor coverings (NWHOF Records, 1, 11). The space included the names of honorees in metal lettering mounted on a marble wall. There were also planters and landscaping, seating, display cases, and museum lighting. As plans for a new library were developed in the new millennium, an area for the Hall of Fame was included. This new library, the Mathewson-IGT Knowledge Center was opened in August of 2008. The old Hall of Fame area in the Getchell Library was demolished along with the rest of that building in December of 2013.

The annual Hall of Fame ceremony itself also involved a great deal of cooperation and collaboration for library staff and the Friends. The first 10 ceremonies were held in the Getchell Library. When space and comfort began to be a consideration due to growing attendance, the ceremony was moved to the Wilbur May Museum, part of the Washoe County parks department. After three ceremonies in the Wilbur May Museum, two additional ceremonies were held again in Getchell. The event was then hosted in 2003 by the Nevada Museum of Art in Reno. Ceremonies from 2004 to 2007 were held at local country clubs. Some of these location choices reflected the Friends' attempts to connect with potential donors. When the Mathewson-IGT Knowledge Center opened in 2008, the subsequent six ceremonies were held in the auditorium there. This was an effective location because the auditorium was adjacent to a gallery and the Hall of Fame exhibit space itself. The growth in attendance, however, soon outstripped the capacity of the Mathewson auditorium. The ceremonies for 2014 and 2015 were held in a ballroom of the student union at the University of Nevada, Reno.

Nevada Writers Hall of Fame Medallion (photography by Theresa Danna-Douglas, courtesy Special Collections, University of Nevada, Reno, Libraries).

The nature of the ceremony has evolved over the years. Many of the early events used a tag-team of speakers, presenters, and hosts. Some of the early events even included a business meeting of the Friends. The first award ceremony had a formal speech by John Irsfeld, a professor and administrator from the University of Nevada, Las Vegas, who was selected as a gesture to reach out to the southern part of the state. Irsfeld was not an inductee at that ceremony in 1988, but was himself inducted in 2003 on the basis of his several published novels. Over time, the event planners stuck with a more formal type of presentation with a master of ceremonies. The master of ceremonies was often drawn from the library or university faculty at both the University of Nevada, Reno and the University of Nevada, Las Vegas. Their ranks also included independent scholars, journalists, attorneys and judges, television news broadcasters, a CEO of a gaming corporation, and a minister. The campus event planning office became involved in the event in 2003 and has taken part ever since.

Another feature that began in 2003 was the inclusion of a silent auction. Sponsorships and donations from local businesses provided prizes that were awarded to top bidders with proceeds going to the Friends of the Library. In many years, the revenue from the auction exceeded ticket sales for attendance. Financial information has not been well-maintained for every year in the Friends archive, but as attendance has grown, the financial viability of the program has become much stronger. Program sponsorships are now the most significant form of financial support.

In 1996, Larry Struve, then the president of the Friends had an idea to expand the awards. He suggested the granting of a "Silver Pen" award for writers in early or mid-career who might not qualify for formal induction into the Hall of Fame. The Silver Pen would be a way to recognize younger authors and to encourage continued literary productivity (NWHOF Records, 1, 25). Since 1996, 35 Silver Pen have been awarded. Seven of those subsequently went on to be recognized with Hall of Fame induction.

From 1988 to 2016, 53 individuals have been inducted into the Hall. The Sagebrush School literary movement was also inducted as a group in 2009. The medallion created for that award was presented to literary scholar Lawrence Berkove, who had studied the movement extensively. The majority of those honored with induction into the Nevada Writers Hall of Fame have been literary authors. Many of the authors work in multiple genres, but 16 have been predominantly poets. Fiction writers have numbered 29. Writers of non-fiction in various forms have numbered 36. With the growth of academic creative writing programs, many, though still literary authors, have had an affiliation with higher education in Nevada. Fifteen inductees have been primarily academic scholars.

The selection of inductees has been the area where the most extensive outreach and collaboration has occurred. Over 78 individuals have served on the selection committee. Nine of those are themselves inductees in the Hall of Fame (five serving on the committee before they were inducted and four after induction). Two Silver Pen winners have also served on the selection committee after being given the award. The faculty of the University of Nevada, Reno (10), the University of Nevada, Las Vegas (five), and Truckee Meadows Community College (one) have been represented. Departments of English, History, Journalism, Geography, and Film Studies have all been reflected. There have been 8 different librarians and library staff on the committee. Community representatives have included booksellers, publishers, journalists, attorneys, public relations professionals, and simply avid readers. One of the great benefits of having such a large and diverse population of committee representatives has been that the reputation of the Hall has been very widely spread. People in many walks of life are aware of the honor and have an interest in attending the ceremonies. It has become a cultural event of real significance in Nevada literary circles. Authors note the award on their websites. Anonymous editors add information about the induction to Wikipedia entries of the writers.

The Nevada Writers Hall of Fame wall in the Mathewson-IGT Knowledge Center (courtesy Steven R. Harris).

Measuring the outcomes and return on investment of programs like these is a difficult task. Certainly, in the sheer number of attendees, the Hall of Fame program has shown continuous growth, even at the current $40 ticket price. Although the event itself is a large and expensive undertaking, its popularity and the integration of sponsorships and auctions have made it financially viable for the Friends of the Library. The fact that it is a Friends-sponsored event makes it more practical and defensible for an academic library that has often had financial difficulties of its own. It is always a positive publicity event for the library, reflected in the participation of staff and sponsorship from KNPB, the local public television affiliate. The popularity of the program is also demonstrated by the frequent attendance of both the President and Provost of the University of Nevada, Reno. They both feel some pride of ownership in the event.

Of greater value to the library and to the Friends organization are the relationships that have been formed over the 28 years of the program. The Nevada Writers Hall of Fame reaches into every aspect of literary culture in Nevada, from readership and book sales to authorship, publishing, criticism, and literary journalism. It has reached a level of popularity where people actively nominate authors they think are worthy. Moreover, many authors now nominate themselves! After the very first induction, members of the

Reno Professional Writers Group wrote a letter of thanks to Marilyn Melton for establishing the Hall of Fame. "Writers aren't used to being honored. We're not even sure we deserve it, but it sure is nice that our efforts to please and teach are welcome" (NWHOF Records, 1, 4). The program continues to provide value for the library, the Friends, and the literary community. As James W. Clark observed in conversation with Lisa Morgan, "our literary culture [is] one of the most lasting features of who we are as a people" (Morgan 2003, 156). The Nevada Writers Hall of Fame is one important mechanism of preserving and promoting the literary culture of the people of Nevada.

A more interesting question might be how the Nevada Writers Hall of Fame succeeded so dramatically, in a small state with a small literary community. Certainly, a series of unrelated circumstances came together in the right place and time, but, more importantly, a motivated and dynamic leader in Marilyn Melton was there at the inception both to create significant hurdles to scale and to insist that they were overcome in the end. By having a grand vision of the NWHOF, she ensured that it would be taken seriously and valued by the whole state. But individuals in other states and locations can look at particular steps to success that might help to create a similar hall in other places.

- Craft a clear vision of what that hall of fame will be, including how the selections will be made, how the awards will be promoted, what the winners will receive, and where the "home" of the Hall will be.
- Cultivate a strong Friends organization that can carry a lot of the work load and contribute financially or help encourage contributions from others.
- Maintain strong connections with the library administration and staff.
- Make sure to serve the interests of the library while promoting the idea of the hall of fame. Do not make it a burden for the library.
- Engage a wide range of the literary community to make selections of inductees. The hall of fame really belongs to them.
- Engage other parts of the community as well. People who otherwise might not have literary connections have cultural interests and thoughts nonetheless. Diversity is valuable.
- Have a succession plan for selection committee participants. Change the membership over time, although not necessarily every year.
- Be genuinely open to selecting the best candidates based on unbiased evaluation and feedback. Avoid cronyism.
- Make sure the literary community knows that excellence is being rewarded.
- Make the award ceremony a celebratory event.
- Make it about the writers.
- Give some tangible reward or memento of the award.
- Have a permanent place where the inductees are memorialized.
- Keep previous winners engaged. Involve them in planning future events (if they are willing). Put them on the selection committee or at least ask them for suggestions of who to honor.
- Create a thorough marketing plan. Make sure to keep the media informed of important dates and events.
- Market towards many audiences: the media, potential winners, potential donors, potential supporters in planning and organization, the organizational administration or local government, and, of course, the reading public.

- To sustain the event year after year, create a calendar of milestones to achieve. Be projecting out a couple of years for planning and selection of winners.

All of these steps may not be possible for every organization, but it is valuable to consider all of these (and many more perhaps) when thinking about creating a hall of fame. A hall of fame is a great way to create connections with a local literary community. It becomes a vehicle for recognizing their importance to society. The Friends of the University Library at the University of Nevada, Reno was successful in creating a hall of fame that has been embraced throughout the state of Nevada.

Works Cited

Friends of the University Library Records, AC 0446. University Archives, University Libraries, University of Nevada, Reno.

Glotfelty, Cheryll, ed. 2008. *Literary Nevada: Writings from the Silver State.* Western Literature Series. Reno: University of Nevada Press.

Harris, Steven R. 2002. "Writers in the Library: Literary Programming on a Shoestring." *College & Research Libraries News* 63 (6): 423–425.

Morgan, Lisa. 2003. "The North Carolina Literary Hall of Fame and Literary Historian's Perspective: An Interview with James W. Clark, Jr." *North Carolina Literary Review* 12: 153–59.

Nevada Writers Hall of Fame and Silver Pen Award Records, AC 0519. University Archives, University Libraries; University of Nevada, Reno.

Nevada Writers Hall of Fame. 2016. http://guides.library.unr.edu/nvwriters-hall-of-fame, accessed June 28.

Ray, Kathlin L. 2012. "Introduction." In *Celebrating 25 Years of the Nevada Writers Hall of Fame.* Reno: University of Nevada Libraries.

Rio, David. 2003. "Robert Laxalt: A Basque Pioneer in the American Literary West." *American Studies International* 41 (3): 60–81.

About the Contributors

Roland **Barksdale-Hall**, library director at Quinby Street Resource Center, Sharon, Pennsylvania, is a faculty member at Writing Success, Stoneboro, Pennsylvania. He has appeared in *Urban Library Journal, Against the Grain* and contributed to *Where Are the Librarians of Color?* and *The Library's Role in Supporting Financial Literacy for Patrons.*

Heather **Botelho** is a youth services librarian at Flower Mound Public Library in Flower Mound, Texas, responsible for the young adult collection and teen and tween programming. She leads a monthly writing group for teens, is a blogger for Comics, Cosplay and Geek Culture in Libraries and is a former blogger for YALSAblog.

Patricia **Brown** is a librarian at Louisiana State University–Eunice. She has published in *The Sixteenth Century Journal, Shakespeare in the Classroom, Progressive Librarian, Louisiana Libraries, Community Greening Review*, and *Modern Haiku*. Her interests include bibliography, pedagogy and ethics and politics in librarianship.

Rita Keeley **Brown** is an author, editor, educator, and speaker with careers in music, education, business, and writing. She is the author of *Good Luck, Mrs. Brown…* and *A Pawn of Fate*. She leads workshops in creative writing and "You Have a Story to Tell." She is vice president of programs for the California Writers Club–San Fernando Valley.

Wendy **Burk**, University of Arizona Poetry Center's librarian, is the author of *Tree Talks* and the translator of Tedi López Mills's *Against the Current*. She is the recipient of a 2013 National Endowment for the Arts Literature Translation Fellowship and a 2015 Artist Research and Development Grant from the Arizona Commission on the Arts.

John C. **Burns** has worked in public and academic libraries and is an assistant professor, reference, and instruction librarian at Dixie State University in St. George, Utah. He has helped develop lecture series and continuing education and info lit courses and works to foster technology within libraries. He teaches courses in research/information literacy, photography and graphic design.

Maura Gage **Cavell**, is a professor of English and director of the Honors Program at Louisiana State University–Eunice. In 1999, she co-founded the *Louisiana Review*. Her poetry has appeared in numerous journals, including *Louisiana Literature, The Storyteller, Chiron Review, Poem, Abbey, Boulevard, Iodine Poetry Journal, Flint Hills Review* and *ICON*.

Sarah **Cissé** is a reference/instructional librarian at the Alvin Sherman Library Research and Information Technology Center at Nova Southeastern University in Fort Lauderdale, Florida. Her publications include *Partnering with Public Library Services, Bringing the Arts into the Library* and *The Fortuitous Teacher*.

Laurel Erin **Fennell** is a reference librarian and an associate professor at Miami Dade College. She is a member of the American Library Association and the Society of Children's Book Writers and Illustrators.

Raúl **Fernández-Calienes** has been in education, ministry and service with minority and indigenous peoples for most of his life. He is a visiting associate professor at St. Thomas University School of Law in Miami Gardens, Florida, senior research fellow at STU's Human Rights Institute, and managing editor of the peer-reviewed *Journal of Multidisciplinary Research.*

Sarah **Fisk** is an events/programs planner at the Orange County Library System in Orlando, Florida, where she specializes in planning author events and writing workshops. She writes young adult fiction under the name Sarah Nicolas (*Dragons Are People, Too*) and romance under the name Aria Kane (*Once Upon a Darkness, Sibilance* and *Chasing Luck*).

Karla **Fribley** is the instruction coordinator and reference librarian at Emerson College in Boston, Massachusetts. She works with students in writing and publishing programs, organizes faculty development opportunities, and presents at regional and national conferences on strengthening information literacy in the curriculum and librarian/faculty collaboration.

Karin **Gillespie** is the author of six novels including the Bottom Dollar Girl series (*Girl Meets Class,* the latest). She's written for the *New York Times, Washington Post* and *Writer Magazine.* She has a book column in the *Augusta Chronicle* and a humor column in *Augusta Magazine.* She was the author coordinator and fundraiser for the Georgia Literary Festival.

John **Glover** is the humanities research librarian at the James Branch Cabell Library at Virginia Commonwealth University. His research includes humanities librarianship, literary horror and research practices of creative writers. As J.T. Glover, he writes fiction and non-fiction, and his work has appeared in *The Children of Old Leech, Underground Voices, Goreyesque, Thinking Horror, The Lovecraft eZine* and *Makeout Creek*, among other venues.

Hagai **Gringarten** is a professor of marketing at St. Thomas University in Miami Gardens, Florida, and coauthored a bestselling book about coffee. He is faculty advisor to the American Marketing Association chapter and is founder and editor-in-chief of the *Journal of Multidisciplinary Research.* He is also cofounder and faculty advisor of the *Journal of Student Research* and serves on the editorial board of the *Journal of International & Interdisciplinary Business Research.*

Vera **Gubnitskaia** is a reference librarian at Valencia College, Winter Park, Florida, and has worked in public and academic libraries in Russia and the United States. She coedited *Marketing Your Library, Continuing Education for Librarians* and *How to STEM.* She has contributed to *Librarians as Community Partners* and *Library Management Tips that Work*, and her reviews appear in *Journal of International Women's Studies* and *Small Press Review.*

Anna Caroline **Harris** is an assistant professor of English and specializes in contemporary poetry. Her poems appear in *Cellpoems, Poetry for the Masses, Mikrokosmos*, and *NakedCity.* She advises *Sand Hills* literary magazine, directs a writers weekend program, facilitates Write to Heal and teaches courses in composition and creative writing on the Summerville campus of Augusta University in Augusta, Georgia.

Steven R. **Harris**, assistant dean of libraries at the University of Nevada, Reno, has management responsibility for collections, technical services, and special collections. He is coeditor of *Teaching Literary Research* and is author of *Sudden Selector's Guide to English and American Literature Resources* for the Association for Library Collections & Technical Services series.

Ava Leavell **Haymon** is a poet whose honors include the Louisiana poet laureateship. She has read and published her work in venues across the United States and overseas, including the Arts Club in Washington, D.C., and the *Southern Review.* Among her awards are the L.E. Phillabaum Poetry Award and the Mississippi Institute of Arts and Letters Award in Poetry. Her book *Why the House Was Made of Gingerbread* was on the 2010 top ten book list of Women's Voices for Change.

Melissa E. **Johnson** is the electronic resources and serials librarian on the Summerville campus of Augusta University in Augusta, Georgia, and the embedded librarian in the English and Foreign Languages Department, where she teaches freshman composition. She is active in NASIG,

American Library Association, Association of College and Research Libraries, Georgia Library Association and Southeastern Library Association, and is an MLA International Bibliography fellow.

Patrick **Jones** is the author of over forty books for teenagers, many of them focused on the criminal justice system. His fiction series *Locked Out* concerns the impact of parental incarceration on teenagers, and his fiction series *Unbarred* explores issues facing teens returning after spending time behind bars. His latest is the nonfiction *Teen Incarceration*. www.connectingya.com

Diane **Kendig** has worked as a poet, writer, translator and teacher for forty years. A recipient of two Ohio Arts Council Individual Artist grants, a Fulbright and an NEH award, she has published most recently in *J Journal*, *Wordgathering* and *About Place*. She taught at Bentley University and the University of Findlay, where she created its creative writing program and a prison writing program. dianekendig.com and http://dianekendig.blogspot.com/

Laurie **Kincer**, a reading communication specialist at Cuyahoga County Public Library, Parma, Ohio, coordinates the new William N. Skirball Writers' Center at the South Euclid–Lyndhurst Branch of CCPL, with free writing workshops, writing conferences and author visits. She has presented on "Libraries Influence Readers, Writers and Communities" at the annual conference of Association of Writers and Writing Programs.

Meg **King-Sloan** is branch manager at Chesterfield County Public Library's North Courthouse Road Library, North Chesterfield, Virginia. She was part of a panel presentation on targeted programming in local neighborhoods at the Virginia Library Association Annual Conference, She has also been a member of ALA's International Relations Round Table International Librarian's Pre-Conference Committee.

Stanley L. **Klemetson** is an associate dean of the College of Technology and Computing at Utah Valley University in Orem. He has published numerous technical articles and has authored or coauthored several technical books and manuals. His literary works have included essays in anthologies and blog posts. He successfully completed NaNoWriMo in 2015 to finish the draft of a light fantasy book and is actively involved in the League of Utah Writers.

Cybele **Knowles** is a communications associate with the Center for Biological Diversity and the University of Arizona Poetry Center's digital media coordinator, where she coordinates the classes and workshops program. Her poetry and prose have appeared in *Fairy Tale Review*, *The Destroyer*, *Spiral Orb*, *Diagram*, *Pindeldyboz*, *The Asian Pacific American Journal*, *Faucheuse*, and *The Prose Poem*.

Sarah **Kortemeier** is the University of Arizona Poetry Center's library specialist, where she assists with the daily operations of the center's library. Her work has appeared in *Ploughshares*, *Alaska Quarterly Review*, *Barrow Street*, *Fairy Tale Review*, *The Feminist Wire*, *The Journal of the Center for Mennonite Writing*, *Folio*, *Sliver of Stone*, *Sentence: A Journal of Prose Poetics*, and *Spiral Orb*.

Diana J. **Lennon** is a Latino services and programs librarian at the Greenburgh Public Library in Elmsford, New York. She was a 2010 ALA Miriam L. Hornback Scholar and is a member of ALA, NYLA, REFORMA and the Westchester Library Association. She contributed to the anthology *Library Services for Multicultural Patrons*. In 2016 she traveled with the first ALA delegation to visit libraries in Cuba.

Jeffrey **Makala** is a special collections librarian and university archivist at Furman University in Greenville, South Carolina. He is a member of the editorial board of *RBM: A Journal of Rare Books, Manuscripts, and Cultural Heritage* and is co–North American book reviews editor for *SHARP News*, the newsletter of the Society for the History of Authorship, Reading, and Publishing. He has published on special collections librarianship, exhibition design and nineteenth century American literature and culture.

Daniel **Marcou** is a librarian in the outreach unit at Hennepin County Library in Minnesota. He has provided library service and programs to incarcerated adults for ten years. In 2009, he was named a *Library Journal* "Mover and Shaker" for "going above and beyond the call of duty in his job." www.danielmarcou.com

Meagan **Marshall**, a poet, performer, and professor, directs the Hugh C. Hyde Living Writers Series and teaches in the Department of English and Comparative Literature at San Diego State University. She also teaches at San Diego City College and works with the Early College High School Initiative. Her poetry has appeared in journals including *The Portland Review*, *Web del Sol*, *San Diego Poetry Annual* and *Poetry International*, and has been performed by San Diego Dance Theater.

Alyssa **Martin** is the reference and instruction librarian at Troy University Rosa Parks Library in Montgomery, Alabama. She has been active in the American Library Association's Instruction Section and has served twice as secretary of the Alabama Library Association. In 2014, she received the Employee Excellence Award for Faculty at Troy University Montgomery. She has been published in peer-reviewed journals and has experience writing and implementing grants.

Robert S. **Means** is an English language and literature librarian at the Harold B. Lee Library at Brigham Young University, Provo, Utah, since 1996. He is coauthor of *Arthur Symons, Critic Among Critics* and a contributor to the *Encyclopedia of Jewish-American Literature*. He has published articles on James Joyce and Great War poets, and is one of the founders of the *Mormon Literature & Creative Arts* database at Brigham Young University.

Tina M. **Metzger** is assistant branch manager of the Midlothian Public Library in Chesterfield County, Virginia. A member of the Virginia Library Association, she has been a librarian in academic and public settings and was event planner and project manager for the Festival of the Written Word 2015.

Julie L. **Miller** is dean of libraries at Butler University, Indianapolis, Indiana. She contributed critical essays about Rita Dove, Alice Fulton and Josephine Jacobsen to *Contemporary Poets*, 5th ed. She has published in *College & Undergraduate Libraries*, *Technical Services Quarterly*, and *Education Libraries*, and served on the ACRL New Publications Advisory Board.

Jennifer **Mitchell** is head of manuscripts processing at the Louisiana State University Libraries. She is chair of the Description Section of the Society of American Archivists and is a member of the Society of American Archivists and Louisiana Archives and Manuscripts Association.

Alda **Noronha-Nimmo** is a professor in the English and Communications Department at Miami Dade College. Her research focus is on developmental reading education and she has published a textbook on reading, *Read Your World*. Her interests include critical thinking and brain development as it relates to learning.

Jen **Park** is the assistant librarian for access and outreach services at Mount Saint Mary College in Newburgh, New York, where she oversees resource sharing as well as creating and promoting the library's programs and services. Previously, she had worked at Western Michigan University Cooley Law School as a head of circulation, where she oversaw resource sharing practices.

James W. **Phillips** is an associate professor of theatre and director of MSMC Theatre at Mount Saint Mary College in Newburgh, New York. He is a professional director, actor and sound designer with credits in theatres from Washington, D.C., to Palm Springs. His scholarly interests include the theory and structure of comedy and commedia dell'arte.

Erin **Prentiss** is a reference/instruction librarian at Augusta University in Augusta, Georgia, where she is a member of the University Libraries' Marketing Committee. Her interests include community engagement, diversity in publishing, leisure in the library, and critical information literacy, and she is a member of the American Library Association and the Georgia Library Association.

Nina Q. **Rose** is an academic librarian with a background in law and publishing. She is an assistant library administrator and outreach librarian at St. Thomas University Library in Miami Gardens,

Florida. She manages the library's social media accounts and designs digital flyers to promote the library and events. She is the book review editor for the *Journal of Multidisciplinary Research* and has edited law book chapters and articles.

Mantra **Roy** is an outreach librarian for humanities at the University of Rochester, New York. Her primary liaison department is English and its concentrations in literature, writing, visual and cultural studies and theater. She develops projects with the Digital Humanities Center, the Andrew W. Mellon Fellows in Digital Humanities, the Rossell Hope Robbins Library, Rare Books and Special Collections, the Humanities Center, and the Writing, Speaking, and Argument Program.

Christopher **Shaffer** is the dean of Troy University Libraries in Troy, Alabama, and previously was director of Troy's Dothan campus library. He has been published in peer-reviewed journals and has experience writing and implementing grants. He received the 2015 I Love My Librarian Award.

Carol **Smallwood**'s experience includes school, public, academic, special librarianship. Publications include *Librarians as Community Partners*, *Bringing the Arts into the Library*, *Library's Role in Supporting Financial Literacy for Patrons* and *Women on Poetry*, which is on the *Poets & Writers Magazine* list of Best Books for Writers.

Aline **Soules**' poetry has appeared in such publications as *100 Words*, *Literature of the Expanding Frontier*, *Kenyon Review*, *Houston Literary Review*, *Poetry Midwest*, *Long Story Short*, *Newport Review*, and *Reed Magazine*. Her poetry chapbook is *Evening Sun: A Widow's Journey*, and she writes *Meditation on Woman*, prose poetry and flash fiction. Twitter (@aline_elisabeth) or http://alinesoules.com

Markel **Tumlin** is the English and American literature librarian in the Research Services Division at San Diego State University. He spent twenty years as a contributor to the *Annual Bibliography of English Language and Literature*. As chair of the SDSU Library Comic Arts Committee, he co-created three recent poster presentations for the Comic Arts Conference and also contributed to *Comic-Con Kids*, an oral history of Comic-Con's founding.

Erin **Vonnahme** is a humanities librarian at Miami University in Oxford, Ohio, where she is subject liaison to the departments of English, Media, Journalism, and Film and Theatre and supports digital humanities research across the community as library representative to the Humanities Center. Her research is on inclusive knowledge organization and public service outreach through interactive programming, like zine workshops and makerspaces.

Index